Publications of the Literary and Linguistic Computing Centre
University of Cambridge

edited by R. A. Wisbey

Volume 1

The computer in literary and linguistic research

The computer in
literary and linguistic research

Papers from a Cambridge symposium

edited with an introduction by
R. A. Wisbey

Professor of German in the University of London King's College
formerly Director of the Literary and Linguistic Computing Centre
University of Cambridge

Cambridge at the University Press 1971

Published by the Syndics of the Cambridge University Press
Bentley House, 200 Euston Road, London NW1 2DB
American Branch: 32 East 57th Street, New York, N.Y.10022

© Cambridge University Press 1971

Library of Congress Catalogue Card Number: 70-152645

ISBN: 0 521 08146 7

Printed in Great Britain by
Alden & Mowbray Ltd
at the Alden Press, Oxford

Contents

Introduction

Computers in literary research – there can be few readers today for whom this concatenation will evoke quite the *frisson* of surprise (and possibly mortification) which would have been their reaction only ten years ago. Since then, whatever the misgivings of their editors, many august academic journals have published accounts of computer applications to learned activities which hitherto had escaped contamination by technology, save in its less intimidating manifestations like the card-index, the typewriter and (indirectly) the Monotype keyboard. Conversely, one may surmise that the face of a computer operator is now less likely to register startled disbelief when a chattering peripheral is found to be printing sentences like 'If all time is eternally present / All time is unredeemable. ...'. In practical terms this means that, today, even the most reluctant scholar has at least an indefinite notion of the computer's ability to store, manipulate and analyse natural language texts, whilst his less wary colleagues are likely to meet with a sympathetic reception if they approach their local computing centre with proposals for literary or linguistic research – some universities, indeed, have set up institutes and departments whose special task it is to facilitate work of this kind.

More commonly, however, the scholar's first steps in computing will be guided by a programmer, skilled in numerical analysis or even in data processing, but lacking actual experience of literary computation. This may well not prove an insuperable obstacle, since the scholar himself should be able to specify his requirements rigorously – or if not, the need to acquire this useful skill will quickly be impressed upon him, by way of patient but searching interrogation. Yet unless he is closely acquainted with the few specialist periodicals in this field, like *Computers and the Humanities* and *Computer Studies in the Humanities and Verbal Behavior* (and this provides no absolute guarantee), the novice has little chance of knowing even whether the text he wishes to analyse is already

vii

available in computer-readable form, still less of directing the programmer's attention to structurally similar projects in progress elsewhere, i.e. to the possibility that usable techniques and programs may already exist for the operations he has in mind. Moreover, the difficulties of adapting or rewriting programs for use with an installation other than that for which they were originally designed are such that, in this sphere, ignorance may in fact be bliss. For a variety of understandable reasons, therefore, there has been a strong situational bias towards a local solution to the computing needs of the literary scholar or the linguist.

In itself this is not to be viewed wholly in a negative light: one of its results has been a gratifyingly rapid increase in the number of computer scientists familiar with the specific problems of research in the humanities. Again, while it is undeniably wasteful for the same basic tasks to be tackled independently by a considerable number of programmers, their varying backgrounds and experience necessarily lead to a welcome diversity of approach and to the fulfilment by the ingenious individual of requirements which most others have failed to meet or which have been rejected in advance as too demanding. Yet this and other positive considerations do not outweigh the obvious disadvantages to a new discipline of a situation in which closely related projects may go on in quasi-tribal isolation, largely cut off from outside scholarship. Published news of such research, furthermore, is correspondingly sparse, tending either to appear as a statement of future intent and thus to be of limited reliability, or to be delayed until a project has reached a successful conclusion: for a variety of good reasons, too numerous to detail here, this may be much later than the beginner originally anticipated. Even when accurate information about a project is available, access to it is impeded by a bibliographical coverage which, although improving, is still sporadic. For his part, a programmer will naturally apply to his work in the humanities standards of originality drawn from computer science in general; he may thus feel no urge to publish an account of methods which he regards as essentially derivative. The scholar engaged in literary computation thus soon discovers that he is far more dependent on immediate personal contacts for information than is normally the case in his more orthodox studies; here he is experiencing in common with many scientists – but without the material facilities these enjoy – the problems of communication in a rapidly expanding field of knowledge, subject to continual technological change.

It was against this background, which is merely adumbrated here, that the present writer, encouraged and assisted by Mr Michael Farringdon of the Department of Computer Science, the University College of Swansea, ventured to organize a symposium which would bring together a representative body of scholars and programmers actively engaged in applying the computer to problems of literary and linguistic research. From the outset, the organizers interpreted the term 'linguistic' narrowly, including by their definition all work directly relating to literary language, but excluding computer-based studies of language in its non-literary aspects. The grounds for this decision were of course practical, not theoretical in nature: to have included all the interests for which the term 'Computational Linguistics' provides a convenient description, many of which are by no means without implications for literary studies, would have been to transform the symposium into a congress and to engulf its central literary preoccupations. Numbers were to be restricted still further, again from practical rather than chauvinistic motives – and not least because an international colloquium was envisaged for a later date – by limiting participation to scholars from the United Kingdom. But here informal channels of scholarly communication demonstrated their efficacy (and resilience) in the most reassuring way, with the result that when the symposium assembled in Cambridge on 23 March 1970 it included a small number of participants from Australia, Belgium, Canada, Germany, Italy, the Netherlands, Norway and the United States – as it proved, much to the benefit of all concerned.

The purpose of the symposium, the first of its kind in Great Britain, required that all those attending it should take an active part. An unusual amount of time was thus allotted for discussion, and while fuller versions of most papers were circulated they were actually presented only in abbreviated form. This volume contains the extended versions of select papers, many of them substantially revised and enlarged for publication. The volume is not intended solely for the specialist: the reader without any previous knowledge of this subject will find, if he perseveres at least up to the final section, which is devoted to computer programming – and even this should not prove totally beyond him – that he has been introduced to the principal ways in which the computer can assist the dictionary-maker, the textual editor, the analyst of style and, surprisingly perhaps, the teacher whose pupils are learning to read literary texts in a foreign language; indeed that he has acquired a sufficiently detailed insight into the limitations of the methods described to conceive and plan related work of his own.

Among applications of the computer in this field the least controversial and the most productive, thus far, have been those designed to give the scholar more ready access to the material he wishes to study. We are still remote from the time when an historian, tracing the reception of popular knowledge about ancient Egypt, might be able, *inter alia*, to instruct a central computer to quote all references to the Sphinx in any book held by the British Museum. (This is perhaps just as well, for the questioner might find himself erecting a prefabricated pyramid in his back garden merely in order to house the computer print-out answering such an enquiry.) Such faintly daunting prospects will become a reality only after the development of omnivorous automatic reading devices on the one hand, and of virtually infinite immediate-access data storage on the other. For the moment the scholar's aspirations are kept in check above all by the cumbersome processes he must follow in converting his literary texts into machine-readable form. Once this has been done, however, the computer will – given the requisite programming – locate for him any elements which he can specify with sufficient exactness, whether it be all the occurrences of a particular name, word, image or linguistic form; alternatively it will list all those vocabulary items which are used (or never used) by author A, as opposed to author B. Thus the computer-readable texts excerpted for the lexicographer may later serve in an infinitude of other ways to reduce the time scholars have traditionally spent in amassing their research material; under these circumstances a change of approach may now involve, not years of additional compilation, but simply a set of additional questions to the computer. The exciting possibilities opened up by such methods are treated at length in this book, particularly in section 1; with equal realism attention is also properly directed to the current limitations of these techniques. As Professor Louis Milic shows in a later contribution, it is relatively easy to jockey a computer into producing a line of *ersatz* Dylan Thomas; interpreting (or identifying) the real thing, however, is a different matter. The machine will supply the evidence needed for a rigorous and delicate semantic distinction, but it will hardly make that decision itself, any more than it can be asked to assist, save by generalized indexing, a study of emotive vocabulary in a literary work, unless the scope of 'emotive' can be specified with greater rigour than will come easily to the propounder of such a subject.

Confronted by an index or concordance to a scholarly edition he has prepared, the textual editor reacts somewhat defensively, for he knows better than most how difficult it is to achieve consistency of practice over a lengthy period. Now this dilemma is being resolved, since the editor himself, if he is wise, will use computer-generated analyses of manuscripts or previous editions as aids in his editorial work; once his own text is finalized he will obtain a concordance to it, and after last-minute adjustments he will publish edition and concordance simultaneously. Some progress has been made in alleviating other aspects of an editor's work, notably in collation, especially of variants established manually. Recent advances hold out some hope that the computer may even be able to contribute something to disentangling contaminated manuscript traditions (see section II). Not unnaturally, a multitude of problems remains: in general, this volume hopes to contribute as much by pointing out where these problems lie as by offering ready-made solutions. In many cases, and textual editing is an instance, there is likely to be a steady rather than dramatic erosion of those areas in which, at first sight, it appears that the computer can render little assistance – the decipherment of heavily abbreviated medieval manuscripts may serve as one example. A brief but determined onslaught on such a problem will suffice to disabuse any scholar who fears that the word 'erosion' in this context is a euphemism for creeping redundancy.

After a taste of computer applications, a more frequent complaint stems from the salutary discovery – in an age of increasing specialization – that a command of one's own field, with its ancillary disciplines, is no longer enough. To start with, computer experts are beginning to display a touching eagerness to develop 'high-level' programming languages tailored to literary and linguistic requirements (see section VII), a delicate hint, perhaps, that the palmy days of the 'chauffeur-driven' computer-user are almost over. Secondly, an acquaintance with computerized approaches to stylistics may lead one to predict a rapid improvement in standards of numeracy in arts faculties or instead perhaps a statistically significant increase in the frequency of marriages between *literati* and the daughters of Professors of Probability Theory. Few of the attempts made so far to apply mathematical methods to literary analysis, admittedly, have led to results which will find much favour with the sceptic or even satisfy the devotee, as will be clear from the reservations voiced in this book (section IV). It would take a brave (or very prejudiced) man, however, to deny the possibility of any future advance along these lines. The history of letters is not without its examples of men of literary sensibility who also possessed mathematical sophistication; if and when a scholar with these dual qualifications successfully accomplishes a major piece of literary interpretation with the aid of mathematical techniques, the question will have been settled once and for all. Meanwhile judgement must be reserved.

Stylistic analysis may be regarded as the most intractable task confronting literary computation, not least because of the notorious difficulty of defining style itself. Amidst such uncertainty it is clearly prudent to reduce the unknowns to a minimum; specifically, there is little hope of successful comparisons between the style of one author and another, until it is possible to establish reliably and in depth the stylistic affinities (or differences) between two or more works undoubtedly written by the same author, perhaps at different periods. Many projects in computational stylistics (see the comments in section IV) have neglected to satisfy this elementary requirement. Significantly, comparative techniques have been more effective in author attribution studies (sections II and III), particularly where it has been a question of arbitrating between the claims of a few rival candidates. Here, reference to a limited number of superficial features may conceivably be adequate to resolve the question of authorship. The relationship between such work and full stylistic analysis is essentially that between the profundity of acquaintance needed to pick out an individual at an identification parade and that required to write his biography. Nevertheless, the progress made in attribution studies is an encouraging indication that the task being attempted by computer stylistics is not insoluble, providing that the range of variation or instability within an individual author's work is explored fully, and that suprapersonal elements are not falsely interpreted as personal. To meet this twofold demand – that the language of an author must be seen both within the overall context of his works and against the perspectives supplied by genre and epoch – implies compilation and analysis on a scale quite beyond the scholar working by traditional means.

Finally we may consider a more mundane, but no less essential way in which the computer can assist scholarship. Library catalogues (see section VI) and the standard bibliographies to humanities subjects, like the card files of the lexicographer, are essentially static instruments designed to serve a particular purpose. With the conversion of these into machine-readable form it becomes possible to reorganize and merge the material they contain at will, so as to obtain, for instance, bibliographies to individual writers, with entries ordered alphabetically by author, by editor, date, country of origin, language or any other criterion identifiable automatically.[1]

---

[1] As there is no detailed treatment of bibliographical compilation in this volume, save for methods of automating input, the following references may be of assistance: L. Sawin, C. Nilon, R. Clark, *The Integration, Storage, and Retrieval of Bibliographic Data in English Studies*: Cooperative Research Project No. 2189, University of Colorado (Boulder, Colorado, 1965); B. R. Pollin, *Godwin Criticism. A Synoptic Bibliography* (Toronto, 1967). As from 1966, the Deutsche Bibliothek, Frankfurt am Main, successfully computerized the compilation and production of its *Deutsche Bibliographie*, see Rüdiger Bernhrdat; 'Computer-Einsatz bei der Herstellung der Deutschen Bibliographie',

A further annotation of the original files would permit compilation of bibliographies to specified works, genres or periods within a national literature or group of literatures. Further variants can be readily imagined, indeed the above example is intended merely as an open-ended illustration of the computer's power to sort, classify and juxtapose, not least for purposes which readers of this volume have yet to devise.

Nachrichten für Dokumentation, XVII (1966), 23–30. The Modern Language Association of America is now applying similar methods to compiling its annual bibliographies. Eventually the resultant data-banks should constitute a major tool of scholarship.

Editor's acknowledgements

I am much indebted to Mr J. G. B. Heal of the Literary and Linguistic Computing Centre, University of Cambridge, for his constructive comments on technical aspects of some of the papers in this volume, and to Mr M. H. T. Alford, also of the Centre, for compiling the index.

I

Lexicography, textual archives and concordance making

Historical dictionaries and the computer

A. J. AITKEN*

A historical dictionary, such as the *Oxford English Dictionary* (*OED*) and
the many other large academic dictionaries of national languages, has the
following defining characteristics. Each of its word-entries is accompanied
by a comparatively copious selection of illustrative quotations and references; these are set out so as to display, as fully as may be, the distributions of the word in question in various dimensions – the linguistic
dimensions of form, sense or meaning and habitual collocation and
syntactical situation, and the extra-linguistic dimensions of time, region
and genre. Thus by its arrangement of illustrative quotations a historical
dictionary purports to display all the available distributional information
about each word, except the purely statistical; and even this can be displayed or at least implied in a rough and ready way, for example by the
proportions of references given under the different heads or by means of
brief explicit statements. The definitions and descriptive notes, which are
also a normal feature of such dictionaries, may be regarded as fulfilling a
somewhat secondary purpose, that of signposts or labels to the particular
subset of quotations which follows. The remainder of this article will be
concerned only with the more essential tasks of collecting and arranging
quotations and the extent to which computer facilities can assist or supersede the purely human (or 'manual') means by which these tasks have
formerly been carried out.

The corpuses of sources from which historical dictionaries have drawn
their collections of quotations have customarily extended to some (in certain cases, many) thousands of volumes, amounting to hundreds of millions
of words of continuous text. *A Dictionary of the Older Scottish Tongue*
(*DOST*), which the present writer edits, is based on a reading of upwards
of 2,000 volumes or at least 200 million words of text. With its book-list of
16,000 volumes *OED* rests on a very much larger corpus still, as do many

* Editor of *A Dictionary of the Older Scottish Tongue*, University of Edinburgh.

other large national dictionaries which embrace the modern period of a national language.

Collections of quotations which took in a majority or even a significant minority of the word-tokens occurring in these vast corpuses would far exceed ordinary human abilities to edit them – or even, for that matter, to store them in the traditional form of paper 'slips'. In assembling their collections, therefore, the compilers of dictionaries of this sort are compelled to limit themselves to a comparatively small but, as they will hope, representative selection of examples of word-use from the immensely larger number theoretically available.

Collections have in consequence numbered between about one and about twelve million examples. From these initial collections a further selection is made in the course of editing the dictionary, leaving, as the number of quotations finally printed, between a few hundred thousand in the case of the smaller works (like *DOST*) up to several millions in larger works (like *OED*). The proportions of redundant material at this stage thus vary from perhaps a third up to about four-fifths or even in some cases nine-tenths. But any considerable increases in these proportions, such as would be occasioned by larger initial collections, would seem to be self-defeating, short of correspondingly large increases in the number of skilled editorial workers (who in practice always seem to be in short supply).

Much larger collections have always been possible, at least in theory; with the help of modern technological aids, such as photocopying and similar devices and computers, they are now easy – perhaps fatally easy – to assemble in practice. Yet the time taken to edit older dictionaries based on no more than a few million quotations has always been measured in decades or generations. As we shall see, there is no reason to suppose that the editing of modern technologically aided dictionaries can proceed any more speedily.

If his selection of slips is to be fully representative, the dictionary compiler must take some steps to ensure that, as well as the more readily noticed uncommon items and uses, all the commonplace uses of the commoner words are included. There are likely to be various means of achieving this, including the conversion into dictionary-usable form of existing concordances and word-indexes, the excerption of grammatical dissertations (which frequently embody numerous typical and atypical instances of common function words), and the incorporation in one's material of the entire contents of any earlier dictionaries. In addition, the compiler of a traditional dictionary might have a very limited number of texts, perhaps chosen to span the dictionary's chronological, regional and stylistic range, excerpted very fully, so as to represent adequately all these commoner uses. When done by traditional human methods, this may remain a selective, not a wholly indiscriminate process. Only a very few typical instances will be taken from each text of the most common words, though an attempt will be made to trap any atypical instances; and a normal limit (perhaps of 15 examples in a text of 100,000 words) may be put to the number of quotations taken for any word. This should restrict the number of excerpts to under 25% of the total number of words in each text.[1]

At the cost of an occasional oversight, consequent on natural human fallibility, this avoids the only real difficulty encountered in employing a computer to undertake this work – its inability to select, except randomly or by crude numerical criteria. Nevertheless, its ability to store large quantities of text and to produce from this complete and accurate concordances in the form of dictionary slips recommends the computer for this relatively indiscriminate part of the dictionary-making process. In effect, this is to use the computer and its line-printer as an unusually versatile multiple copying device, with the further bonus that the computer can also sort its output alphabetically. Methods can be devised to compensate for its incapacity for rational selection (see below, p. 12).

For very copiously excerpted texts, this is manifestly more efficient than the traditional method of manual copying and manual sorting. Its advantages over the systems involving copying by office duplicator or by photographic and xerographic apparatus? are less clear cut and depend on

---

[1] See R. Busa, A. Zampolli in J. Štindlová, *Les Machines dans la Linguistique* (Prague, 1968) (hereafter cited as *Les Machines*), pp. 33–4 and 137, where it is estimated that some 600 word-types, representing less than 1% of the total of these, supply more than 60% of the word-tokens of a Latin text totalling 2,000,000 words. Similar calculations on some Older Scottish texts yield not dissimilar results. More precisely, in one text, assumed to be typical, having in all 6,155 form-types (i.e. orthographic 'words') and 88,067 form-tokens (i.e. occurrences of orthographic words), 1% (61) of the types, having frequencies of occurrence of 220 or more, supply 54.6% of the tokens (48,107). In the same text 5% of the types (325), having frequencies over 30, supply 78.5% of the tokens (69,114). Restricting the normal allowance of examples for any given form to below 30 for this text would thus restrict the total number of examples to a maximum of 28,703 (or 32.5% of the total); restricting this allowance to 15 would bring this maximum down to 22,442 (or 25.5%). Equally, even with somewhat less stringent limits on the normal allowance of examples for high-frequency forms (those occurring, say, over 30 times), it would of course still be possible to maintain the same limits on the total yield of examples, if some corresponding reduction were made in the allowance for middle-frequency forms (these occurring between, say, 11 and 29 times), according to a more complex, but in principle feasible, calculation.

[2] A simple technique employing an ordinary office duplicator and a manual guillotine is in effective use in several major Scandinavian dictionary projects (including *Nynorsk*

the density of excerpting aimed at: the more nearly total the excerption, the greater the advantages of the computer method. But the latter does always score in simplicity of operation and the convenience of its filing and sorting facilities.

This is one part of the work of dictionary compilation for which we may be glad to accept the computer's help. The thirty or fifty or hundred or so volumes thus fully excerpted will furnish the basis of the dictionary's collection and may be assumed to account adequately for all the more common phenomena. Any usages which are at all common may then be ignored in excerpting – much more selectively – from the very much larger body of the remaining sources, the remaining 1,470 or 1,950 or 9,900 volumes or whatever it might be. In dealing with these the excerptors will confine themselves to specially informative or interesting examples and to quite unusual words, forms and word-uses.

The mere reading of the corpus of sources covered by large national dictionaries like *OED*, and even by smaller specialist dictionaries like *DOST*, would occupy several lifetimes. So this selective part of the excerpting process can only be carried out by a team of excerptors – a small number of professionals or a larger number of amateur volunteers. Ideally, it demands of the excerptor, among other things, much knowledge of the language, so that he has a feeling for the likely distributional range and frequency of incidence of particular forms and usages at different points in the corpus. Only thus can he predict what must be added to the files and what, conversely, may safely be assumed as already adequately represented. Certainly, when in doubt (and this will often be the case) he will tend to err on the side of inclusiveness – but with restraint, if he is to avoid accumulating an intolerable bulk of redundant material. In practice, few excerptors, whether professionals or amateurs, are likely to reach these exacting standards. But excerptors' habits and predilections differ, in the features which their selection exemplifies most adequately and in overall fullness or scantiness of coverage; by assigning similar texts to two dissimilar excerptors the idiosyncrasies of one may be allowed to complement those of his colleague; the same text may of course be assigned to several excerptors whose habits will complement one another in this way; published glossaries, annotative commentaries and the like, which will naturally be incorporated in the material, may also be allowed to complement or to

Ordbok and Det Norske Litterære Ordboksverk) in Oslo and Copenhagen. A much more complex technique, employing microphotographic and xerographic apparatus and electromechanical sorting machines, is described by A. Duro in *Cahiers de Lexicologie*, VIII (1966), 95–101 (hereafter cited as *Cahiers*), also *Les Machines*, pp. 285–91.

take the place of the work of the excerptor; and the dictionary editor is of course not debarred from using his own knowledge and acumen to make good hiatuses, either in vetting the excerpting or when he comes to edit the dictionary. By expedients of this sort the margin of error inescapable in this method of selective excerpting may be reduced, though not of course wholly eliminated.

It seems highly unlikely that any practicable automatic method of overcoming the built-in uncertainties of this part of dictionary compilation will become available in the foreseeable future. The only methods of computer simulation which suggest themselves to this writer (which would depend on the matching of collocates of given keywords) seem so jejune in their potential achievements and so costly in human time to develop them (and perhaps also in computer time once in operation)[1] as not to be worth pursuing. So this selective process must remain a purely human task. Even in computer-aided dictionary projects it must be undertaken at some point in the course of compilation if a fully worked out dictionary of the sort defined at the head of this article is to be feasible.

The sorting stage of dictionary-making, which, in a traditional manually compiled dictionary, would normally follow that of collection, may be regarded as the sum of three processes – alphabetic or 'approximate' sorting, 'lemmatization' or the grouping of orthographically and morphologically related variants under a single headword (thus the quotations for *ran* and *running* would be grouped below those for RUN), and the separation of homographs (thus the quotations for *lead* (the verb) would be grouped separately from those for *lead* (the noun)). In most dictionaries the second at least and perhaps also to some extent the third of these processes will have been anticipated at the collection stage, the collectors having marked each slip with its headword (thus the slips for *ran* and *running* will bear the headword RUN). Any omissions or errors in the attributions of the headwords can for the most part be made good in the course of sorting by intelligent sorters with some knowledge of the language concerned.

This operation, when carried out manually on a collection of a million or two quotation slips, might be expected to occupy several sorters for a number of years (at a rate, perhaps, of 250,000 slips per sorter per year). Of the three main stages in a dictionary's compilation (respectively, of collection,

---

1 Not to mention the cost of key-punching the vast corpus of texts covered at this stage of the work. Though not impossible (see p. 14 for a project (TLF) accomplishing just such a feat), this would by itself greatly exceed the cost of selective excerpting by traditional methods (cf. the figure proposed for the latter on p. 10). But an efficient OCR device (see pp. 10–11) might resolve this issue at least.

of sorting and of editing) this is much the smallest. In contrast, we may note that to assemble the collection of upwards of 10 million slips, until recently not yet alphabetically sorted, for one large dictionary (the *Dictionary of Sanskrit on Historical Principles*) took 40 or more excerptors almost 20 years. Sorting ought not to take anything like this amount of labour. Editing a collection of this size, on the other hand, will certainly take far longer.

The order of skill required for sorting is modest (but it does require some knowledge of the language under study); hence labour cost need not be high. Even so, for these large collections it is clearly far from negligible. This is also probably the most repetitive and mindless of all dictionary-making operations; here, most of all, is the 'drudgery' traditionally associated with dictionary-making. Any help towards its accomplishment by computer or other mechanical means can be justified on both these scores. The larger the collection the truer this becomes. The mammoth collections envisaged for some of the new computerized dictionaries (see below, pp. 11–14) could scarcely have been contemplated without the sorting facility offered by the computer.

But whereas the computer can far outstrip the human sorter in simple alphabetic sorting, it has no such advantages in the other processes requiring to be executed at this stage – lemmatization and homograph separation. In the parts of a dictionary's collection which are being handled by computer, as much as in the manually treated parts, these processes will continue to require human intervention, either by 'pre-editing' the data or by 'post-editing' the output (see pp.11–13). Specially large computerized collections might even justify the trouble of providing the computer with 'dictionary look-ups' to enable it to execute automatically part of the task of lemmatization (see p. 14).

While we are right to accept what help the computer and other machines can give us in these essential collecting and sorting procedures, we must not suppose that the computer is serving as more than an aid in the most 'mechanical' and least demanding chores of lexicography. The transformation of a collection of broadly arranged examples, of which we have so far been talking, into a finished dictionary follows from the much more exacting and delicate tasks which make up the editorial stage in historical dictionary-making. At this stage the dictionary's editors subdivide the quotations for each lemma by 'sense' (in effect by common context),[1]

---

[1] A refinement and continuation of the process of homograph-separation, mentioned above (p. 7) as taking place at the collection and sorting stages of the dictionary's compilation – but demanding, as a rule, a rather higher order of knowledge and skill.

excogitate definitions for each sense and select for printing those quotations which best illustrate the word's formal, semantic and grammatical histories and the distributions of each form and sense in time, space and genre. As yet practicable and economic means of simulating by computer these subtle analytical procedures remain a distant and perhaps impossible dream. This, however, is the heart of the lexicographical process.

It is also much the most difficult and time-consuming part of lexicography. In carrying out these editorial tasks, with all the innumerable and complex decisions they involve, a reasonably skilled lexicographer might hope to work through no more than 10,000 to 15,000 quotation slips per annum. The largest number of slips for a single lemma which I ever had to edit myself ran to about 4,000 and occupied about three months – this after many years' editing experience. Thus the editing of a collection of 10 million slips might occupy 1,000 'lexicographer-years' or, to be more realistic, 10 lexicographers 100 years. We have only to think of the histories of the great nineteenth- and twentieth-century national dictionaries to see that these figures are of the right order. Hence, also, the editing of large historical dictionaries invariably takes far longer than the preliminary collecting and sorting of their raw material.[1] Might this not prove even more true when collecting can be accelerated and collections enormously enlarged by using computers, while, conversely, no means yet present themselves of speeding up the mental activities of dictionary editors? So efficient are the computers at total excerption and inefficient at selection that they present a strong temptation to accumulate more examples than are strictly necessary. One outcome of this may be a more nearly perfect dictionary; another, certainly, will be higher editorial costs.

At contemporary British values and salaries (assuming these to remain stationary for the 60 years at least which, with an editorial staff of nine or less, such an enterprise would be likely to occupy) the labour costs of producing a (wholly imaginary) dictionary based on a collection of 2 million slips excerpted from 3,000 volumes of 100,000 words each, might be

---

[1] *OED*, which began with 3½ million slips assembled in 16 years, though it disposed ultimately of many more (perhaps to a total of 6 millions), took 50 years to edit with an editorial staff of varying sizes but numbering for a time between 20 and 30. It was accomplished in much less time than any of its contemporaries on a similar scale: for example, the *Woordenboek der Nederlandsche Taal*, which recently (1964) celebrated its centenary, and the Swedish Academy's *Ordbok öfver svenska språket*, begun in 1882, are both expected to take several decades still. The main collections for the *Thesaurus Linguæ Latinæ* seem to have been completed between 1883 and 1900; editing has since (1970) proceeded to letter O. The much smaller *Oxford Latin Dictionary* seems to have taken 6 years (to 1939) for the gathering of its collections; but 30 (to 1969) to edit.

roughly estimated at £728,000. This consists of: at least £120,000 as the cost of professional collection (by at least 5 persons over 15 years); £8,000 as the cost of sorting (by 4 persons over 2 years or *pro rata*); £600,000 as the cost of editing (by 5 scholars and perhaps 3 or 4 clerical assistants[1] over 40 years). Considerable savings could be made by employing unpaid volunteers for the bulk of the excerpting (£60,000 perhaps). So long as the charges for data processing are merely notional or nominal,[2] some saving might be made by employing a computer for the excerpting of, say, 30 basic fully excerpted texts (see pp. 4–5); this might work out at £2,000.[3] Savings could perhaps also be effected by taking advantage of mechanical sorters for the quotations from the selectively excerpted texts (these quotations would then have to be written or otherwise copied onto punched cards)[4] – conceivably half or more of the remainder of the sorting costs. These methods might thus reduce the total by around £5,000, or, using volunteer excerptors, £65,000 – less than one-tenth of the total cost, which, as always, is chiefly that of editing. To this saving the computer's contribution is quite modest.

The advent of a really versatile and economic Optical Character Reading device[5] could, however, materially alter this balance of costs in the computer's favour and outdate some at least of the preceding discussion. Conversion of text into computer data would then become wholly automatic and the delays and errors at present consequent on the key-punching process eliminated. Not only would this greatly simplify the treatment of the

---

[1] To carry out, for example, final arrangement of the material, control of accuracy, incidental research, press-preparation, first checking of proofs.

[2] An important proviso. In Britain and some other countries, computer services to academic users (including lexicographers) are available at 'notional', or at nominal, cost. While we applaud this, we ought also to remember that if we had to meet the cost of computer time (on a time-sharing system of computer use) and, *a fortiori*, of the programming services we enjoy, any savings in cost to lexicographers obtained with the help of computers would be, at best, very substantially reduced.

[3] Ignoring the cost of key-punching and correction (rather optimistically assumed to be roughly equatable with whatever method of text-reproduction is employed in the non-computer methods) and of multiple copying (for which various efficient non-computer methods are also available; see, e.g. note 2, p. 5, above), and, conversely, ignoring the costs of computer programming and processing (see the previous note), this saving is to be attributed only to the computer's sorting facility. The figure given assumes that 700,000 slips are produced by a computer technique like that discussed on pp. 11–12 of this article, and that some manual labour will also be called for, for example, in lemmatizing many of the computer-derived slips and sorting them into the remainder of the dictionary's collection.

[4] For example, as described by A. Duro in *Cahiers*, pp. 95–101.

[5] For a recent and optimistic account, published while the present paper was in the press, see Richard S. Morgan in *Computers and the Humanities*, v (November 1970), 75–8.

basic texts selected for very full excerption, it would also increase the advantages of handling by computer the selectively excerpted texts. The selected keywords might be marked in the original source with some symbol which the OCR device and subsequently the computer could recognize, and the machines then left to carry out on their own the copying, sorting and print-out of slips. Or, if this proved impossible, the text might first be converted through the OCR device into computer-readable form; the computer could then be supplied with a list of the references of the selected examples, as well as, where necessary, codings which would enable it to lemmatize and to distinguish homographs; automatic sorting could follow and the results would be printed out as slips without further attention. In this way the clerical, photographic or xerographic copying which occupies so much time in present-day dictionary-making would be very largely eliminated.

As things are at present, however, cost-saving must remain only a minor motive for enlisting the aid of computers in this kind of lexicography. As we have seen, larger savings can be achieved by rather different expedients. The real benefit of the computer to this area of scholarship lies not so much in its direct contribution to dictionary-making as such, as in a by-product of this – the computer-readable textual archive. Though perhaps not yet fully realized, this may turn out to be the most important justification for the extensive employment of computer techniques in historical dictionary projects in progress today.

On one of the most recent of these – the Accademia Della Crusca's *Historical Dictionary* – the overall aim has been to assemble a very large and exhaustive collection of dictionary slips with the least possible human effort in copying and sorting. Only a fraction of the corpus of sources for this dictionary is to be treated by computer. The bulk of its sources are excerpted more or less selectively by other methods.[1]

The limited body of sources – 'some hundreds of volumes' is the number specified – selected for computer processing are presumably those which will provide the dictionary's basic collection, like that described on pp. 4–6. In return for the single punching (and proof-correction) of its corpus the computer can produce a complete concordance in the form of quotation slips and deliver these already alphabetized according to the spellings of their keywords.

For these slips produced by means other than the computer, lemmatiza-

---

[1] See Duro, *Cahiers*, pp. 95–101. The following paragraphs are based on the remainder of the same article, pp. 101–12 (see also Duro in *Les Machines*, pp. 201–20).

tion and homograph-separation will perforce be accomplished partly or wholly by manual methods. Even for the computer-generated slips, it may at first sight be hard to see any great advantage that any computer-aided technique could have over the traditional methods of subdividing bundles of slips by hand and, when necessary, of manually shifting bundles of slips from one position in the files to another. In the Italian project, however, it appears that this reshuffling of quotations is executed by the computer by one or other of two similar methods. One of these requires a re-reading of the initial computerized text after it has been printed out with each successive word numbered in sequence by the computer; the computer is then informed of the headwords and numbers of those items which it is desired to re-address (thus any occurrences of *ran* would be re-addressed to their headword RUN and the instances of *lead* [verb] would have a separate address from those of *lead* [noun]); thereafter the computer can re-sort and lemmatize the material accordingly.[1]

The other lexicographical problem inherent in any exhaustive computerization of large sections of text is that of reduction to a manageable number of the many thousands of examples of high- and middle-frequency words which the computer, if it is permitted to do so, will pour out on the hapless lexicographer. The simple and at first sight attractive solution originally proposed for the Italian dictionary was to accept a random selection of each of the high-frequency words, balancing the likely loss of some specially revealing examples against this method's advantages in speed and simplicity. While this may be acceptable in some cases, there must be others in which this would also risk the loss of certain rare (and therefore important) homographs of the high-frequency words; in Older Scots, for example, three of the commonest items all have less common homographs, *and* (breath) beside *and* (the conjunction), *the* (thigh) beside *the* (the article) and *the* (the pronoun), and *he* (high) beside *he* (the pronoun). One way of overcoming this difficulty would be to have the computer-treated sources carefully re-read by human excerptors, but only for exceptional examples of the high- and middle-frequency items (these being the only items omitted from the computer's otherwise exhaustive concordance); a handy alphabetical list of these items could easily be provided in advance by the computer. This procedure might be combined with the reading for lemmatization mentioned in the preceding paragraph.

Various expedients for selecting from the high-frequency words and for lemmatization can thus be applied after the textual corpus has been con-

[1] See Duro, *Cahiers*, pp. 103, 106–9; *Les Machines*, pp. 213–16.

verted into computer-readable form. It is also possible to anticipate these problems when the text is being prepared, before it has been punched for delivery to the computer. Some pre-editing is of course always necessary before any text is prepared for processing, if only to settle details of reference and the treatment of diacritics, manuscript abbreviations, punctuation and the like. But, in addition to this, one could also pre-edit the text by adding notations or codings which would identify to the computer particular examples chosen for excerption, the length of excerpts prescribed and the headword under which it is desired to enter any given example. From a text prepared in this way the computer could deliver an output resembling a fully sorted collection for a traditional dictionary (already ordered and lemmatized) without further human attention. Only the stage of analytic editing would then remain; and even before this was done the material for each word would already be available in the most convenient form possible for any user, short of its final subdivision into senses and other appurtenances (such as definitions) of the finished dictionary.

If this procedure were intended merely to produce a dictionary collection, there would of course be little point in key-punching the dictionary's total corpus, even if this were practicable. It would be desirable to produce a full computerized text of only the most copiously excerpted part of the corpus, that designated as the basic collection. For the rest, it would suffice to deliver to the computer only those small stretches of text which included selected keywords. The key-punching of this should prove only moderately more costly than the equivalent copying by pen or typewriter which would be required by traditional methods. And such difference in cost as there was would be partly or wholly recompensed by the filing and sorting facilities supplied by the computer.

This very attractive method seems to combine in a single operation both the provision of a selected dictionary collection, already sorted and lemmatized, and the creation of a fair-sized computer-readable textual archive, the value of which, beyond that of the dictionary, is discussed below (p. 15f.). The latter purpose – that of establishing a computer archive – would of course be served still better, funds permitting, by key-punching in full much larger stretches of text than were strictly required for the dictionary. Something on these lines is understood to be in progress for *The Historical Dictionary of the Hebrew Language* in Jerusalem.[1]

---

[1] This doubtless rather oversimplified account represents my understanding of an oral description given me in 1968 by Prof. Z. Ben-Hayyim: see also his 'A Hebrew Dictionary on Historical Principles' in *Ariel* (A Review of the Arts and Sciences in Israel), no. 13, 1966. A method involving pre-coding for lemmatizing purposes doubtless has special

The methods of lemmatization with computer help so far mentioned necessitate informing the computer explicitly of the destination in terms of headword of every single instance of each word which it has to treat. Another possibility is to provide the computer with a single general list of many of the forms it will encounter and to specify for each of these the headword to which it is to be assigned and the place it is to occupy in a pre-determined arrangement under the headword. Once the computer is equipped with such a list it can allocate to its particular lemma any single instance of any form listed.[1] This is the means chiefly relied on by the Centre de Recherche pour un Trésor de la Langue Française (TLF) of Nancy, for ordering its vast collection of 250 millions of word-examples.[2] In addition, TLF also has a computer 'look-up' which in effect lists certain predictable collocations of certain common function words so that the computer can subdivide its examples according to those collocations and deliver separately the non-predictable ones: a step towards mechanizing the selection of examples of high-frequency words, and a simulation, in this one instance, of the more advanced editorial processes of lexicography. Beyond this, however, it is not clear what is to be the means of selection from these immense numbers of examples: methods similar to those proposed above (p. 12) would, however, seem possible. For all the very large resources in personnel, equipment and money of which TLF disposes, it does seem inescapable that some such means must be applied, if indeed a fully worked out dictionary is to be distilled from this vast archive.

Unfortunately the creation of such lists must demand very considerable expenditure in human knowledge, skill and labour, justified, perhaps, only for really vast undertakings like that at Nancy. Short of collocate-matching methods which are probably impracticable for lexicographical purposes (see above, p. 7), all homographs must be excluded. For a language with a fairly 'fixed' spelling, such as Latin, these may amount to 12% of the total

advantages for a language such as Hebrew, for which simple alphabetic sorting, useful enough for many other languages, including most European ones, is of little value.

[1] For a clear account of a look-up list of this sort and how it may be compiled from an older dictionary or dictionaries, see Busa, *Les Machines*, pp. 251–69. An alternative method, of course, is to derive such a list from a preliminary manual lemmatization of the forms found in part of a text, the computer being programmed to apply the same lemmatizations to all subsequent occurrences of the same forms in the remainder of the text; as I have learned from Professor Ben-Hayyim, this method has been used with some success in Jerusalem, the small percentage of residual errors resulting no doubt from undetected cases of homography. Perhaps such a list will justify the trouble of compiling it and the cost of using it only for very large dictionary collections (or, of course, a very large computer archive)?

[2] See *Centre de Recherche pour un Trésor de la Langue Française* (Paris, 1967), especially pp. 27–31.

number of form-types.[1] But some medieval languages with variant spelling systems – such as medieval Italian[2] and Older Scots[3] – display much higher proportions of homographs and for them, accordingly, the useful applications of this look-up technique are further limited.

In these various ways the computer's facilities for storage of data, sorting and multiple copying, in association with the exclusively human capacity for rational arrangement and selection, can be harnessed to more or less selective, if at the same time monumental, dictionary projects. And yet, for all the ingenuity displayed in these enterprises, the net result is only to enable the computer to replace the human drudge who, traditionally, copied out, sorted and filed his dictionary's slips preparatory to their editing by its scholarly staff. The really essential work of the lexicographer, that of analysing and selecting the material so compiled, remains a purely human prerogative.

In the end, perhaps, the essentially selective aims (so far as concerns particular occurrences of words) of the conventional historical dictionary and the computer's lack of discrimination remain fundamentally incompatible. In the nature of things the contributions to saving in time and cost which the computer can offer are limited and, as we have seen, remain at present quite small; and such improvements in accuracy and completeness as computer-aided methods can facilitate will also continue to be limited by the fallible human judgements on which ultimately they will always depend.

Where a language already possesses, as many do, an adequate historical dictionary of the older kind, it must then be very doubtful if the limited advantages offered by these new techniques are enough to justify new enterprises with essentially the same aims. The really important innovation in historical lexicography which computers have made possible results from a less restricted and selective approach; and its effect is to complement rather than to supersede the older type of historical dictionary. This is the computer-readable textual archive. On such an archive each of the three dictionary projects just glanced at is partly or wholly based. But an archive of this sort, whether primarily created as a repository of dictionary quotations or not, also has its own autonomous usefulness.

Unlike the fully worked out dictionary, the computer archive is potentially exhaustive: it offers access to all instances of given forms or groups of

[1] Busa, *Les Machines*, p. 258.
[2] Cf. Duro, *Cahiers*, p. 104; *Les Machines*, p. 205.
[3] In Older Scots, for example, the form *leid* might represent any one of four distinct nouns, the present tense of one verb or the past tense of another.

forms which occur within its corpus. Also unlike the dictionary, however, it must leave the detailed analysis or final arrangement of these to its users. Thus there is no likelihood that either of these two kinds of lexicographical resource will entirely replace the other. Eventually, no doubt, both archive and dictionary will become available for general consultation at remote terminals so that dialogue communication with both, perhaps using a screen outlet, will become possible. As things are now, for a scholar whose needs transcend the information supplied in a conventional dictionary and who is prepared to take the pains to work out his own analysis of the exhaustive material he can obtain from a computer archive, the dictionary may still be helpful in laying out the guidelines of his investigations. At the same time, the existence of computer archives would often seem to remove the need to burden library shelves with still larger dictionaries filled with still more detailed information of interest to only a few people.

To establish and maintain a small archive of this sort, running to perhaps a few million words of continuous text, need not be exorbitantly expensive. A single key-puncher could complete its data-preparation in a few years and supervision and programming would require only one or two more persons. The example of TLF shows that a fairly rapid conversion to computer-readable form of much larger corpuses is also feasible, given much larger resources in staff: the 2,500 volumes being punched by TLF's 38 key-punchers approximate to the total corpus covered for *DOST* and for some other of the smaller historical dictionaries of the past. Many of us, however, are likely to be limited to a much more gradual increase in the size and scope of our archives, beginning perhaps with those sources for which there is immediate demand. In addition to the material it provided from its own resources in this way, the value of such an archive would increase if it became also a central repository for all computer-readable texts relevant to its field which individual scholars had prepared separately for their own private researches.

As the archive grows, so the practicability of publishing concordances and word-indexes to all its contents must diminish. In my own view such publications should be directed only to those texts which are known to be of quite general interest, leaving it to the specialist to seek out his particular requirements direct from the archive. This makes convenience of access doubly important. Pending the time when this may be possible on-line from remote terminals, the present aim might well be to make the archive accessible at least by post, with the centre which holds it providing also a selection of general-purpose programs for generating concordances, word-counts and collections of dictionary slips for specified portions of the archive (such as all the works of a particular author) or for specified words or word-elements. We hope soon to begin realizing this aim for the Older Scottish Archive,[1] by the methods outlined by Mr Hamilton-Smith later in this volume. By some such means we may approach the desirable goal of supporting a large historical dictionary with the powerful reinforcements supplied by a computer-readable textual archive.

[1] See A. J. Aitken and Paul Bratley, 'An Archive of Older Scottish Texts for Scanning by Computer', *English Studies*, XLVIII (1967), 60–1, and *Studies in Scottish Literature*, IV (1966), 45–7. This small archive, begun in 1964, runs to something over one million words of text and takes in several important early literary collections and single works most of which have hitherto lacked any word-index. Among other users, *DOST* itself has benefited in various more and less obvious ways: in the availability of concordances and word-lists for casual consultation and by using the archive's resources as a partial substitute for a specially cumbersome part of its own system.

B

Publications from an archive of computer-readable literary texts

ROY WISBEY*

During the past decade our ideas about the nature and function of a lexical archive have undergone a significant transformation. Many participants in the Tübingen colloquium on the mechanization of lexicography and literary analysis (November 1960)[1] were lexicographers who had come, perhaps in sceptical mood, but with laudable openmindedness, to explore new methods which seemed to promise a lightening of their traditional burdens. For those of their number who represented large-scale historical dictionary projects which were nearing completion, or which were already at an advanced stage of material collection and hence were irrevocably committed to conventional card archives, the computer had little to offer but, perhaps, a sense of having been born too early. Under the circumstances it was natural for them to emphasize the more intricate aspects of their work, the slow, analytic processes of scholarly selection, classification and interpretation of which lexicography consists; processes in which – and there has been little change in this situation since then – a private army of graduate assistants, like the one employed by the *Dictionary of Sanskrit on Historical Principles*, still constitutes a more desirable ally than any electronic siege-machine. Yet, granted the necessary awareness, this particular generation of lexicographers had good reason to consider itself singularly unfortunate.

Not, of course, that the ultimate success of their venerable projects was in any way jeopardized; nor primarily because, like all their predecessors, they had undergone the rigours inseparable from the manual compilation of an archive, only to lose the consoling if faintly malicious certainty, available in all previous ages, that any future rivals would have the same weary paths to tread. The truly bitter insight, for those to whom it was given, concerned rather the nature of the archive which had been amassed

* University of London King's College; formerly Literary and Linguistic Computing Centre, University of Cambridge.
1 For a brief report on this colloquium see *Modern Language Review*, LVII (1962), 167.

at such material and human cost. For compared with the flexibility and versatility of an archive based on computer-readable texts, the traditional apparatus of the lexicographer in all its reassuring tangibility, is claustrophobic in its narrowness; ironically, moreover, the more scrupulously it has been designed with its original purpose in mind, the more inescapably rigid it is likely to be. No broadly based dictionary project of the past, save one dealing with a period where written evidence was scanty, could, for example, have countenanced a policy of complete excerption for the very common words of a language, even where major works of literature were concerned.[1] The implications of this wholly defensible, indeed essential, selectivity may perhaps not be very serious for certain types of research. The published dictionary will quote verbatim only those instances which best illustrate the range and historical development of a concept; nevertheless the researcher can always have recourse to the original archive for complete occurrences of words of moderate frequency. If prepared to go to sufficient lengths in collecting elements possibly scattered over millions of cards he will be able to attempt other tasks, such as analysing the spectrum of verb forms in use during a particular century, or tracing the fortunes of a diphthong. But there is a point, all too soon reached, beyond which the labour of manually searching the archive effectively rules out its use. In addition there may be a large category of questions which the archive, owing to its inherent limitations, will be incapable of answering; questions, for instance, as to the exact proportions of nouns employing the suffix -*ness* in texts from successive historical periods, general statements of this kind having been precluded by the only partial excerption of certain very common words.

Most dictionary projects inaugurated or recast during the last ten years have transcended these traditional limitations, at least to some degree; for the application of computers to the compilation of lexical materials – primarily implemented for its saving of time and money – creates as a by-product a dynamic tool of research that, if it is adequately conceived and administered, can serve scholarship in much more depth than the static card-index, which is capable of extension and supplementation but not of metamorphosis. However, the establishment of a computer-readable archive requires both resources and determination, particularly in the continued

---

[1] Old High German and Early Middle High German are examples of earlier periods for which the complete excerption of all preserved vernacular texts is both possible and justifiable, since the relative paucity of evidence confers importance even on sub-literary material. But it will be obvious that no such procedure could be followed by a lexicographer concerned with nineteenth-century Germany, for example.

absence of versatile optical character recognition devices (here the decade has produced its disappointments). It is perhaps hardly surprising, therefore, that much, although by no means all, of the solid progress in this direction has been achieved by centres orientated first and foremost towards a specific national language, whether it be French, Italian, Hebrew, Czech, Dutch or the Older Scottish tongue, while any such undertaking as the contemporary frequency dictionary projects in America and Sweden naturally commends itself to local support. This is a logical development; yet it would be quite wrong to imply that all or even most machine-readable textual archives follow this pattern, indeed it would be regrettable if they did. Cambridge, for instance, possesses more computer-readable texts in contemporary Arabic and medieval German than the respective nationals.[1]

In any case I wish to concern myself here not so much with the way in which a computerized archive is used to provide working material for the compilation of a dictionary, whether national or not, although this may be the primary reason for its existence, but rather with its long-term function, namely to be at the service of scholarship in general. Obviously these two aspects cannot be divorced from each other, least of all at the planning stage, for the lexicographer will sensibly refuse to be overwhelmed by complete material for very frequent words; on the other hand scholarship will demand that all major literary works in the field concerned should be present in the archive in their entirety, together with at least representative sub-literary texts. Fortunately there is no absolute conflict of interest here, provided that the more restricted needs of the lexicographer are not allowed to dictate the form of the archive. On the other hand, an archive designed to meet all conceivable needs of literary and linguistic research will be able to regard the lexicographer as only one of its many users, a user, incidentally, who should perhaps be encouraged to consider whether his work really requires the creation of a traditional card file at all, when specified items, identified from vocabulary listings, can be retrieved from magnetic tape at will.

---

[1] Cf. *Les Machines dans la Linguistique*, ed. J. Štindlová (Prague, 1968), for descriptions of various projects, some national, others international in character and inspiration. Nevertheless it must be recognized that few (if any) of the centres mentioned are engaged *exclusively* in work on a national language. See also H. Kučera and W. Nelson Francis, *Computational Analysis of Present-Day American English* (Providence, Rhode Island, 1967), and the survey by A. J. Aitken in the present volume. For Arabic, cf. R. D. Bathurst, *ibid.*; for medieval German, R. Wisbey, 'Ein computerlesbares Spracharchiv des Frühmittelhochdeutschen', *Jahrbuch für Internationale Germanistik*, I, no. 2 (1970), 37–46.

In practice, of course, it may be sounder policy to make no such suggestion, but instead to deluge the lexicographer with the cards for which he is clamouring, in the hope that he will then depart and make no further demands on the archive for at least a quarter of a century. This is only one of many essentially practical considerations: one recurring problem is to satisfy both those who wish to study a particular text in depth and those whose work depends on tracing specific elements through a succession of texts. An example of the former is the textual editor, whose requirements illuminate the fundamental dilemma facing the compiler of a lexical archive. However great his misgivings, he must rely on previous scholarship for the provision of his material, since he and his collaborators cannot become involved in editing or re-editing all the texts they propose to incorporate. For the medievalist the dilemma may resolve itself into a choice between several options, one or other of which may not be available in a particular case: the direct transcription of manuscripts, resort to conservative, near-diplomatic texts where these exist, or (thirdly) the use of critical texts. Each of these alternatives will be considered wrong by a particular class of user, while by providing adequately for the needs of one category the compiler may be reducing the range of the service he can offer to others.

The textual editor with a medieval bias may be inclined to advocate the first alternative, namely that of basing the archive directly on the manuscripts. The needs of such an editor, with his own specialist research, will be met fully only by a scrupulous analysis of scribal usage, to distinguish all the minutiae of calligraphy, abbreviation, word-division and variant orthography. But much of this detail will be irrelevant to general users of the archive and, for various reasons, may be positively misleading, particularly if the sole manuscript of a work is a late one. On the other hand dozens or even hundreds of manuscripts of a given text may be extant. The scholar preparing a new edition of such a work will have to come to terms with this fact; in doing so, moreover, he will be well advised to enlist the aid of the computer, not least because his meticulous transcriptions of the principal manuscripts will be invaluable additions to a separate, highly specialized archive of machine-readable manuscript 'facsimiles' for use above all by textual editors. But such luxuries must be firmly excluded from the general archive with which we are concerned here. The same considerations hold true for more modern studies: here too the efforts of textual critics will gradually amass for each major author a computerized archive containing transcriptions of holographs, autograph manuscripts and all significant editions, compiled in such a way as to avoid any serious loss of orthographical or bibliographical detail. Equally clearly, this material cannot all be accepted into a generalized archive.

In the case of a medieval text preserved in only a single manuscript the adoption of a semi-diplomatic edition, if available, is a rational compromise, yet it is difficult to see how resort to a critical edition can be faulted when a work is more copiously transmitted (unless it is seriously suggested that the eighty or more complete and fragmentary manuscripts of Wolfram von Eschenbach's *Parzival* should all be received *in toto* into a general computerized collection of German – even of medieval German – texts). Each such decision must be made on its merits, but for the majority of works, of whatever period, the archive will commit itself to the edition most widely favoured by scholarly research in the field concerned. At the same time, the archive should contain at least the most significant variants listed in the critical apparatus of the chosen edition. A full discussion of the difficulties inherent in this process of selection would exceed the bounds of this article; it will be evident, however, that the compiler must not fall into the trap of attempting to be all things to all men. An archive designed with the needs of textual editors or of phoneticians in mind is likely to be substantially different from one intended to provide material for an historical dictionary – and the latter will almost certainly be of greater utility to the general user, providing that his interests have been kept firmly in view from the outset. Essentially this means, within the limits described, an 'objective' transcription of each text, i.e. the determination to record all the information the edition conveys, regardless of whether the compiler himself considers particular features important or not. A single example must suffice: Early New High German printed books use a variety of orthographical conventions to indicate the mutation of certain vowels ('Umlaut'). A thoughtless decision, dictated by expediency, to replace this mutation uniformly by a single sign (as in modern German) might make these texts more legible and subtract nothing from their content; however, it would necessarily destroy evidence vital to the study of printers' dialects in the period.

The first publication required of a computer-readable archive should thus be a list (or more likely a periodic list) of sources, together with a clear statement as to the fidelity with which these sources have been transcribed. Yet to provide such a list is to do little more than tantalize the scholar unless access can be provided to the archive itself. If the material it contains has been converted at some stage into lexical cards these can of course be consulted in person by a fortunate few, although even they will probably suffer the limitations inherent in alphabetical ordering. At the same time the advent of microfilm has made feasible the duplication of a card archive; leaving aside the practical difficulties of consulting microfilms randomly, this procedure records the machine-readable archive only as frozen at a particular point in time, thus reducing it to the condition of its traditional, 'static' counterpart.

This objection applies only in part to the provision of duplicates on magnetic tape although these will not be fully useful unless programs as well as data tapes can be exchanged; experience shows that the outside user may have to surmount formidable problems of compatibility here. Even if the compiler and his sponsors can overcome their natural reluctance to hand over the product of many years' labour and of heavy expenditure, the existence of the archive (in an obsolescent form) at a number of scattered computer centres will hardly have solved the problem of universal accessibility. Certain academic users may nevertheless find that by this means use of the computerized archive has become a local university facility, with the convenient financial implications of that status. This does not alter the fact that it would be both more economic and more satisfactory for the parent archive itself to carry out any computational work based upon its holdings, however thoroughly the complexities of inter-university finance may obscure this fact.

In favourable circumstances it is already technically feasible for a user hundreds of miles from such an archive to consult it direct via a teleprinter console linked to the computer concerned, indeed a few privileged scholars already enjoy such facilities for a restricted range of operations.[1] At the moment, however, this solution fails even more markedly than those above to satisfy the criteria of being flexible, inexpensive and (thus) universally available. A more mundane but realistic course is to divide probable requests to the archive into two classes: those which cannot readily be foreseen in advance and those which can. The latter, again, can be separated into those which, although highly specific, are likely to recur (e.g. those for the complete occurrences of a group of words), and others, perhaps no less specific, which will be less frequent (e.g. the provision of word-cards with extended contexts as a basis for the preparation of an author lexicon). It is prudent to provide for the forseeable recurrent needs by publishing reference books based on the archive; these will anticipate the more obvious demands of research and will forestall a host of *ad hoc* requests.

---

[1] The Literary and Linguistic Computing Centre, University of Cambridge, possesses an 'on-line' link, which is used primarily for program development and activation; such

Such volumes will each deal intensively with a relatively homogeneous body of text (possibly confined to one work or a group of related works). Above all they must provide a key to the word material present in the chosen corpus: this is best achieved by means of a concordance which lists the complete occurrences of each word and supplies an illustrative quotation for all save possibly the most frequent (Fig. 1).[1] A simpler, but less informative type of key is the word-index, which provides location references, but not quotations. Of the two a concordance is undoubtedly the more useful aid, since the presence of a textual illustration facilitates the recognition and separation of homographs, the detection of formulaic elements and, to a limited extent, the study of syntactic patterns. With the aid of a concordance the scholar can quickly trace all the passages where a philosopher employs a specific concept or a poet a particular image. Merely to group such elements in a concordance is a creative act which renders inescapable certain insights into the linguistic preferences of an author. At the same time it adds enforced rigour to critical decisions by ensuring that inconvenient evidence is not simply overlooked, one of the most frequent means of scholarly self-deception.

The concordance, as this implies, is not an end in itself, indeed its role may be compared to that of a classified telephone directory; it should provide just enough information for the user to decide whether a particular entry is germane to his interests or not. The adequacy of the mechanically delimited quotations supplied must be judged in the same light: they are not intended to replace the text, but merely to guide the reader to it without too high a proportion of false starts. Here again the compiler faces a practical decision, namely whether the scholarly community will be best served by a large number of 'austerity' concordances which require the reader to search for the occurrences of a verb under its conjugated forms and to delve among the quotations given under ROOT for any mathematical references concealed among other usages of the noun and the verb; or whether to classify the concordance fully according to the best principles of

facilities are now becoming increasingly common, see the references in this volume, *passim*, particularly in the contribution by A. Jones.

[1] The Figures are all drawn from reference works in preparation by various scholars at the Literary and Linguistic Computing Centre, Cambridge. See also the following volumes already published by the present writer: *Vollständige Verskonkordanz zur 'Wiener Genesis', mit einem rückläufigen Wörterbuch zum Formenbestand* (Berlin, 1967); *A Complete Concordance to the Vorau and Strassburg 'Alexander'* (Leeds, 1968 = COMPENDIA, 1); *A Complete Word-Index to the 'Speculum Ecclesiae'* (*Early Middle High German and Latin*) (Leeds, 1968 = COMPENDIA, 2); *A Complete Concordance to the 'Rolandslied'* (*Heidelberg Manuscript*) (Leeds, 1969 = COMPENDIA, 3).

TROWEN   (1)

F6, 1 ich entgilte mîner trowen:

TRÛBE   (1)

1075 trûbe von weinen,

TRÛCH   (1)

F7, 7 und trûch sî verholnlîche

TRUCHSATZE   (1)

F3, 33 Der truchsatze manete

TRUCHSÊZE   (1)

1733 sprach der truchsêze

TRÛG (16)

318 der scuzzele he doch nicht en
       trûg,

893 daz her ein gût swert trûg.

1077 ûz der stad in daz hûs trûg.

1661 daz he an sîner hant trûg:

2971 und trûg sie verholenlîche

3530 der mâne trûg den schaten dare

4165 die her an sîme herzin trûg.

4520 sîme hêren ze samene trûg,

7569 die sie zu iren vrûnden trûg!

7577 des trûg sie jâmers vil,

7701 daz sie daz hêrîn hemede trûg:

7900 die sluzzele he ((dâ)) selbir
        trûg.

8621 trûg dannen vor tôd.

8722 he trûg einen kolben grôz

8789 sînen kolben he gar hôhe trûg,

8998 sînen kolbin trûg er hô

TRÛGE (2)

1097 und trûge in in ein schiffelîn:

7323 daz hêrîn hemede trûge;

TRÛGEN (5)

856 die ros sie zu samen trûgen,

1133 dô sie in trûgen an den sê.

2084 des trûgen wêrlîche

5875 die scharfe swert trûgen

8233 trûgen die garzûne.

TRUGENE   (1)

2838 dez was die meiste trugene

TRUGENÊRE   (1)

8946 daz der trugenêre

FIGURE I. Specimen from a concordance (ed. R. A. Wisbey) to Eilhart's *Tristrant*

manual compilation. Clearly the latter course is preferable, although there are more objections to it than are immediately apparent;[1] this situation may be reduced to a simple equation in which, given the finite resources of the compiler, the effort added to one side by way of grammatical classification is subtracted from the other in the form of delay or of a reduction in the number of aids published. Moreover, those whose ideas on the subject have been formed solely by acquaintance with manual compilation may overlook the highly relevant fact that any re-ordering of the 'raw' alphabetical material according to grammatical criteria will have at some stage to be converted into instructions for the computer. Without this, the final manuscript of the reference work could not be printed automatically, a crucial disadvantage, since conventional typesetting would introduce error as well as being prohibitively expensive. The development of automatic parsing programs is of course a possibility the compiler will consider, more especially if his chosen corpus is both very large and relatively homogeneous: the effort is clearly worth-while when an archive consists of materials in a major contemporary language employing a standardized orthography. But here and elsewhere the theoretical possibilities have to be weighed against the resources available.

Frequency counts, on the other hand, can be provided without undue difficulty and there is no reason why they should not be a standard feature in publications from a computerized archive. The frequency of occurrence should be given for each entry in a concordance (see Fig. 1); when dealing with a lengthy modern text, perhaps a novel, it may even be advisable to publish a frequency count alone, without accompanying quotation and location references, for extremely frequent items like the definite article. The scholar who is studying the author's use of such a word is best advised to work from the text itself: to provide a quotation for each occurrence of *the* in our concordance would be virtually to reprint the edition in any case. It must be stressed, however, that the exclusion of such a word (as a headword) from the published concordance, save in the form of a frequency count, does not mean its exclusion from the archive, as with its manually compiled equivalent. Indeed, it will appear quite normally in the contexts provided for less frequent words in our concordance; equally it is available for retrieval by computer at any time, e.g. if a scholar wishes to study its use in combination with other vocabulary items. Counts of *all* words must be

---

[1] The semantic, and even grammatical ambiguity of many older linguistic forms, for instance, is such that to parse them is tantamount to providing a detailed commentary on the text concerned. Any error of interpretation may lead to an important occurrence of a word being 'lost' under an inappropriate headword.

1.	DAZ	790	4.932	790	4.932
2.	ER	657	4.101	1447	9.033
3.	DER	492	3.071	1939	12.104
4.	VNT	385	2.403	2324	14.508
5.	DIE	282	1.760	2606	16.268
6.	SI	250	1.561	2856	17.829
7.	DEN	226	1.411	3082	19.240
8.	DO	225	1.405	3307	20.644
9.	ÎN	221	1.380	3528	22.024
10.	DA	181	1.130	3709	23.154
11.	DEM	180	1.124	3889	24.277
12.	VON	171	1.067	4060	25.345
13.	EZ	161	1.005	4221	26.350
14.	ÎM	155	0.968	4376	27.318
15.	SO	151	0.943	4527	28.260
16.	NICHT	140	0.874	4667	29.134
17.	MÎT	135	0.843	4802	29.977
18.	DES	134	0.837	4936	30.813
19.	AN	133	0.830	5069	31.644
20.	VIL	128	0.799	5197	32.443
21.	WAS	126	0.787	5323	33.229
22.	SEÎN	120	0.749	5443	33.978
23.	ZE	107	0.668	5550	34.646
24.	GOT	105	0.655	5655	35.302
25.	DÎV	98	0.612	5753	35.914
26.	SICH	95	0.593	5848	36.507
27.	EÎN	93	0.581	5941	37.087
28.	DAR	92	0.574	6033	37.662
29.	IST	86	0.537	6119	38.198
30.	DIV	85	0.531	6204	38.729
31.	WOL	84	0.524	6288	39.253
32.	OUCH	83	0.518	6371	39.772
32.	VNS	83	0.518	6454	40.290
34.	MAN	78	0.487	6532	40.777
35.	ÎR	77	0.481	6609	41.257
36.	WAN	73	0.456	6682	41.713
37.	ALS	70	0.437	6752	42.150
37.	WÎR	70	0.437	6822	42.587
39.	ICH	69	0.431	6891	43.018
40.	SPRACH	67	0.418	6958	43.436
41.	WAERE	65	0.406	7023	43.842
42.	GOTES	63	0.393	7086	44.235
43.	HET	62	0.387	7148	44.622
44.	WIE	59	0.368	7207	44.990
45.	IN	54	0.337	7261	45.327
46.	IR	53	0.331	7314	45.658
47.	WART	50	0.312	7364	45.970
48.	ALLE	45	0.281	7409	46.251
48.	DURCH	45	0.281	7454	46.532
48.	OB	45	0.281	7499	46.813
48.	WOLDE	45	0.281	7544	47.094
52.	GVTE	43	0.268	7587	47.363

FIGURE 2. Specimen from a ranking list (ed. B. O. Murdoch) to the *Anegenge*

provided, for it is often precisely the items of high frequency on which statistical studies of style choose to concentrate. Such work can be facilitated by the provision of a ranking list (Fig. 2) which prints an author's vocabulary in descending order of frequency: it may also conveniently indicate the percentage contribution of each item to the whole text, and provide a cumulative sum of all the elements preceding it in the list. This latter figure will, for instance, tell the compiler at a glance what saving of space will result if he restricts himself to frequency counts for the ten most frequent items in a text. In practice these ten may amount to 20% of the whole. A small band of these very frequent word-forms will be followed by a larger section revealing the predilections of the author as well as the contours of his subject matter. Such lists constitute raw material for use in word distribution and authorship attribution studies, in the editing of texts and even in the design of language courses.[1]

We have been concerned here with frequency analyses for complete texts so that we can safely ignore the thorny problems posed by the application of sampling techniques, as in compiling a frequency dictionary.[2] Some difficulties are inherent in any frequency list, however, since the compiler cannot avoid deciding *inter alia* whether all the different conjugated forms of a verb are to be listed under the infinitive and treated as a single item and whether the singular and plural of nouns are to be counted together. Such amalgamations presuppose that a complete parsing of the text has been carried out; moreover they may obscure interesting insights, like the penchant of a particular author for the present participle. Under the circumstances the provision of raw lists based on the orthographical forms occurring in a specific corpus has much to recommend it: the user can then make what correlations he wishes according to any consistent procedure, without straining his mathematics beyond the processes of addition and subtraction, and with the certainty that his figures will permit valid comparisons between one text and another.

Many requests to the archive will be obviated by consistently providing reverse indexes of word forms, i.e. indexes in which the scheme of alphabetization operates from right to left instead of from left to right, so that *zebra* will precede *cobra* (Fig. 3). The reverse index is a relatively un-

---

[1] See the section 'Vocabulary Studies and Language Learning' in this volume.

[2] Despite the careful theoretical study of these problems which prefaces A. Juilland's *Frequency Dictionary of Spanish Words* (The Hague, 1964) the work itself is open to numerous objections; the methods used may be compared with those employed by H. Kučera and W. Nelson Francis for modern American English (note 1, p. 21, above), by Sture Allén for contemporary Swedish (*Les Machines dans la Linguistique*, pp. 78–81), and by R. D. Bathurst for Arabic (in the present volume).

BEMERCKEN	GEBROKEN	TOONEELEN
GEHEIMNISMERCKEN	INGEBROKEN	SPEELEN
PERCKEN	UITGESPROKEN	TAFEREELEN
STARREPERCKEN	ONGEWROKEN	STREELEN
STERCKEN	VONCKSKEN	TEELEN
WERCKEN	GETALEN	KASTEELEN
BEWERCKEN	VEREEDLEN	VOORTTEELEN
MEDEWERCKEN	KABAELEN	VEELEN
ZEDEWERCKEN	DAELEN	BEVEELEN
WONDERWERCKEN	SCHANDAELEN	TAFELEN
UITWERCKEN	NEDERDAELEN	SNUFFELEN
ZERCKEN	FAELEN	DOORSNUFFELEN
JEUCKEN	NACHTEGAELEN	TWIJFELEN
KREUCKEN	HAELEN	NAGELEN
SPREUCKEN	OPHAELEN	SPIEGELEN
BYBELSPREUCKEN	HERHAELEN	BESPIEGELEN
WONDERSPREUCKEN	ACHTERHAELEN	REGELEN
PLUCKEN	MAELEN	BEZEGELEN
RUCKEN	PAELEN	ENGELEN
DRUCKEN	BEPAELEN	VLEUGELEN
ONDERDRUCKEN	AMIRAELEN	TEUGELEN
VERDRUCKEN	PRAELEN	BEHIELEN
UITDRUCKEN	STRAELEN	.KIELEN
KRUCKEN	BESTRAELEN	NEDERKNIELEN
VERRUCKEN	LETTERSTRAELEN	VERNIELEN
ONTRUCKEN	TAELEN	VERVIELEN
STUCKEN	METAELEN	ZIELEN
SCHELLEMSTUCKEN	DWAELEN	ORAKELEN
HONDEKEN	VERDWAELEN	EECKELEN
STEEKEN	ZAELEN	WANCKELEN
GEBLEKEN	MIDDELEN	ENCKELEN
GELEKEN	WINDELEN	SPRENGKELEN
BOEKEN	DEELEN	KRINGKELEN
GEBREKEN	TEGENDEELEN	STAMELEN
BEREKEN	VERDEELEN	HEMELEN
TREKEN	HEELEN	WEMELEN
TEKEN	SCHEELEN	KRIOELEN
KENTEKEN	VERSCHEELEN	KOELEN
VOORTEKEN	GEHEELEN	MODDERPOELEN
TEIKEN	KEELEN	STOELEN
WONDERTEIKEN	KRACKEELEN	VOELEN
WIJKEN	BEKRACKEELEN	GEVOELEN
GETROKKEN	SCHOOLKRACKEELEN	WOELEN
GEDOKEN	KRAECKEELEN	STAPELEN
BEWIEROOKEN	PANNEELEN	MOMPELEN

FIGURE 3. Specimen from a reverse index (ed. P. King) to Vondel's *Bespiegelingen van Godt en Godtsdienst*

```
TOHTER    (1)    228 suester

SUESTER   (1)    227 tohter

UINSTER   (1)    2276 winster

WINSTER   (1)    2275 uinster

IR  (2)   1699 mir 2416 mir

DIR  (14)    535 mir   567 mir   649 mir
             721 dir   722 dir   757 mir   853 mir
             860 mir   880 mir   965 mir   972 mir
            1465 mir  1635 mir  2132 mir

MIR  (15)    536 dir   568 dir   650 dir
             758 dir   854 dir   859 dir   879 dir
             966 dir   971 dir  1466 dir  1636 dir
            1700 ir   2131 dir  2415 ir   3003 ire

SCÛR · (2)    1884 gemischtiu 2188 uiur

UIUR  (1)    2187 scûr

GRAS  (2)    1891 wás 2199 was

WAS  (12)    209 was   210 was   233 gesach
            1375 besaz 1584 destebaz 1858 daz
            1892 gras 1897 ulahs 2200 gras 2662 daz
            2675 gesach 3247 daz

NEWAS  (1)    187 sach

JÂCOBES  (2)    500 chunnes   728 chunnes

DES  (7)    117 Ramasses 1147 ellendes
           1512 landes 1749 Zambres 2215 Moyses
           2355 Moyses 2401 uehes

LANDES  (1)    1511 des

ELLENDES  (1)    1148 des

CHUNIGES  (1)    2660 lebenes

ISAÂCHES  (2)    497 Abrahâmes
            725 Abrahâmes

UEHES  (1)    2402 des

ABRAHÂMES  (2)    498 Isaâches
            726 Isaâches
```

FIGURE 4. Specimen from a rhyme index (ed. R. A. Wisbey) to the *Millstätter Exodus*

familiar but extremely versatile aid. It groups together compounds with the same terminal element (*relay*, *mislay*, *outlay*), collects all words featuring the same suffix, unites all instances of the present participle in English, and shows a textual editor at a glance the possibilities for completing a word of which only the final letters have been preserved. Less obviously, it makes the grammatical reorganization of a concordance a less urgent task, since it brings together related but alphabetically separated words like *honour/ dishonour, enquire/inquire*. In fact reverse alphabetization is so helpful a device in assembling material for research into morphology and word formation that for this reason alone it is difficult to understand why philologists in many disciplines have been so slow to recognize its value. Every dictionary, for instance, should include an appendix listing its headwords in reverse alphabetical order. Apart from the applications already discussed, and popular ones like the solution of crossword puzzles, this would again be of value in language teaching: thus the appendix to an English dictionary, in grouping all words ending in *-ough*, would facilitate systematic comment on their pronunciation.

The reverse index to works from the archive may be supplemented by an index of rhymes where relevant (Fig. 4). This can be compiled automatically by computer if a regular rhyming scheme (or a specifiable alternation of rhyming schemes) is employed, or with the help of an initial manual classification if it is not. The headwords of the rhyme index should be arranged reverse alphabetically, for this brings them into rhyming order, while each entry is followed by all the words with which it rhymes, together with location references and a frequency count. By this means one secures raw material for the study of an author's rhyming habits – and with a medieval author these may provide the only firm basis for establishing the phonology and morphology of his poetic language in general.

It will be apparent that none of the aids mentioned so far, concordances, frequency counts, reverse indexes and rhyme indexes, should be viewed in isolation: used in conjunction with each other they constitute a powerful instrument for the study of a single text, or of trends within a whole genre or epoch. Taking as our starting point the casual observation that a specific author has a strong predilection for abstract nouns we might first consult the ranking list of frequencies for rapid confirmation that there is substance in our general impression. By scanning the reverse index we can then obtain a complete list of all the abstracts used by the author, conveniently arranged in groups according to suffix. The concordance is then used to establish the whereabouts, frequency and textual environment of each relevant form. Following this, the rhyme index (if applicable) will allow conclusions as to the frequency of abstract nouns in the rhyming position and the extent of their use as rhymes to other abstracts. All these findings may then be compared with those for other authors, genres or epochs; it will be relatively easy to calculate the percentage contribution of abstracts (or of any subset) to the work as a whole, since a total word-count for the text will accompany the ranking list. In practice, use of the reference work will of course not be as linear as this example may suggests, but the method will be plain.

How much further is it reasonable to go in extending the range of the reference works we have described? If the metre of a text obeys exactly specifiable rules, or if the metrical units have been labelled manually, the computer can effect an automatic metrical analysis,[1] the findings of which will open up a further dimension of study. Grammatical analyses can also be carried out if the basic elements of the text have been identified by special parsing programs or by way of pre- or post-editing. It will then be possible to print lists of nouns, adjectives, adverbs, conjunctions, or of any combination of these. In its turn, this facility may have implications for the arrangement of the concordance (see above). *Mutatis mutandis* the occurrences of phonemes, morphemes or certain syntactic structures can be listed and analysed. There are many areas of study, like that of syntax, where we shall encounter marked divisions of opinion as to what matter is of sufficient generality to merit publication: analysts of style might think it desirable, for instance, to state the mean sentence-length of a work, or to list those words with a given number of letters; more significant, however, may be the sequence of sentences of varying length, or the sequence of words of varying length in a sentence. Yet will most users of the volume look with favour on the desolate strings of numbers which would convey this information? Special indexes could be compiled to cope with the problem of multisyllabic words: these could group items containing internal letter matches, ignoring initial and final elements which have been provided for already. This method would bring together *woe**be**gone* and *un**be**known*, but also, in the absence of sophisticated safeguards, *rever-**be**rate*, *de**be**nture* and *lum**be**ring*. The textual editor or bibliographer may wish to know exactly where a specific diacritic or ligature occurs in a text, but will this knowledge be of sufficiently general interest to warrant publication; or is this not one of those cases where the computer should be called on to ransack the archive in discreet anonymity?

---

[1] For a stimulating recent example, cf. W. Ott, *Metrische Analysen zur 'Ars Poetica' des Horaz*, Göppinger Akademische Beiträge, 6 (Göppingen, 1970).

Fortunately one's publisher may be relied upon to inject an element of realism into this debate, unless of course one has decided that books are in any case outmoded and that an archive's contact with the outside world is best maintained by use of reference material on microfilm or microfiches. My own attitude to microfilms, in this role, is tinged, however heretically, by the belief that the best insights may come when, remote from all mechanical or optical paraphernalia, one is pursuing an intuition, aided by all the resources of printed and bound reference works. As a cheap, handy, portable, reliable and essentially democratic random access device the printed book still has no rival. For its author, moreover, there is one other relevant consideration: that of public recognition for his labours. But who knows – the day may not be too far distant when a scholar can expect an enthusiastic reception for the statement: 'I have also published 2,000 feet of microfilm' or when, opening the *Times Literary Supplement*, I may read: 'With this brilliant microfiche, Professor W***** has once more . . .!'

The production of concordances from diplomatic transcriptions of Early Medieval German manuscripts: some comments

BRIAN O. MURDOCH*

R. A. Wisbey has described as one of the aims of the Literary and Linguistic Computing Centre of the University of Cambridge 'the creation, on computer magnetic tape, of an archive including all the principal German texts written between the mid-eleventh and the late twelfth centuries'.[1] He has stressed too the value – overlooked by some recent scholars – of this 'seminal period' in vocabulary studies in medieval German, and indeed, interest in Early Middle High German literature has in recent years been concerned with thematic studies as much as with specifically philological problems.[2] This interest – and it is linked, one presumes, with the fact that scholarly editions of much of the material are now becoming readily available – makes the need for lexicographical aids to the study of the period the greater. Publications from the archive consist, broadly speaking, of concordances (for the poetic monuments) and word-indexes (for the prose texts).[3] Production of these is well under way, having commenced with

---

* German Department, University of Illinois at Chicago Circle.

[1] R. A. Wisbey, *A Complete Word-Index to the 'Speculum Ecclesiae'* (Leeds, 1968), p. vii. That an *archive* of the entire corpus of EMGH is planned appears to have been overlooked by reviewers such as J. W. Marchand, who in a review of the concordance to the *Speculum* wonders about the wisdom of choosing for treatment a relatively little known text: *Journal of English and Germanic Philology*, LXIX (1970), 128. For the philologist, of course, the prose *Speculum Ecclesiae* might well be of as much or greater value than the poetic monuments.

[2] See Wisbey, 'The Analysis of Middle High German Texts by Computer – Some Lexicographical Aspects', *Transactions of the Philological Society 1963* (Oxford, 1964), p. 28. Recent thematic studies in the period include for example X. von Ertzdorff, 'Das "Herz" in der lateinisch-theologischen und frühen volkssprachigen religiösen Literatur', *Beiträge zur Geschichte der deutschen Sprache und Literatur* (Halle), LXXXIV (1962), 249–301; D. Wells, *The Vorau 'Moses' and 'Balaam': A Study of their Relationship to Exegetical Tradition*, MHRA Dissertation Series, 2 (Cambridge, 1970); B. O. Murdoch, 'The Fall of Man in the Early Middle High German Biblical Epic' (diss., Cambridge, 1968).

[3] See Wisbey, 'Analysis', pp. 30–48. An attractive compromise is the concordance-cum-index which provides an illustrative quotation only for words of relatively low frequency. For some further possibilities in work of this nature, see Ilpo Tapani Piirainen, 'Glossarherstellung mit Hilfe des Computers', *Neuphilologische Mitteilungen*, LXIX (1968), 677–84.

Wisbey's own concordance to the *Wiener Genesis*, and continued with his COMPENDIA series, a number of volumes of which are either in print or projected.[1]

Wisbey has himself described some of the problems that he had to face in the production of the earlier concordances.[2] Several of the more technical limitations involved have since been overcome, thanks, for example, to improved keypunch facilities, an important consideration when rendering a language with a fairly wide range of diacritics. The COMPENDIA volumes, moreover, are produced by an offset-lithographic process from computer-generated typescript, and it is thus essential to obtain hard copy of high quality. Fresh problems, or intensified forms of problems already encountered are, however, continually arising, and it is with some of these that the present paper is concerned. More specifically it is a working report on the measures necessary when the text taken as a basis for a concordance or a word-index is a diplomatic transcription of a manuscript, rather than an edition prepared by a scholar as a critical text. In the cases I shall describe, only one manuscript of each work is extant – the most common state of affairs in this period. While this makes things more difficult for the critical editor, it simplifies matters if one is concerned with concordance production: further complexities arise, of course, when *varia* from several different manuscripts have to be taken into account.[3]

The advantage of taking as a basis the manuscript form of a text is clearly that this is of greater validity than a version printed in an often tacitly 'normalized' language – in this case the Middle High German 'static literary esperanto' which may so easily be thought to represent 'the phonological system of the text itself rather than an editorial convenience'.[4] Every emendation, however small, is potentially one stage further away

---

[1] Roy Wisbey, *Vollständige Verskonkordanz zur 'Wiener Genesis'* (Berlin, 1967). The COMPENDIA series contains concordances or word-indexes by Wisbey to the Vorau and Strassburg *Alexander* (Leeds, 1968 = vol. I), to the *Speculum Ecclesiae* (Leeds, 1968 = vol. II), and to the *Rolandslied* (Leeds, 1969 = vol. III).

[2] 'Analysis', *passim*. See also the comments in Wisbey's own paper in the present volume: 'Publications from an Archive of Computer-Readable Literary Texts'.

[3] See R. Wisbey, 'Concordance Making by Electronic Computer: Some Experiences with the *Wiener Genesis*', *Modern Language Review*, LVII (1962), 170.

[4] See (although his comments refer to a later period) P. F. Ganz, 'On the Text of *Meier Helmbrecht*', *Oxford German Studies*, II (Oxford, 1967), 40. A nice illustration of the questions at issue is provided in the recent edition of the Cambridge 'Yiddish' codex, which is written in Hebrew characters in a language close to Middle High German. A 'normalized' version of this text – and this has been attempted – would be, as the recent editor points out, tantamount to a 'translation into Middle High German'. See Heikki J. Hakkarainen, *Studien zum Cambridger Codex T.S. 10. K. 22* (Turku, 1967), p. 25.

from the authentic medieval form. It would seem desirable to preserve in
the concordance or word-index an inconsistent and unfamiliar orthography
rather than to work from an even slightly emended form.[1] I propose to
describe here my own experiences with two such pieces of work. The first
is a concordance, now in its final stages, to the Early Middle High German
Anegenge, a poem of the late twelfth century dealing with the Fall and the
Redemption. The second is a rather more problematical and long-term
project involving the production of word-indexes to some eleventh- and
twelfth-century German sermons.

The basic point, then, about working from a manuscript text in transcription is that the language will not be as familiar as 'normalized' Middle
High German. In addition to this, however, the manuscripts are, at this
early period, frequently corrupt. Orthography and word-division may be
inconsistent or confused. The manuscript may be damaged physically,
leaving *lacunae* and incomplete words. Haplography and dittography may
have given rise to problematical readings. The diplomatic transcription
requires a great amount of preparation – of pre-editing – from the scholar
before it is ready for the computer. Such is the nature of this work that
even with the hoped-for developments in the use of optical scanners –
and there are varying degrees of optimism on this score[2] – quite extensive correction tapes would still be necessary for the text before it could
be treated.

The major consideration is to keep as close to the printed diplomatic as
possible. It is not always easy for the scholar to keep separate in his mind
the quite different processes of scholarly editing and pre-editing for the
computer, but the urge to make sometimes quite obvious emendations has
to be resisted if any degree of consistency is to be achieved. Even so, it is
impossible to be entirely consistent. Much depends, of course, on the
printed version of the transcription available to the scholar. For the
Anegenge, the task is made easier by the recent appearance of an edition by
Dietrich Neuschäfer, which prints a painstaking diplomatic transcription
synoptically with a critical text.[3]

It is impossible to take the manuscript itself as a basis when the aim is a
work for publication. Even where a published facsimile exists it would be

---

[1] For some interesting comments on this point, see the review of the first three COMPENDIA
volumes in the *Times Literary Supplement* of 26 March 1970, p. 344.

[2] See R. S. Morgan, 'Optical Readers', *Computers and the Humanities*, III (1968/9), 61–4
and David Paisey, 'British Germanists and the Computer', *German Life and Letters*, XXII
(1968/9), 155–63, as well as a number of other papers in the present symposium.

[3] Dietrich Neuschäfer, '*Das Anegenge*'. *Textkritische Studien. Diplomatischer Abdruck.
Kritische Ausgabe. Anmerkungen zum Text* (Munich, 1966).

extremely difficult to set up a workable system of reference. As regards purely scribal features, the ultimate value of listing these has so far not seemed to justify the attendant difficulties. The *Anegenge* is written in a fairly uniform single hand, and considerations of this sort do not arise with this work. A computer analysis of scribal variations might be of use in other medieval German texts, however, such as the Old High German Tatian-translation.[1]

Certain problems that arise are of a purely mechanical nature, and some of them are encountered also in the treatment of critical texts. The manuscript in which the *Anegenge* is found (Wiener Sammelhandschrift 2692) has, for example, capitals of double-line depth. It was an easy decision to ignore these for the purpose of the concordance and to treat them as regular upper case letters, as they may readily be picked out in the printed text. These capitals are furthermore preceded in the manuscript by small raised guide-letters placed by the scribe for the benefit of the rubricator. These too could be omitted, as they have little value for the concordance, would make for unnecessary complication, and may be identified from the text with ease. Other problems with the *Anegenge* could be treated according to already established precedents: the resolution of the digraph *æ* into *a + e*, the replacement of *ſ* with *s*. There were no difficulties with diacritics, beyond an idiosyncratic use of a double diacritic (*î̭* or *i̭̭*), and for this the *ad hoc* decision was made to render them consistently as *î*. The existing keyboards could not cope with the double superscript, and the solution is a philologically acceptable one. Cases were few enough for them to be listed in an introduction.

The bulk of pre-editing was concerned, for the *Anegenge*, with the division and joining of words, a point in which the manuscript is particularly haphazard. With Neuschäfer's text to hand, it was convenient to compare the diplomatic with the critical version, and indeed, Neuschäfer's decisions regarding word-division were very often followed. That there were exceptions to this, however, demonstrates that it is not possible to exclude scholarly intervention with complete consistency. There are of course cases where some adaptation of the manuscript is necessary. As far as word-division is concerned, cases occur in the *Anegenge* where, for example, a preposition and a following article have been run together: *Anegenge* 81 *Inder helle = In der helle*. *Ze* is frequently joined to the following word, and it was decided to separate this throughout. Here, however, the result was in

---

[1] Wisbey has commented on this point in the introduction (p. viii) to his word-index of the *Speculum Ecclesiae*.

one case slightly odd: *Anegenge* 166 *zdem* (as against the expected *zedem*) = *z dem*. *Ze* in this case appears in the concordance simply as *z*, but although the researcher looking for *ze* would find and recognize the contracted form, the seeker after *dem* might not look under *zdem*. It must be conceded at this point that the provision of a reverse index of word forms, such as that used in Wisbey's concordance to the *Wiener Genesis*, and later in the COM-PENDIA series, would enable the user to find the word easily. But since these cases are unlikely to occur too frequently, a certain consistency may be preserved without undue difficulty, and things are made slightly easier for the user, who can find the words he wants in the concordance proper.

There are also cases where joining is necessary. Thus *Anegenge* 170 *unrech tes tûn* = *unrechtes tûn*. The appearance in this case of *unrech* alone would be nonsense, that of *tes* alone, confusing, as it might just be an unusual form of the definite article. Prefixes and enclitics, such as the *ge-* of the past participle, or the negative *en-* may be added to the appropriate word to give a consistent pattern, and some pre-editing of this type is needed even with verbal and nominal compounds. This, it is to be hoped, might at least prevent the repetition of a notorious nineteenth-century misreading of a passage of the *Anegenge*. *Anegenge* 906 *sam die zwelf poten taten* contains what is in fact the nominal compound *zwelfpoten*, 'dis-ciples'; it was misread as containing the compound *potentaten*, 'potentates', by a critic who did not, presumably, recognize *taten* as a verb. He confesses with regret his inability to find a source for the introduction of twelve potentates into the New Testament narrative![1]

Provided the conventions adopted are made plain in an introduction, any decisions made on matters of this sort should lead to a greater facility in the use of the concordance. The scholar preparing the text for the computer must, however, be on his guard against emendations which would mean changes to the diplomatic text other than simple joining or division. Thus in line 2725 of the *Anegenge* we find *hintern list*, which the critical editor rightly emends to *hinderlist*. Merely to join the two elements would give a form **hinternlist*, which would not be acceptable philologically, and so the elements must be left as they stand. The same must apply even with mani-festly corrupt passages (and indeed a consistent policy of pre-editorial word-division can sometimes bring these to light)[2] even when this again

---

[1] V. Teuber, 'Über die vom Dichter des *Anegenge* benutzten Quellen', *Beiträge*, XXIV (1899), 280. This was, of course, recognized by later research: A. Leitzmann, 'Zum *Anegenge*', *Zeitschrift für deutsches Altertum*, LXXVII (1940), 104.

[2] Thus in the *Anegenge* 1928 we have *ern thielt*: the first element looks like the negative *-n* combined with the pronoun *er*. But this is rather a case of the prefix *ent-*, and the

results in some rather odd entries in the final concordance. Thus *Anegenge* 3176 *nu hôre die ir sch* yields the entry *sch* in the concordance.[1]

The existence of a diplomatic transcription as good as that by Neuschäfer as a readily accessible and highly suitable base is a fortunate chance. The scholar is less well-off, however, where the sermon-literature of the Early Middle High German period is concerned. In spite of its somewhat esoteric air, this material is of enormous importance to the linguistic evaluation of the period, as it provides a body of prose in the vernacular, at a time when many of the extant monuments are in verse. For grammatical and syntactical studies this is, of course, of great relevance.[2] As a repository of popular theology in the 'age of belief' the sermons are of equal value as cultural documents. But apart from the researcher dealing with the sermons in their own right, the scholar whose concern is with, say, a thematic study in the period, might be forgiven if he finds the great majority of these works rather soporific. Concordances and word-indexes are therefore of great value in a situation of this sort. There are, however, few modern editions of these texts; the conservative, but nevertheless text-critical edition of the *Speculum Ecclesiæ* is a rare exception.[3] Most scholarly work on the sermons was done during the nineteenth century, and while there are good editions to be found here, too (A. E. Schönbach's *Altdeutsche Predigten*, I–III (Graz, 1886–91) – on tape at the Cambridge Centre – is a good example), many texts are found only in imperfect diplomatic versions without commentary or critical text, in rare editions or in nineteenth-century issues of periodicals. In point of fact, one suspects that a little research among German manuscript collections would bring to light rather more material than is known at present. The first difficulty, then, for the would-be compiler of a word-index to these texts is the availability of materials.[4] A number of editions are, it is true, being reprinted by the Deutsche Wissenschaftliche Buchgesellschaft in Darmstadt,

---

words must be divided as *er nthielt*, in spite of the 'beheaded' entry *nthielt* in the concordance. The appendix of critical *varia* will, of course, direct the user to Neuschäfer's correct emendation to *enthielt*.

[1] I understand that it may be possible to use the computer to assist in the solution of passages like this, which involve broken words. The critical editor's task would, for instance, be made easier by the automatic supplying of all feasible endings.

[2] For comments on this point, see Märta Åsdahl Holmberg, *Exzipierend-einschränkende Ausdrucksweisen* (Uppsala, 1967), p. 7.

[3] '*Speculum Ecclesiæ*: *Eine frühmittelhochdeutsche Predigtsammlung*, ed. Gert Mellbourn (Lund/Copenhagen, 1944). This is the basis of the COMPENDIA word-index.

[4] J. Leighton, in this volume ('Sonnets and Computers'), mentions similar difficulties of material collection. The problem is heightened when one is concerned with a word-index designed for publication rather than with a stylistic analysis in which the results are the important factor.

or by reprint companies, but others remain difficult of access outside the larger libraries. The problem is the greater with texts that appeared in the first instance in periodicals, especially as these may be rare in their own right. A major collection, for example, is found only in volume VIII of F. J. Mone's *Anzeiger für Kunde der teutschen Vorzeit*, which appeared in 1839; apart from the British Museum, the Cambridge University Library and the Bodleian there can be few university libraries in Great Britain which can provide this text. A large number of sermon fragments from the eleventh and twelfth centuries are, moreover, scattered over a number of different journals. The problems, then, are not only of availability, but also of reference. With single-volume texts there seems to be little alternative but to use the existing edition *nolens volens*, hoping that the user will have access to a copy. For the collections in periodicals, however, some other solution seems necessary. An obvious answer is the large-scale re-editing of the material. But this would be an enormous, and somewhat daunting task. It might well mean considerable delay in satisfying the requirements of scholars concerned with linguistic or thematic questions relating to the entire Early Middle High German period. Ironically, too, it is precisely this work of re-editing that could best be done *after* the appearance of a number of word-indexes has simplified comparison between different texts. A possible answer lies in the reprinting of the relevant periodical articles (most of which are well out of copyright) followed by the word-index in its printed form. This would ensure that the texts are available, and an internal reference system could then be set up.

With the sermons, the problems of pre-editing encountered with the *Anegenge* are intensified. Several questions, such as those of word-division remain the same, but the sermons have frequently survived in a very fragmentary form. A single example (from an admittedly extreme case) should suffice to illustrate the point:

> ungeuuissa
> uissa peha
> nda riuuesa
> tiger.   zi diu so
> mest ze dere
> urteila.   daz tu
> end& neuuer
> r daz tu. . . .[1]

---

[1] J. Keinz, 'Althochdeutsche Bruchstücke', *Sitzungsberichte der . . . Akademie der Wissenschaften*, phil.-hist. Kl., 1 (Munich, 1869), p. 542. The fragment is in fact probably of the eleventh century. Of the twenty potential concordance or word-index entries in the

Apart from the resolution of abbreviations such as the ampersand ($= et$) there is little one can do in these cases except to take the text as it stands. Any emendation is in any event likely to be highly conjectural in a fragment of this sort.

The problem of abbreviations is a major one. The medieval scribe abbreviated frequently, and this is true especially of Latin and even vernacular biblical quotations in the sermons. The poetical monuments are relatively free of this problem: the *Anegenge* has a few simple abbreviations which Neuschäfer resolves quite adequately, and his readings could be taken over with little more than a general reference to the fact in the introduction. As far as the sermons are concerned, though, the problem is best brought home with another illustration:

daz er ſine gnade uon eu niht ker. Alſo dˢ | *wiſſage giſpro*hcin hat. Abſcondā faciē meā ab eiſ ꞇ ō ſu . . | .o. . . ſubt . . . anciā g̊cie mee ꞇ aparruit atꝗ exitū opaeoꝓ p̣ | ducet.[1]

Once again the case is an extreme one. But on more frequent occasions a biblical verse will be rendered by a list of letters alone:

Er spricht ovch anders wo.   ecce ego sto ad host. et pul. siquis aper. mi. in t. ade. et ce. se. et ip. m.[2]

In these cases, the verse must be identified by the time-consuming process of selecting a recognizable word and then referring to the various occurrences of it in Dutripon's concordance to the Vulgate until the correct verse is found. The verses involved are frequently easily identifiable. Frequently again they are not. An added problem is that they do not always coincide with the Vulgate exactly, and this too the pre-editor must face, even if this might more properly be considered the work of the critical editor.[3] Once

fragment, thirteen may be picked out on sight as possible full words, although without reference to the manuscript itself this cannot be checked.

[1] J. M. Wagner, 'Predigtentwürfe', *Zeitschrift für deutsches Altertum*, xv (1872), 441. Wagner's notes resolve the passage as Deuteronomy 32. 20. This may be correct, but it does not cover the entire reference. Moreover, notes of this kind are the exception rather than the rule. It is apparent from the italicised portion that the transcription has been edited to some extent, for the German at least.

[2] *Deutsche Predigten des 13. und 14. Jahrhunderts*, ed. Hermann Leyser (Quedlinburg/Leipzig, 1838 and Darmstadt, Wissenschaftliche Buchgesellschaft, 1970), p. 96. The verse is probably Apocalypse 3. 20: 'Ecce ego sto ad hostium et pulso: si quis audierit vocem meam et aperuit mihi ianuam, intrabo ad eum et cenabo secum et ipse mecum.'

[3] Dr W. Ott, of the Zentrum für Datenverarbeitung at the University of Tübingen, informs me that a computer-generated concordance to the variorum Vulgate is in process. This should make this particular task considerably easier. See *Computers and the Humanities*, iv (1969/70), 127, where the project is described in detail.

the abbreviations are resolved, the pre-editor can provide the person punching the text with a key; the abbreviations are then punched as full words, and appear in the word-index as such. The user may then compare the pre-editorial decision with the diplomatic text as it stands and make his own decision.

These then are some of the problems of producing a concordance from a diplomatic text – problems that must be faced well before the work is even ready for punching. The concordance or word-index produced in this way is not, however, without its disadvantages as a working tool. The corruptness of a manuscript text *will* be mirrored in the concordance, and one has a right to enquire about the value of the meaningless *sch* in the *Anegenge* work. To overcome difficulties of this sort, full use must be made in a published concordance from a diplomatic, of certain refinements that have appeared in the COMPENDIA volumes, and indeed, in the concordance to the *Wiener Genesis*.

An appendix of critical *varia* and *addenda*, for example, can be a valuable aid for the user of the concordance in cases where a critical version exists. For the *Anegenge*, the synoptic arrangement of the versions made it fairly simple to prepare an appendix of this sort. Such an appendix would not, of course, list mere 'normalizations', but it would list any major emendation which might not easily be found in the body of the concordance. Thus Neuschäfer's emendation of *sch* to *schephære* would be listed here. This type of appendix would take account too of postulated lines in the text – of anything, broadly speaking, that the critical editor had had set in italics. This fact of course makes it easier to prepare this appendix by hand. A reverse index of forms – also used in the existing concordances – is of assistance in cases where pre-editorial word-division or joining might lead to difficulties for the user.[1] A feature that has been supplied by Wisbey in his concordance to the *Rolandslied* is also of great value where the basis is a diplomatic transcription: a finding-list of verb forms. This is a hand-compiled list of all the verb-forms in the text, grouped under 'normalized' head-words. In this way, the problems caused by an inconsistent orthography may be overcome to some extent. This verb-list, which, it might be added, involves the compiler in no little amount of work, requires some-

---

1 Wisbey, *Verskonkordanz zur 'Wiener Genesis'* contains in addition to a reverse-index of forms, an appendix relating Dollmayr's text, the one taken as a basis for the concordance, to a then unpublished edition of the *Wiener Genesis* by Dr Kathryn Smits ('Die frühmittelhochdeutsche *Wiener Genesis*. Kritische Ausgabe'. Diss. Freiburg/Br., 1966); this has now appeared as volume 59 in the series Philologische Studien und Quellen (Berlin, 1971).

thing rather more than mechanical decisions. But questionable readings may, of course, once again be checked against the text itself by the user of the concordance.

I have tried to touch on a number of specific problems of pre-editing. It is worth noting, however, that the work with which I am concerned is only a small part of the larger programme of research under way at the Cambridge Centre in the circumscribed field of Early Middle High German alone. From this, it should become clear that the building up and exploiting of an archive of Early Middle High German is a team task, the individual portions of which must interlock with each other before the value of the whole is fully realized.

II

Textual editing and attribution studies

The computer and literary editing: achievements and prospects

HAROLD LOVE*

The computer has already been of great assistance to individual editors of literary texts and it would seem that the time is approaching when the applications they have pioneered will be passing into wider use. It will be my aim in this paper firstly to indicate what some of these applications have been; secondly to foreshadow a number of further applications which seem likely to be attempted in the near future; and thirdly to raise the question of whether adding the computer to the traditional tools of the editor is likely to have any effect on the nature of the editing process as such – whether we are merely streamlining old methods, or beginning to evolve new ones.

As much of what I have to say is going to be very hypothetical, I think it will be helpful to anchor it as firmly as possible to a particular field of editorial activity and a particular kind of editing endeavour. I must therefore warn the reader that most of my remarks will apply primarily to the editing of English texts of the sixteenth, seventeenth and eighteenth centuries, and to the production of what is known as the critical old-spelling edition as defined in the writings of McKerrow,[1] Greg,[2] and Bowers.[3] For this reason, not all my generalizations about editors are going to make sense when applied to the classical or medieval fields. I must make it clear at once that I am not claiming any special pre-eminence either for the period or for the type of edition, except in so far as this is the area in which most of the classical demonstrations of Anglo-American textual bibliography have been made and one that seems to be exceptionally rich in opportunities for the

* Department of English, Monash University, Australia.

[1] R. B. McKerrow, *Prolegomena for the Oxford Shakespeare* (Oxford, 1939).
[2] Sir Walter W. Greg, 'The Rationale of Copy-Text', *Studies in Bibliography*, III (1950–1), 19–36. Reprinted in O. M. Brack, Jr. and Warner Barnes (eds.), *Bibliography and Textual Criticism: English and American Literature 1700 to the Present* (Chicago, 1969), pp. 41–58.
[3] Fredson Bowers, 'Current Theories of Copy-Text, With an Illustration from Dryden', *Modern Philology*, LXVIII (1950), 12–20. Reprinted in Brack and Barnes, pp. 59–72.

computer. The critical edition, as conceived by the writers I have mentioned, aims to ascertain not only the author's words – whatever *substantive* readings may be in doubt – but also, where this is possible within the range of editorial choices allowed by the witnesses, to recognize and preserve his accidentals: spelling, punctuation, layout and the rest. It is for this reason that the editor, if faced with a substantively corrupt first edition and a reprint embodying authorial corrections, will today normally prefer to use the first as the basis of his edition, and will in fact modify the accidentals of those readings from the corrected text which he chooses to incorporate in his final text, whenever they are in conflict with the prevailing style of the copy-text. (The assumption is that, however superior the substantive readings of the second text may be, its accidentals must be less authoritative simply because it is one copying further removed from the lost autograph. In practice, of course, one may find compositors treating the accidentals of manuscript additions to printed copy with a fidelity they do not exhibit towards the body of the text.) To evaluate and modify accidentals in this way demands a thorough command of textual detail and the availability, ideally, of a complete concordance of the author's writings, separate concordances of his holographs, of the copy-text, and of the corrected text, and detailed information concerning the habits of contemporary scribes and compositors. These things the computer can give us. Indeed, until the computer was available to give them, the demands of the Greg–Bowers approach could only be fulfilled in a very hit-or-miss way.[1]

To consider what the computer has already done for the editor and what it is likely to do, it will be useful to look one by one at the principal stages in the preparation of an edition. The first stage is that of locating and consulting the witnesses. As far as the locating is concerned, there is already an immense amount of hand-accumulated information available in library catalogues, in the various national union catalogues, and in published bibliographies and finding-lists. The task of the computer will be, with the aid of such programs as that described by Miss Wilson later in this volume, to expedite the compilation of the eventual world union catalogue, but this will have to wait until the individual libraries have succeeded in putting their card-catalogues into machine-readable form. In the meantime, we can draw solace from such lesser enterprises as W. J. Cameron's HPB (Hand-Printed Book) project which aims to list locations for all individual

[1] I should make clear that the editor working in this tradition will still see himself as the editor of the text as transmitted by the physical records and thus will not be inclined to introduce accidentals which he may know, on the basis of evidence extrinsic to the text being edited, to be characteristic of the author.

copies of books surviving from the handpress era – roughly up to 1830. As regards the problem of consultation, we need to bear in mind that the good editor has always been internationally minded, has always seen himself as a user of the world corpus of catalogued books rather than of any one library. A hundred years ago a particular page in a particular manuscript might be a month and the price of a steamer ticket away. Today – providing one is not dealing with the government, which is to say the British Museum, the Library of Congress, or the Bibliothèque Nationale – it is a fortnight and the cost of an airletter and a microfilm exposure. This is reasonably satisfactory and one can hardly see the computer closing the gap at this stage, except perhaps by marginally speeding the delivery of the airletter.

Having assembled his texts, the editor will next want to list the points at which they vary so that he can establish their stemmatical relationship and relative value as witnesses to the substantives of the archetype. If he is working with printed books, he will have the additional task of verifying the readings of any given copy by comparison with a number of others from the same setting of type. In this second enterprise, he can call on the help of the Hinman collator which allows him to juxtapose the images of pages from two separate copies and then, by rapidly alternating those images, draws his attention to the points at which they differ. The collator can compensate to a degree for the differences in page size caused by paper-shrinkage or the distortions of photocopying but cannot be adjusted to cancel out the effect of type movement during the printing-run except over parts of a page. (The bibliographical scholar, of course, would not want it to be; the fact that it reveals such things being its main advantage for him over naked-eye collation where they can be established only by elaborate measurement.) The necessity of copy-collation is a consequence of the unfortunate proneness of printers to make alterations to composed type during and between press-runs. One of the most fervent wishes of editors of early printed books is that this task of comparing near-identical type-impressions, whether conceived simply as images or as arrays of characters, could be handed over to an optical scanning device. This would require that the computer first identify the point of maximum 'fit' of the two images, as the collator does, and then locate and list the pages or areas of pages where significant disparity is encountered. The main practical problem would be that any device sensitive enough to register a substitution of, say, lower case 't' for 'r', two letters which are very similar in most seventeenth-century founts, would also pick up quite an amount of typographical 'noise' – smudging, imperfectly impressed letters, type-batter,

C

under- or over-inking, ambiguous punctuation marks, bleed-through, and so on. However, these objections do not apply nearly as strongly to stereo-printed books and, since scholars are now beginning, with hard-won but often quite significant results, to read twentieth-century novels for press-variants, this might be the most fruitful area for a pilot project. My impression is that such an application is within the range of existing technology but well beyond that of any conceivable editorial budget.

The other aspect of collation is the listing of variants between separate texts of the work, a field where we are able to report a quite heartening degree of activity. The pioneer here, as in several other fields, was Vinton Dearing, who in 1962 completed a collation program in collaboration with Ronald Bland for use in the California edition of the works of Dryden.[1] This program was originally written in MAP and has since been rewritten in FORTRAN. It uses card input and can handle up to ninety-nine texts; however, it relies on manual pre-sorting to bring corresponding lines together. Following Dearing's lead, a number of other programs of this kind have been written. I helped produce one myself in collaboration with Georgette Silva which uses tape input and makes its own decisions as to which lines correspond.[2] A further collation program has been developed at Cambridge; for others see the descriptions by Miss Widmann (in this volume) and by Dom Froger.[3] There has also been a general discussion of the problems of machine collation by M. Cabaniss.[4] The most elaborate program of this kind currently in working order would seem, according to report, to be that developed by William M. Gibson for comparing two texts of a novel by Henry James. This has been copyrighted with a view to commercial use and has been described in a volume of essays on modern editing techniques.[5] The ideal collation program should be able to deal with an unlimited number of texts. (There are over ten thousand catalogued manuscripts of the Vulgate.[6]) It should be able to deal with prose as

[1] Described in his *Methods of Textual Editing* (Los Angeles, 1962); reprinted in Brack and Barnes, pp. 73–101.
[2] Georgette Silva and Harold Love, 'The Identification of Text Variants by Computer', *Information Storage and Retrieval*, v (1969), 89–108.
[3] See note 2, p. 51 below, and 'La collation des manuscrits à la machine électronique', *Bulletin de l'Institut de Recherche et d'Histoire des Textes*, XIII (1964–5), 135–71.
[4] 'Using the Computer for Text Collation: Problems, Studies and a Method for Solution' (unpubl. diss., University of California, Los Angeles, 1968).
[5] *Art and Error: Modern Textual Editing*. Essays compiled and edited by Ronald Gottesman and Scott Bennett (Indiana U.P. and London, 1970). See also George R. Petty, Jr. and William M. Gibson, *Project Occult* (New York U.P. and London, 1970).
[6] Figure quoted by J. W. Ellison, 'Computers and the Testaments', in Edmund A. Bowles (ed.), *Computers in Humanistic Research* (Englewood Cliffs, 1967).

well as verse, should be able to print variants in footnote as well as in Manley and Rickert format, and should require no pre-editing of copy beyond the minimum necessary to make the tapes usable by other workers who may have different projects in mind. (In a dramatic text, for instance, it is a helpful courtesy to code for speakers as well as act and scene. Bibliographical analysis requires reference by page.) None of the programs with which I am acquainted at present does all these things but no doubt developments will follow as users require them.

While mentioning Dearing's work in this field, I must not pass over his method of proofreading input, which is to have the text punched-up by two different operators and then use the computer to spot discrepancies. Hill tried out the same method on Shakespearean texts and found that he was getting 'a rather large number' of identical misreadings – but this may have been partly due to the rather special problems posed by late-sixteenth-century accidentals.[1] Luckily, punching for collation is to a degree self-proofing. The vulnerable archaism has to be transcribed correctly on only one occasion for it to show as a variant, when it would, of course, be referred back to copy. The same applies to any reading shared by more than one copy.

Having identified the variants, the editor has next to establish the relationship of his texts and evaluate their relative worth as witnesses to the archetype (*recensio*). The basic logic of stemmatology was first spelled-out in detail by Greg in *The Calculus of Variants* (Oxford, 1926) and has recently been the subject of valuable studies by Dearing, Froger, and Hrubý.[2] All four agree in isolating two stages – one, non-temporal, in which the essential linkages between the manuscripts are expressed by means of lines of transmission and hypothetical intermediaries, and a second, directional, in which qualitative change is indicated as movement from an archetype at the top to the various terminal texts at the bottom of the tree. (It is a point frequently overlooked by novices that any point in a stemma can be taken as the topmost without changing its essential relationships.) The second of these stages relies on the ability to distinguish between correct and incorrect readings and must therefore be left to the editor, though the further stage of determining where these good readings

[1] T. H. Howard Hill, 'The Oxford Old Spelling Concordances', *Studies in Bibliography*, XXII (1969), 159. See also Dearing in *Literary Data Processing Conference Proceedings* (MLA, 1965), pp. 204–5.
[2] See Vinton Dearing, *A Manual of Textual Analysis* (Berkeley and Los Angeles, 1959) and 'Some Routines for Textual Criticism', *The Library*, 5th series, XXI (1966), 309–17; Dom. J. Froger, *La critique des textes et son automatisation* (Paris, 1968), and Antonín Hrubý, 'A Quantitative Solution of the Ambiguity of Three Texts', *Studies in Bibliography*, XVIII (1965), 147–82.

come to a node can be safely handed over to the machine. For cases where such discriminations cannot be made, Hrubý has opened up new possibilities by proposing that statistical methods be used to determine the location of intermediaries. The first stage of stemma building is purely classificatory and is thus admirably fitted for computerization. Greg's method is based on the distinction between simple variation, in which there are only two textual alternatives, and complex, where there are more than two. He gives three rules for using simple variations to determine the nature of links between manuscripts, and Dearing has complemented these with three routines which deal with complex variations by transforming them into what he calls 'synthetic simple variations'. Programs are stated to exist for all these procedures, and Dearing has also published a set of instructions for carrying them out on the abacus.[1] Froger describes a number of programs and has also expressed his stemmatological procedures in terms of set-theory. Because of the detail and clarity of his exposition, his work should be of greater use to novices than Dearing's.

Greg's *Calculus* is based on the somewhat limiting assumption that likeness between texts is the result of copying. In practice, textual traditions are frequently found to be contaminated, i.e. readings from one line of transmission have been introduced into another, as happens when a scribe consults a second manuscript (or his memory) to help him over a difficulty. Textual critics in the past have tended to sidestep this problem either by relying on conjecture alone without genealogical controls or by favouring the readings of a single manuscript beyond their known worth. Dearing's routines deal with irregular agreements by rewriting them as variants, but still require that they should be identified as such by qualitative means. Hrubý proposes a solution by 'mechanical dissolution of conflicts'.[2] Froger describes some useful diagrammatic aids for locating conflict and has proposed an arithmetical technique for determining the *proximity* of manuscripts in case the genealogical relationship should prove irrecoverable. A forthcoming study by Lambertus Okken, which I have been able to consult through the kindness of Dr Wisbey, proposes a more revolutionary method based on a rigid separation of the manuscript as variant carrier from the variant or textual component transmitted.[3] This approach looks

---

[1] Vinton Dearing, 'Abaco-Textual-Criticism', *Papers of the Bibliographical Society of America*, LXII (1968), 547–78. See also his 'Some Notes on Genealogical Methods in Textual Criticism', *Novum Testamentum*, IX (1967), 278–97.

[2] Antonín Hrubý, 'Statistical Methods in Textual Criticism', *General Linguistics*, v (Supplement, 1962), 100–22.

[3] Lambertus Okken, *Ein Beitrag zur Entwirrung einer kontaminierten Manuskripttradition* (Rijksuniversiteit te Utrecht, D. Litt. dissertation, 1970). The problem has also been

extremely promising; however, I would not at this stage consider myself qualified to evaluate it. A way in which the computer could contribute in this area would be through the generation of artificial textual traditions whose stemmatical relationships would be known in advance and which could thus serve as a testing-ground for currently available techniques.

Having established (or attempted to establish) the relationship of his texts and listed his variants, the editor is now faced with the task of reconstructing the original. (Many of the choices involved will already have been made while establishing the stemma.) The technique he employs is ultimately an intuitive one, a delicate balancing-out of plausibilities – the difference between the 'scientific' and the naïvely eclectic editor being that the former, through his stemmatological, palaeographical and biblio-graphical knowledge, will possess a much keener awareness of the dimen-sions of the field of choice within which intuition may legitimately be exercised. When such an editor can call on the aid of the computer, his advantage in this respect may be magnified enormously; however, final editorial decision must remain in all but the simplest cases with himself, not only because the kinds of discrimination involved are so complex but also because the edition is ultimately to be used by human beings for a human end, and editorial choice will in some instances quite properly be governed by such a consideration. (The issues involved may be seen in macroscopic form by considering the situation of an editor faced with the problem of whether to print an early or a late text of a James novel, the 1805 or the 1850 *Prelude*, a version of a play as acted or as later revised for readers. The matter has been taken up more philosophically by James Thorpe.[1]) What the computer can contribute, and what makes it invalu-able, is linguistic data, especially the kind of data made available by concordances. Without this, the recurrence of the rare word or the eccen-tric spelling may still be noticed as the editor re-reads his text. But the slightly suspect turn of phrase, the slightly unusual prepositional usage, may not be verifiable unless the full range of the author's usages, and ideally those of some of his contemporaries, is available in a form that permits ready consultation. Nor will it be possible to ask such questions as, in the case of lacunae, what characters are most likely to follow in a particular context (one which has been successfully asked with the aid of

considered by Humphrey Palmer in *The Logic of Gospel Criticism* (London and New York, 1968), pp. 97–106, and by N. Morcovescu in a forthcoming study of the logic of variant groupings.

1 'The Aesthetics of Textual Criticism', *Publications of the Modern Language Association of America*, LXXX (1965), 465–82. Reprinted in Brack and Barnes, pp. 102–38.

the computer of a text from the Dead Sea scrolls[1]). Techniques of bibliographical analysis can also be applied far more effectively than would be possible by hand. Compositor discrimination, for instance, may be carried out through an adjustment to standard programs for producing alphabetical word-lists by which locations are replaced by a forme-identification number and a search made of adjacent entries for mutually exclusive distribution patterns (on the assumption that most significant variants will be neighbours). In the past editors have simply had to do without these aids. Now they are increasingly in the position of being able to make them themselves, or get them made for them, and it is essential that they take full advantage of this opportunity. Impressionism and the random instance are no longer enough. Neither is textual inertia masquerading as conservatism.

A special problem is raised by texts which show evidence of authorial revision: that of distinguishing between authoritative variations and those contributed by the scribe or compositor. In certain cases, as Friedman[2] has shown, these readings can be either accepted or rejected *en masse*. In others, the only recourse is to a detailed investigation of the habits of the scribe or compositor involved, or of others of their kind at the same place and time – preferably when reproducing the writings of a dead author. Analysis of the handwriting of the seventeenth-century scribe Ralph Crane is one of the projects reported from the Oxford Shakespeare and it is to be hoped that a proper analysis will also be made before too long of the reprint variants of such vital agents in the transmission of literary texts as the Tonson shop at the turn of the eighteenth century and the great mid-Victorian printing-houses.[3] There is also a wonderful field for computer analysis in the scores of manuscripts surviving from the clandestine scriptoria of Restoration London. It is good to see that each year more of the texts that must form the basis of such studies are being put into machine-readable form; however, it is necessary to point out that the kinds of normalization for the purposes of concordance-making which are described by Dr Murdoch in this volume, by removing scribal or composi-

[1] See P. Tasman, *Indexing the Dead Sea Scrolls* (International Business Machines, 1958).
[2] Arthur Friedman, 'The Problem of Indifferent Readings in the Eighteenth Century, With a Solution from *The Deserted Village*', *Studies in Bibliography*, XIII (1960), 143–7. Reprinted in Brack and Barnes, pp. 188–93.
[3] The issue under discussion is quite separate from that of what a printer will do at any given period with an author's *manuscript*, but this too is something about which we need to have much more precise information. May I also make a plea for studies of the evolution of house-style among the major printers and publishers, not omitting those of our own century?

torial peculiarities, are putting severe difficulties in the way of those who may wish to use the same tapes for bibliographical analysis. If, for example, in preparing a concordance for a sixteenth-century work it is decided that 'to morrow' shall become 'tomorrow', it is possible that a useful compositor discriminant will have been obliterated. Keeping a record of all editorial changes made to a textual document prior to punching could save a subsequent user of the archive much unnecessary proofreading.

I promised at the beginning of this paper that I would try to distinguish between areas in which the computer was simply being used to streamline existing methods and those in which the editing process itself was beginning to show fundamental modifications. Most of the cases I have so far considered have been of the former kind; however, when we come to the stage where the editor prepares his emended and annotated text for publication we may be on the verge of a more far-reaching change. I refer to the possibility, so far to my knowledge untested by an editor, of the text being assembled on magnetic tape and set by the computer itself. The editor using the computer for collation or for concordance generation is going to have his copy-text on tape, and providing his edition is of the type I described at the beginning of this paper in which alterations to the text are relatively sparse, there is no reason why he should not record his emendations in the form of corrections to the copy-text tape. This would have the added advantage that, as each of these emendations was made, the computer could also be generating, measuring and filing the necessary footnotes. (In practice the correction tape would probably be the full historical collation as it would appear at the end of the volume, with individual records coded as demanding or not demanding the emendation of copy-text.) To make this kind of operation work, two separate editing programs would be required. The first would introduce a number of minor symmetries customary in editions of this type – regularization of speech-prefixes, assignment of stage-directions to margin or centre, adjustment of punctuation marks following words in italic, and the like. As it did this, the program would decide whether to insert these alterations among the page footnotes and a separate list of accidental variants, depending on whether or not they were declared silent. The second program would make up the book into pages of text and textual footnotes, justify prose, add line numbers and head titles, and prepare the tape for typesetter output.

The revolutionary element in this procedure is that the editor would not see his text, except in print-out form, until it finally appeared in type. The magnetic tape would have become his palimpsest. The main advantages would be to eliminate the whole process of preparing and correcting a typescript and to simplify the task of proof-correction. One would also expect some reduction in the cost of the edition. The only drawback is that one would not in the present state of printing technology end up with quite so handsome a piece of book-production, and if any feel, as I do myself, that this is an excellent reason for not following up my advice in this matter, there would still be advantages in taking the process as far as the correction tape stage and using paper-tape output fed back through a tape assembly to produce printer's copy.

The computer in historical collation: use of the IBM 360/75 in collating multiple editions of *A Midsummer Night's Dream*

R. L. WIDMANN*

As the special editor of the New Variorum edition of *A Midsummer Night's Dream* (*MND*), I am faced with the monumental task of collating some 80 to 120 editions of the play. When I chanced to describe the problem to a physicist in January 1969, he assured me that a computer could provide effective assistance in this work. So began my nodding acquaintance with the intricacies of computation. After further discussions with Dr Joel Cohen of the Department of Physics and the Laboratory for Research on the Structure of Matter at the University of Pennsylvania, and after consultations with a systems engineer from IBM, I adopted the working methods described below.

There were several possible ways of accumulating the data for the computer; eventually I chose to use punched cards, mainly because of their durability. Various systems involving the transfer of data direct to magnetic tape, whether on-line or off-line, were ruled out, not least because of the inordinately high costs involved. After deciding to use punched cards, Dr Cohen and I processed a small sample in the spring of 1969. We key-punched the first forty-five lines of six editions, namely Q1 (the quarto of 1600), Q2 (the quarto of 1619), F1 (the First Folio of 1623), the old Kittredge, the New Cambridge, and the new Pelican editions. Our successes with these samples encouraged us to pursue the use of the computer with the prepared text handling program, FORMAT, written by Gerald M. Berns. In the sample run of April 1969, a + sign indicated that a capital letter followed in the original text. An asterisk was placed before and after italicized forms in the text. Collation by eye would have been somewhat difficult, employing these symbols: we are now using upper case and lower case letters, while underlining indicates italics in the final print-out. I chose to use FORMAT because it provides output in both upper and lower case as one of its standard features. Since the IBM card records only in

* Department of English, University of Pennsylvania, Philadelphia.

upper case, the FORMAT codes are incorporated in the text as it is punched. For print-out the IBM 1403 printer is used with a special print train.

Other features of my working methods were also dictated by the desirability of having print-out approximate as nearly as possible to the final copy which will be sent to the printer of the MND edition; the New Variorums, under the general editorship of James G. McManaway, will be published by the University Press of the University of Pennsylvania. Guidelines for the Variorum special editors will appear in the forthcoming handbook in preparation by Professors Richard Hosley, Richard Knowles and Ruth McGugan.

The Variorum volumes will have two sets of numbering. In one margin will appear the act, scene and line numbers. Consecutive line numbering by intervals of ten lines will be provided in the other margin. The Through Line Numbering (TLN) has been established by Professor Charlton Hinman in his Norton facsimile of the First Folio. So I decided that each punched card should be identified by this latter numbering and that each card would contain one line of verse. Because my copy-text[1] is a quarto, rather than the First Folio, the prose line numbering has been established by using the Hinman TLN for the line containing the last word of the prose line in the Norton facsimile First Folio. These numbers, which go up to 2,223 for *MND*, are punched into the first four columns of the eighty-column card. We reserve columns five and six in case subscripts or superscripts become necessary. These columns, i.e. five and six, are also used for cards which are blank except for the characters 'plus' and 'one', i.e. $+1$. (Such a card is necessary where one or more editions happened to have a line longer than the eighty columns available. The continuation card for such a line must be matched in other editions (in which the lines are shorter typographically) by a blank; we call these blanks 'plus 1' cards.) Column seven is always blank; with column eight the punching of the text begins. One line of verse goes onto each card. Should a line, such as a stage-direction, be longer than eighty columns,)L is not punched in columns 78

---

[1] Here, I am using 'copy-text' in the sense originally discussed by W. W. Greg, 'The Rationale of Copy-Text', *Studies in Bibliography*, III (1950–1), 22, where he says, '[t]hus in the case of printed books, and in the absence of revision in a later edition, it is normally the first edition alone that can claim authority'. Paul Baender, 'The Meaning of Copy-Text', *ibid.* XXII (1969), 311, expands Greg's terminology by pointing out 'the two most common meanings of copy-text. Sometimes it clearly means printer's copy . . . At other times copy-text means entire editions that serve as basic texts, presumably after due assessment of press variants and other discrepancies among all extant or representative copies'. G. Thomas Tanselle, 'The Meaning of Copy-Text: A Further Note', *ibid.* XXIII (1970), 191–6, points out numerous fallacies in Baender's article and correctly criticizes Baender's first definition of 'copy-text'.

and 79 of the card;)L indicates completion of a line in FORMAT. The words are continued on a second card, which is called 1234 + 1 or whatever the appropriate number may be; the text begins again in column eight.[1]

Because the punched cards record data only in upper case, the symbol ¢ must be punched directly before a character which is capitalized in the edition. FORMAT then provides upper case print-out of the character following a cent sign and a lower case print-out of all other letters. Italics are achieved by punching)U before and after the word or portion of a word which is italicized. Frequently, the speech prefixes are only partially italicized in early editions. Hence, there must be some way of indicating T*he*. or H*ip*. for Theseus or Hippolyta.

I have incorporated two special symbols. The signs ./ and :/ are equivalent to . and : in early editions. I am interested in finding out exactly where and why these diamond periods and colons appear. In general, these variant punctuation marks tend to occur near the ends of either the outer or inner formes. In the first quarto, printed in 1600, the method was imposition by formes and not seriatim; sheet B was the first printed.[2] The marks also tend to appear more frequently in the lower halves of pages. A simple sorting program will be used in order to see how many of these punctuation marks appear, where they actually are, and why the compositors might have chosen to use them.

Because I have employed the TLN to identify cards, I have not used columns 73 to 78 for sequencing numbers. However, each edition does have a cover card with the abbreviated name of the editor, such as *Warb* for Warburton or *Han3* for the third edition prepared by Hanmer. And, in order to prevent irremediable confusion, should the cards be dropped, each edition has a coloured stripe along the right or left side of the cards. Felt nibbed pens are used in six colours; a single-coloured line is drawn either

---

[1] We use an IBM 029 key-punch. I have rented one of these, at $62 a month, for use by my three part-time student assistants, who are paid $2 an hour; professional key-punchers cost $4 an hour. Punched cards were chosen as an input medium since I anticipated difficulties in correcting paper tape or magnetic tape without the help of professional staff.

In general, all costs are higher than I anticipated. Indicative of the charges involved is the sum estimated by Professors Lawrence and Noel Stern at Drexel University in Philadelphia; they are supervising the preparation of concordances to the Milton Prose Works, published by the Yale University Press. They estimate that an editor needs funds of $30,000 per volume; charges for computer time are not included. My own project has cost about $5,000 to date, not including my own time. No doubt another similar sum will be expended before I finish.

[2] See Robert K. Turner, Jr., 'Printing Methods and Textual Problems in *A Midsummer Night's Dream* Q1', *Studies in Bibliography*, xv (1962), 34–8; he points out that sheet B was the first composed and machined.

one, one and a half, or two inches from the tops of the cards on either the right- or left-hand sides.

Approximately sixty important editions, each involving about 2,300 cards, will be key-punched. All seventeenth-century editions will be included; these are the two *MND* quartos and the first four folios. Most eighteenth-century and many nineteenth- and twentieth-century editions, all of which have been suggested for complete (rather than just partial) collation by those New Variorum special editors who have already finished the textual parts of their volumes, will also be key-punched. Assessments of textual relationships by these editors are published elsewhere, notably in *Shakespearean Research and Opportunities*.[1] Commentary by some of these editors will also appear in the handbook for Variorum editors. I do not plan to have any of those editions key-punched which will be only partially collated,[2] simply because the expense of key-punching does not warrant it. A student key-puncher takes about twenty to twenty-eight hours to punch and proofread the cards for one edition.

After the editions for complete collation are key-punched, they will be put into the computer via magnetic tape, since the core is too small to contain the 11,040,000 characters in 60 editions of 2,300 cards each. Once the data is available inside the computer, comparisons for variants will be made. Print-out sheets will provide several kinds of information. First, each edition will be printed out, giving lines 1 to 2223; the earliest edition will come first and the most recent last. Then the computer will print out all versions of the individual lines together; i.e. all versions of line one will be printed out, then all versions of line two, three, and so on. Next, the computer will print out only the copy-text, in this case, Q1 of 1600, in its entirety; directly underneath Q1, only those words or punctuation marks

---

[1] Edited by William R. Elton, The Graduate Center, CUNY, 33 W. 42nd Street, New York, New York 10036.

[2] 'Partial collation' means that only cruxes, generally semi-substantive and substantive variants, will be checked in an edition, rather than comparing all its lines with previous editions. The special editor of any given New Variorum volume determines what the cruxes are for his play. W. W. Greg, 'The Rationale of Copy-Text', defines types of variants as follows: 'But here we need to draw a distinction between the significant, or as I shall call them "substantive", readings of the text, those namely that affect the author's meaning or the essence of his expression, and other, such in general as spelling, punctuation, word-division, and the like, affecting mainly its formal presentation, which may be regarded as the accidents, or as I shall call them "accidentals", of the text.' In his footnote to this statement, he elaborates: 'It is also true that between substantive readings and spellings there is an intermediate class of word-forms about the assignment of which opinions may differ and which may have to be treated differently in dealing with the work of different scribes' (p. 21). It is this latter group which has become known as 'semi-substantives'.

(preceded by a word in order to provide context) which vary from Q1 will be printed for successive editions. The line number in Q1 is indicated by the TLN, while successive editions are designated by an abbreviation. Thus, collation by eye is greatly facilitated, as the following sample shows.

```
2178   +1
q2
f1
f2
f3
f4
r1
r2
r3
p1
p2
t1
t2
h1
wa          And this ditty after me
j1
ca
h3
ma
```

```
2179   And this dittie after mee, Sing; and daunce it trippingly.
q2                     Ditty      me, Sing    dance
f1                     Ditty      me, sing    dance      trippinglie.
f2                     Ditty      me, sing    dance      trippinglye.
f3                     Ditty      me, sing    dance
f4                     Ditty      me, sing    dance      trippingly.> w
r1                     Ditty      me, Sing    Dance
r2                     Ditty      me, Sing    Dance
r3                     Ditly      me>w
p1                     ditty      me>w
p2                     ditty      me>w
t1                     ditty      me>w
t2                     ditty      me>w
h1                     ditty      me>w
wa          Sing, and dance it trippingly.>w
j1                     ditty      me>w
ca                     ditty,        me,>w
h3                     ditty,        me,>w
ma                     ditty,        me,>w
```

```
2179   +1
q2
f1
f2
f3
f4
r1
r2
```

r3	Sing, and Dance it trippingly.			
p1	Sing, and dance it trippingly.			
p2	Sing, and dance it trippingly.			
t1	Sing, and dance it trippingly.			
t2	Sing, and dance it trippingly.			
h1	Sing, and dance it trippingly.			
wa				
j1	Sing, and dance it trippingly.			
ca	Sing, and dance it trippingly.			
h3	Sing, and dance it trippingly.			
ma	Sing, and dance it trippingly.			

2182	Hand in hand, with Fairy grace,		
q2			
f1	hand	Fairie	
f2			
f3			
f4			
r1			
r2			
r3	Hand,		Grace,
p1		fairy	
p2		fairy	
t1		fairy	
t2		fairy	
h1		fairy	
wa		fairy	
j1		fairy	
ca	Hand,	fairy	
h3		fairy	
ma		fairy	

2183	Will we sing and blesse this place.		
q2			
f1			
f2			
f3			
f4		bless	
r1		bless	Place.
r2		bless	Place.
r3		bless	Place.
p1		bless	
p2		bless	
t1	sing,	bless	
t2		bless	
h1		bless	
wa		bless	
j1		bless	
ca	sing,	bless	
h3	sing,	bless	
ma	sing,	bless	

The first editor to separate TLN 2179 into two lines was Rowe, who did so in his third edition, here designated 'r3'. His capitalization of 'Dance' is not followed by any other editor. This kind of accidental variant can be easily ignored when preparing my copy for the printer. Of more interest is Capell's capitalization of 'Hand', in TLN 2182; his source is the third Rowe edition. The use of the caesura in TLN 2183 also shows how Capell relies on an earlier edition, here Theobald's first edition, which is abbreviated 't1'.

But, for the textual editor, the real interest in the sample comes with the substantive variant found in the Fourth Folio, 'f4'. Here, the text (line 2179) omits the 'it' which is found in all the other nineteen earliest editions. (The symbol > w is a feature added to my program in order to indicate a difference in line length. The causes of such differences are then examined.) It will be interesting to see if such a variant is picked up by any later editor.

In addition to the visual ease in collation provided by a computer printout, the main attraction of machine assistance obviously comes in its ability to work so swiftly, efficiently, and tirelessly. I see my project as employing the computer in the role of a high-grade clerical assistant, a 'heedful slave' (*The Comedy of Errors*, II. ii. 2) which has now freed the human editor from many tiring tasks of visual collation. It is the uniting of human efforts to machine capabilities which makes us see that there is indeed something remarkable left beneath the visiting moon.

A method of 'author' identification

ALASTAIR MCKINNON and ROGER WEBSTER*

This paper describes a method which has served to establish a hierarchy among eight of Kierkegaard's most important pseudonyms.[1] It is written for the information of those interested in the problem of author identification and is based on the assumption that a method capable of discriminating between the various writings of a single author might have other applications in this surprisingly varied and complex field. This paper gives a general account of the method with particular emphasis upon the role of the computer; those wishing more detailed information about the problem, method or results are invited to consult forthcoming reports dealing with these particular aspects.

I

The problem with which we are concerned is a reflection of the complex nature of Kierkegaard's authorship which, in turn, is a reflection of his underlying aim and strategy. Briefly, his aim is to lead his reader to authentic existence or, in another terminology, to psychological and spiritual maturity. In this connection the role of his acknowledged and generally 'religious' works is obvious, while that of the pseudonymous, 'aesthetic' works requires some explanation. In fact, the latter works reflect his conviction that, as he put it, his contemporaries lived in aesthetic or, at most, in aesthetic-ethical categories and that it was his task, as a religious author, to find and meet them on their own ground. Indeed, it is this conviction which explains the nature and shape of the pseudonymous

---

* Department of Philosophy, McGill University, Montreal.
[1] Prospective readers are warned of the following difficulties in this method, at least as applied in this particular instance. (a) The last acknowledged selection (SK8), unlike all others, is taken from three separate sources; hence its odd and misleading scores. Such composite or synthetic selections are clearly to be avoided. (b) Two of our pseudonymous selections (PS6 and PS7) are from the hand of a single pseudonym. This, combined with the use of exclusive pair vocabulary as the basis of our final test, has naturally lowered their respective standings in our final hierarchy.

We hope to recover the data for use on the IBM 360 and to reprocess it omitting SK8 and, most probably, PS6. (A. McK., April 1970).

authorship. In Kierkegaard's view, the illusions of his contemporaries could be effectively dispelled only by a specially constructed authorship consisting of works which, viewed individually, present alternative points of view and, taken together, present a genuinely dialectical progression from one life-view to the next. Hence the use of his many pseudonyms which, as he says, are 'poetic creations' or, again, literary personalities whose distinctive life styles are perfectly expressed in their individual works. For example, A, the pseudonymous author of volume I of *Either-Or* perfectly expresses the aesthetic point of view not only in what he says but, equally, in the way in which he says it. Similarly, B, the pseudonymous author of volume II, is the perfect embodiment of the ethical attitude. Indeed, each has an internal consistency which, as Kierkegaard points out, would be impossible and even inappropriate for 'any actually existing author'. This seems also to be true for each of his other pseudonyms.

It would be entirely wrong to regard Kierkegaard's use of the pseudonyms as mere eccentricity or perversity; they are, in fact, a perfectly natural part of an entirely rational if very subtle strategy. But it would be equally wrong simply to identify Kierkegaard with any or, *per impossibile*, all of his various pseudonyms. As he repeatedly insisted, they are ideally consistent personalities each with his own distinctive point of view. In fact, Kierkegaard went even further. He noted that there were obvious contradictions between the different pseudonyms. He pointed out that anyone could make him look like a fool by placing quotations from different pseudonyms side by side. He begged that anyone quoting from a pseudonymous work would do him the favour of citing the name of the responsible pseudonym. At one point he even suggested that a current confusion regarding one of his own fundamental categories was due to the fact that people had, 'as a matter of course', confused his own view on the subject with those expressed in the pseudonymous works. Plainly, then, the pseudonymous nature of these works is a matter of great importance and must be taken seriously.

There would seem to be two obvious solutions to this problem. One might disregard these warnings altogether as many commentators have actually done. Alternatively, one might dismiss the pseudonymous writings and in defence thereof cite Kierkegaard's own protest – 'So in the pseudonymous works there is not a single word which is mine.' But the former will not do and the latter involves discarding many of Kierkegaard's most interesting writings. Further, this latter course is ruled out by two other considerations. Both logically and on his own account the pseudonyms present and canvas every significant life-view from which, as from other considerations, it follows that some must be closer to the real Kierkegaard than their fellows. Also, Kierkegaard himself later came to see that certain of his pseudonyms were more intimately related to him than others. The problem then is to discover a method which will enable us to plot the relations between Kierkegaard and his various pseudonyms. Very crudely, it is to find a way of determining which are closer to him and which are more remote.

2

Of course, there are already a number of author identification methods which might have been adapted to solve our problem; those of Ellegård, Morton and, notably, Mosteller and Wallace are but the most obvious possibilities.[1] But in my view there are strong considerations against the use of any 'thumb-print' tests in this case. While the pseudonyms appear clearly distinguishable from one another there seemed no good reason to suppose that each would have his own distinctive 'thumb-print'. Further, it seemed clear that the distinction between the pseudonyms went far beyond one of mere 'style'; indeed, their works really overcome all facile versions of the style/content dichotomy. It was therefore important to find a method able to take advantage of this fact and, not being restricted to a few grammatical connectives, able to afford a comprehensive picture of the different text selections; in short, a method possessing the formalism and rigour of statistics and offering at the same time insight into the nature of the works themselves. In this connection I can report that this procedure yields two or, in the case of the pseudonymous works, three separate vocabulary lists for each selection. These are, respectively, the total vocabulary, the exclusive vocabulary and, for the pseudonyms, the vocabulary shared exclusively with the acknowledged selections. Preliminary examination of these lists suggests that at least one may serve as the basis for a useful and simple abstracting procedure. They have already provided significant confirmation of some of our findings and, hence, support for our method.

In its present form our procedure consists of two separate stages, each with its own particular role. The first stage has two parallel parts: a comparison of the text densities of the pseudonymous (PS) and acknow-

[1] For full references to the relevant work of these and other scholars, see 'Problems of Chronology and Disputed Authorship' in *An Annotated Bibliography of Statistica Stylistics*, ed. Richard W. Bailey and Lubomír Doležel (Ann Arbor, 1968), pp. 75–9.

ledged (SK) sets and, secondly, a comparison of their internal coherence or homogeneity by means of the vocabulary connectivity method. The purpose of these comparisons is to show that, both individually and collectively, the PS selections are significantly different from the SK. The second stage of the procedure is a pair-vocabulary test, the purpose of which is to establish a hierarchy of the pseudonyms in relation to the acknowledged Kierke- gaard. We shall explain these steps in greater detail below, but first we must deal with the preparation of text and the use of the computer.

3

At the outset we chose eight selections from the pseudonymous and the same number from the acknowledged works. Each of these selections was substantial and the sets totalled 496 and 483 pages respectively. Four of the selections represented an original work in its entirety while the remainder were carefully selected samples necessitated by the size or, in certain cases, by the nature of the original. SK8 was a synthetic selection and, it may be noted, proved nearly disastrous on this account.

Each of the sixteen selections was pre-edited by marking all nouns with a 1, all verbs with a 2, all adjectives with a 3, and all adverbs with a 4, a procedure which permitted the subsequent recovery of all instances of each class of our content vocabulary. The entire text of each selection was then key-punched in free format along with the markers for these four types of words. A master word-list was produced and manually canonized (i.e. all variant forms of all words of these four types were reduced to their dictionary or root form). All further processing was carried out at the McGill University Computer Centre on the IBM 7044, equipped with 32K words of memory, of which approximately 20K were available for programming, and each 36-bit word was capable of storing six alphabetic characters. This computer was then used to canonize all marked words in the various texts and from this to produce canonized word-lists for each of the individual selections. It should be noted that our concern was restricted to these four types of words or content vocabulary and that they constituted the basis of our subsequent measures of text length and vocabulary size.

Having thus been reduced to machine-readable form, and one in which the content vocabulary could be easily distinguished, the entire text was copied onto magnetic tape. The first program then filtered from the tape the content vocabulary of the sixteen selections, keeping track of the fre- quency of occurrence of each vocabulary item. Due to memory limitations it was necessary further to subdivide the vocabulary of each selection not only into the four vocabulary types, namely nouns, verbs, adjectives and adverbs, but each type was also divided alphabetically from A-L and M-Z, making a total of 128 blocks of data. Two computer words were allocated to each vocabulary item, so that only the first twelve characters of each text word were retained. Subsequent checks revealed that the number of items lost in this way was negligible. Finally, each of the 64 blocks was reduced to alphabetic order.

A second program then integrated this data to produce an alphabetical master list of the entire vocabulary under consideration, and at the same time assigning a relative number to each vocabulary item. The purpose of this was twofold:

(1) to replace the two-word vocabulary items by a single word identifier containing the relative number of that item, so that both memory space and comparison time would be conserved in subsequent operations;

(2) to enable variants to be canonized to their root forms. This was accomplished by manually scrutinizing the list and associating with each variant the relative number of its root form. The original vocabulary consisted of some twenty thousand items. After canonizing, this number was reduced to approximately ten thousand.

The entire output of the first program was then reduced to its canonized numerical format. At this point the observed vocabulary partitioning was immediately evaluated. At first it seemed that this might prove to be a prohibitively time-consuming task, for it required that each word of each selection be compared with all the words of the remaining seven selections for each of the eight type-alphabetic subdivisions, and that this be repeated $2^8 - 1$ times! In fact, the result of one comparison through all the selections was sufficient to establish an ordered 8-bit pattern indicating in which selections the word did or did not occur. The pattern was retained in the low-order region of the word after shifting the identifier the requisite number of places. Thus, for example, the following word:

35	0
0 . . . 0100	10010000

indicates that the fourth vocabulary item is present in selections 1 and 4. The number of items in a given partition can then be found by summing the number of occurrences of the corresponding bit pattern. The derivation of the calculated values is explained in the next section.

4

The first stage in our method involves a comparison between the PS and the SK selections. The first step in this stage consists of a comparison of the vocabulary densities of these selections, the statistics for which are given in Table 1. The text lengths of the SK and the PS sets are of the

TABLE 1. *Text-vocabulary relationship*

| | Text length | Vocabulary | log V |
	N	V	log N
SK1	11,181	2,176	.825
SK2	14,408	2,807	.829
SK3	8,588	1,732	.823
SK4	10,114	1,940	.823
SK5	11,285	2,074	.818
SK6	12,845	2,180	.810
SK7	6,548	1,262	.813
SK8	7,701	2,144	.860
PS1	10,519	3,132	.869
PS2	9,380	2,258	.845
PS3	8,639	2,229	.851
PS4	9,771	2,868	.865
PS5	7,759	2,057	.851
PS6	13,549	2,509	.824
PS7	15,432	3,032	.831
PS8	9,062	1,854	.827

same order of magnitude and, this being so, we assume that they constitute comparable samples. We also assume that the individual selections are sufficiently large to permit the use of the log V/log N ratio[1] as a means of comparison. Now, as this table shows, the ratio for both the individual PS selections and for the PS set is in general much higher than that for the SK selections and set. In fact, the average for the PS set is .845 while that for SK is .825 or, deleting the synthetic SK8, .819. In brief, the PS authors have a much richer vocabulary than SK. It would seem that this is clear evidence of a significant difference between these two sets; certainly it appears to support the claim that the PS authors are quite distinct from the acknowledged SK.

[1] The ratio in question is that of the logarithm of the number of vocabulary items in a particular selection to the logarithm of the total number of its content words. We use this ratio because our own detailed empirical investigations revealed that, for our selections at least, vocabulary size grew with text length according to a bi-logarithmic relationship.

This same general conclusion is suggested by the vocabulary connectivity method which is best regarded as a parallel step in the first stage of our procedure. In essence this method consists of a comparison of the observed and calculated values for both the SK and the PS sets taken separately. In earlier versions of this work the calculated values were produced from a formula employing the number-frequency distribution of the set and the text length of the individual selections. This was found to be inadequate and in the present version these values are derived instead from a naive model or formula incorporating both individual text lengths and the rank-frequency distribution of each selection. Hence this model, unlike the earlier one, permits one to take account of the differing vocabulary densities. The application of this formula gives the number of vocabulary items which would belong exclusively to a given selection on the basis of this model. The corresponding observed values were produced by the computer by comparing the vocabulary of all selections within each set. As this is a test of approximation to a purely chance distribution, the differences between the calculated and observed values in each case indicate the degree of homogeneity within each of these two sets. The results of this comparison are given in Table 2. This table shows that the SK set is much more coherent or homogeneous than the PS. This is most evident from a com-

TABLE 2. *Vocabulary connectivity values*

	Vocabulary exclusive to given selection		Difference
	Observed	Calculated	
SK1	447	412	+35
SK2	664	649	+15
SK3	268	281	−13
SK4	302	337	−35
SK5	352	375	−23
SK6	407	404	+ 3
SK7	170	164	+ 6
SK8	644	428	+216
PS1	944	583	+361
PS2	406	315	+ 91
PS3	383	311	+ 72
PS4	669	495	+174
PS5	401	274	+127
PS6	522	362	+160
PS7	765	516	+249
PS8	339	218	− 78

parison of their respective differences. The magnitude of the differences for the SK set is 346 while that for the PS set is 1,312. Further, of SK's total of 346, 216 or approximately two-thirds comes from our synthetic SK8. If this difference were removed the total of SK differences would drop to a mere 150. Clearly, therefore, the SK selections are in general much more like one another than the PS.

It is perhaps also worth pointing out that whereas the SK differences contain an approximately equal mixture of positive and negative values, all the PS differences, except that of PS8, are high and, particularly, positive. This means that seven of these eight selections have a substantially larger number of exclusive vocabulary items than are predicted by our chance model. In short, these selections have a markedly large and rich vocabulary. Of course, this is also implied by the ratios in Table 1.

TABLE 3(a)

	Exclusive vocabulary		Ratio
	Observed	Calculated	
PS1	269	304	.8854
PS2	139	165	.8426
PS3	123	163	.7546
PS4	156	258	.6047
PS5	102	143	.7134
PS6	155	192	.8073
PS7	237	273	.8682
PS8	116	115	1.0087

TABLE 3(b)

Selection	Ratio	Pseudonym	Work
PS8	1.0087	Anti-Climacus	*Sickness Unto Death*
PS1	.8854	A	*Either-Or*, vol. 1
PS7	.8682	Johannes Climacus (2)	*Concluding Un-scientific Postscript*
PS2	.8426	B	*Either-Or*, vol. 2
PS6	.8073	Johannes Climacus (1)	*Philosophical Fragments*
PS3	.7546	Johannes *de silentio*	*Fear and Trembling*
PS5	.7134	Vigilius Haufniensis	*Concept of Dread*
PS4	.6047	Constantine Constantius	*Repetition*

The final stage in our method is the pair-vocabulary test. This involves three distinct operations. The first is the determination of the number of observed vocabulary items each PS selection has *exclusively* in common with SKn. The second is the calculation of the number of such items which might be expected on the basis of chance alone using our naive model for the nine relevant selections (i.e. PS1, PS2 ... PS8 *and* SKn) and hence making the necessary corrections for the differing lengths and densities of each selection. The third is the finding of the ratio between the observed and calculated values. These values, together with their ratios, appear in Table 3(*a*). The resulting hierarchy is given in Table 3(*b*) together with the final ratios for easy comparison.

It is evident that these results suggest a quite different and very interesting interpretation of Kierkegaard but it is not our purpose to explore such matters here. Those interested in this question are invited to consult other forthcoming accounts of this work. In the present context, it is perhaps more relevant to point out that the differences between certain of these ratios are sufficiently small that they may be the result of mere chance. Specifically, taking the arbitrary figure of 5% as a minimum difference, there might be individual interchanges between the second and third, the third and fourth, and the fourth and fifth pseudonyms in this list. However, using this same standard, all remaining placings and priorities can be regarded as statistically well established.

5

It would be interesting and no doubt important to discuss the various assumptions underlying this method but it is perhaps more relevant to conclude with a comment concerning its further application.

That Kierkegaard's pseudonyms can be discriminated in this way is certainly surprising but not at all inexplicable. He insisted that they were distinct literary personalities and we have simply assumed that, if this were so, they would also have distinctive vocabularies. In fact, our investigations have shown this to be the case. Nor is it simply that certain key words such as *Absurde, Paradox, Stadier*, etc. are apparently reserved for the pseudonyms as such, though this is, I suggest, both startling and important. Rather, each pseudonym clearly has his own distinctive vocabulary. Table 2 shows that each has a very large number of vocabulary items peculiar to himself. Similarly, Table 3 (*a*) shows that each has a surprisingly large number which he shares exclusively with the acknowledged

Kierkegaard; which items, according to a preliminary survey, are largely independent of the subject matter under discussion. Hence, in one sense, our method worked because Kierkegaard was a supreme literary genius. Whether it would be equally successful with another author will perhaps depend upon whether he has similar intentions and, equally important, comparable skills.

This research was supported by grants from McGill University and the Canada Council to both of which I express my thanks. I am also grateful to Dr Gustav Herdan for advice during the early stages of this work, and to Professor Floyd R. Horowitz, Co-Editor of *Computer Studies in the Humanities and Verbal Behavior* for permission to reprint this article, which was originally published in vol. II of that journal (March 1969). (A. McK.)

III

Vocabulary studies and language learning

Computer assistance in language learning and in authorship identification

M. H. T. ALFORD*

For the past four years work has been in progress at the University of Essex for developing new methods of learning to read foreign languages. The problems have been treated primarily as psychological and only secondarily as linguistic. In the psychological sense, learning is a process which occurs throughout life in response to stimulus. The process is composed of initial learning and the refreshment of past learning. Without refreshment the effects of forgetting will overtake those of learning. The student's task is to obtain at least an equilibrium between the two. Both the student and the native have to maintain the level of performance by experiencing sufficient stimuli. Educational definitions of learning do much to obscure this situation.

Experiments have mostly been conducted with Russian texts. This has no psychological significance apart from the relation between this language and the learner's previous linguistic experience. Reference is also made to scientific literature. In the matters described, this is essentially the same as *belles lettres*, although some features tend to greater exaggeration of the phenomena. If a discipline is simply equated to a subject and a sub-discipline to a topic, the information will relate quite well to literary affairs.

A large amount of language information must be known in order to comprehend any significant body of literature. To establish the native's performance and the student's target, the textual details have to be quantified within the limits of each person's experience. The data then requires rearrangement in numerous ways so that it will facilitate the student's learning when presented to him. In particular, the rearrangement must take into account the individual's history of past learning and his future prospects at any moment, since these factors have a major influence on the efficiency of his current activity.

* Literary and Linguistic Computing Centre, University of Cambridge (formerly of the Language Centre, University of Essex).

Only the computer can carry out these complex tasks. In consequence, the Essex Project has been committed to Electronic Data Processing for the solution of research problems and for the production of instructional materials. As it is inefficient to organize any technology simply to satisfy initial requirements, programming has been planned to achieve the greatest flexibility in data processing.

Unannotated text is the only first-stage input and the programs perform various manipulations which are not tied to any specific purpose. For example a count derived from one text might be used for such widely different subjects as:

   (i) learning problems (high and low frequencies);
  (ii) educational administration (size of vocabulary);
 (iii) social studies (presence, absence and popularity of given words);
 (iv) determining authorship (idiosyncratic frequencies).

Singly and in combination the programs allow access to a considerable range of data. In cases where this does not cover new needs, the existing subroutines can be employed to make up a substantial part of the programs required. Since the manipulations which have been used for psychological analysis can be applied to other problems, it is worth considering them in some detail. They can be classified broadly as follows:

1. Identification

Text words can be identified as:

  (a) occurrence forms (graphic forms providing exact matches of text words);
  (b) paradigm members (occurrence forms equated with dictionary forms);
  (c) scatter-group members (words of different parts of speech varying only in grammatical meaning);
  (d) morpheme combinations.

Identification provides a programming location either for the retrieval of amplifying information or for later-stage instructions such as parsing routines.

2. Counting

This can be carried out with any form of identification and in any specified circumstances. Computation of such things as percentages, averages and distributions can be based on the figures thus acquired.

3. Comparing

Lists or texts can be compared (at any level of identification) to ascertain the common and the different elements in each. Uses range from the determination of new learning problems to checking the influence of one author or speaker upon another.

4. Amplifying

Identification can indicate the storage location of any information which may be required. Commonly sought forms of information are:
- (*a*) a dictionary entry appropriate to the identified word;
- (*b*) the morphemic segmentation of the identified word and the dictionary word;
- (*c*) the frequency of occurrence of the identified form according to any programmed system of reckoning;
- (*d*) the percentage text-coverage of any word;
- (*e*) its history of previous occurrence as bibliographic or concordance data.

5. Merging

Counts, lists and other data often have to be merged. This function makes possible counts larger than can be kept in the computer memory at one time. It also serves various editing requirements.

6. Ordering

Words may be ordered in various ways such as:
- (*a*) left-to-right alphabetically;
- (*b*) right-to-left alphabetically;
- (*c*) alphabetically commencing with any morpheme;
- (*d*) by any calculated frequency;
- (*e*) by reaching a specified number of occurrences.

7. Concordancing

Key words can be retrieved with their contexts. The keywords may be in:
- (*a*) alphabetic order;
- (*b*) text order.

The former serves to illustrate the usage of one word. The latter can contrast the usage of different words.

8. Formatting

The position of data on each page of print-out can be regulated:
 (a) to separate different types of information into selected fields;
 (b) to restrict print within a certain field.
The former has uses extending from the separation of stimulus from response, for psychological purposes, to assisting access to different data, for any form of investigation. The restriction to certain fields is important for photographic reproduction of print-out.

9. Editing

 (a) adding new information to reference files (such as dictionaries);
 (b) deleting information from files.
It will be noticed that the programs are able to analyse words in considerable depth but do not analyse word combinations. Lack of the latter facility was not found to be important in this type of work. Ample information about individual words allows humans to deduce nearly everything they wish to know about combinations. Furthermore, deduction processes improve learning and it is desirable that the form of the instructional material should promote this. It would have been quite simple to program the analysis of sentences for parsing or for identification of lexical items consisting of more than one word, but this would have taken up much space in core store and would have slowed down the program's speed of operation. Instead, by carrying a high-frequency dictionary in core, a very economical standard of operation has been achieved. The dictionary look-up program, for example, can find and print out the entries appropriate to 840 text words every minute. For this performance a low-level language (PLAN, available on the ICL 1900 series) was used and only 16 K (of 24-bit words) of core store were required. A similar program written in COBOL has achieved 330 words per minute. It would not be difficult to increase both these speeds substantially.

Computer programs can be applied to text to obtain data for two different types of analysis which determine 'author psychology' and 'reader psychology'. With authors, the purposes of analysis may be to establish personal identity, characteristics or sources of influence. With readers, it is the linguistic learning resulting from exposure to given texts, or to literature of a certain type, which can be assessed. Since the research at Essex has been concerned with readers, this subject will be dealt with first. The paper will conclude with some observations on author psychology.

The concept of 'a language' has little relevance in lexical learning. A modern developed language may have a vocabulary of about half a million words and at this size only representative terms from chemistry, biology, mineralogy, technology and other subjects would be included. The lexical requirements of individuals are a small fraction of this. Even the vocabulary of a single discipline reflects the linguistic habits of its individual scientists extremely poorly. Russian physics texts, for example, are almost completely covered by 60,000 different words. A large proportion of these would rarely if ever be met by any particular physicist in the course of his work. Specialist vocabularies generally run to about 10,000 words and differ a great deal from each other both in content and in the frequency of particular items. With each reduction in the size of the social group the more appropriate the vocabulary becomes to the needs of individual members. All the same, even a small social group remains a prescriptive and inaccurate classification of native lexical performance. There are many different interests within a group and members have different combinations of them. All this is reflected in vocabulary.

Since a group is only a psychological approximation to an individual, data relating to it must always be treated with reserve when formulating learning instructions. In the past, linguists have used group data because it was not feasible to provide individual data. The computer has completely changed this. It is now possible to take the texts which an individual will read and analyse them in terms of his personal learning experience. Whether a single text or many are taken for a count, one feature will remain constant: a small number of higher-frequency words will cover a large proportion of the text. In tabular form the data appears as follows:

No. of different words	Approx. % text coverage
4	10
50	34
100	45
350	70
1,000	86
2,750	96

D

These figures are taken from Russian physics.[1] If there is a spread of subject-matter, the text coverage declines for greater numbers of different words. Coverage can be up to 10% lower[2] for the higher figures.

It is advantageous to learn the high frequency (HF) words. A person who can recognize the 1,000 most common words in a particular subject will, on average, only meet one or two new words per sentence. The chances of being able to deduce the meanings of these will be quite high. At the same time the number of reference searches will be kept as low as possible for the amount of text read. When about 3,000 HF words are known, only about one word in a paragraph presents a problem. By this time the chances of being able to deduce its meaning are very good and further learning can mostly take place from profitable and extensive reading.

Most existing word-counts add the vocabularies from numerous different subjects. These combinations often fail to match the experience of individuals either by including unwanted subjects or by taking the wrong amounts of text from each. Some counts are very large and have the intention of finding a core HF vocabulary common to all subjects. This is illusory. Apart from two or three dozen grammatical words, 80–90% of HF words are lexical items which vary greatly even between the specializations in one subject. If an individual learner does require to read a number of different subjects, a general count is still only of limited use in learning. It describes a remote state of affairs and the count data can only properly be applied when that stage of experience is reached. It does nothing to trace the progression of events from which intermediate learning actually takes place.

Words which appear as low frequency (LF) in a general count are often high frequency in a local count. Computer[3] data shows that once a general low-frequency word has occurred in a text, its immediate future text-coverage is likely to be more than ten times that predicted by the general count. When a person reads, the local high frequency of words is often more than enough to cause learning with long retention. In consequence, it is currently studied literature which is of major importance in the learn-

---

[1] Sources (a) A. S. Kozak, 'High Frequency Words and Occurrence Forms in Russian Physics', RAND Corporation (Santa Monica, 1962); (b) Scientific Language Project data, University of Essex.

[2] E. Steinfeldt, *Russian Word Count* (Progress Publishers, Moscow), p. 53.

[3] The computer dictionary used at the University of Essex had the 800 most common Russian physics words in core store and lower frequency words on disk. When disk words were transferred to core, they were retained there. Core dumps could then be compared with text-coverage data from count programs.

ing process. In quantitative terms this can be considered in batches of 5–15,000 text words.

Besides high frequency, there is another psychological phenomenon which is formative in learning. This is the fact that items experienced and forgotten will be relearnt more quickly than completely new data. It is, therefore, advantageous to keep check of low-frequency vocabulary in a learner's past. When the cumulative influence of past ineffectual learning can be traced, relearning can be efficiently applied.

In practice, vocabulary learning is of two kinds, context-free and contextual. At Essex, each is assisted by different computer print-outs. For context-free learning, any required Russian texts are used as input and the outputs provide a word frequency count accompanied by a complete Russian – English dictionary entry for each word. Before reading the texts, learners check their knowledge of the high-frequency words and memorize as many as may be necessary to ensure a high-percentage text-coverage of known words. This increases reading fluency and, consequently, more past learning is refreshed. New learning is helped by improved chances of deduction and by the greater spacing of items requiring memorization. After having read the texts, learners check their knowledge of lower frequency words and see where relearning can most profitably be applied.

Text is read with a print-out in which the whole text is in a single column on the left margin and every word has a complete dictionary entry against it. This reduces reference search-time to almost nil and eliminates the distraction of finding unwanted data before the correct answer. These forms of assistance are of the greatest importance since vocabulary learning by frequent manual reference to dictionaries is appallingly inefficient. The psychological background to this and other learning activities does not come within the scope of the present paper. Those who are interested in these matters or in the details of the programs should read 'A Computer-Assisted Method of Learning to Read Foreign Languages' (M. H. T. Alford, Language Centre Report, University of Essex).

Author psychology can be considered in group and in individual form. Computer analysis provides the same type of data for both, but different interpretations have to be made. Groups can be defined as people sharing a given interest over a given period of time. A field of interest can be determined by the relationship between general high-frequency vocabulary and local high-frequency vocabulary. When the relationship is close the field is specialized, when it is more distant the field less specialized.

Experiment is needed to establish a satisfactory measurement of relationship. The two factors involved are (1) frequency and (2) presence/absence. A text is more specialized than the literature with which it is being compared when its high frequency words have a much lower frequency in a general count. But the local high-frequency words may not always provide an adequate distinction between closely related subjects. The common vocabulary of all branches of theoretical physics is mathematics. In experimental science the connection is the vocabulary of methodology. Consequently, related subjects have also to be distinguished by the presence or absence of typical vocabulary at medium frequencies and above.

Word frequencies change over long periods of time. In science this is apparent over decades. Words representing new concepts rise sharply from zero frequency or rarity to high frequency and then gradually decline as interest shifts away from their focal point. In most physics counts, for example, the word 'atom' is now less common than 'meson' or the other elementary particles. The frequency of the word 'meson' has itself declined in favour of the named types of mesons. It should, however, be noted that the term meson has been current for more than thirty years. Lexical frequency change is slow even when the ideas represented by the symbols undergo constant modification.

The historical period from which any frequency data is drawn is clearly important. With an individual, the point in his biography must also be considered. Psychological analysis can make a distinction between the products of habit, which can be changed, and ability, which is subject to less variation. An example of the former would be the use of particular conjunctions, and of the latter the total size of the vocabulary in a large amount of text. In the psychological analysis of the writings of individual authors, it must be borne in mind that measurements of performance and ability only classify. They do not distinguish unique features. There are, however, very many different ways in which language performance can be assessed. The combination of classifications applicable to a particular person should make it possible to identify authorship with a high degree of certainty. But the matter is complicated by the fact that each classification establishes the likelihood of adherence to a mean performance. In consequence, working out the reliability of any identification is not a simple statistical problem.

There is already some detailed literature on this subject[1] and, in the

[1] G. U. Yule, *The Statistical Study of Literary Vocabulary* (Cambridge, 1944) and Alvar Ellegård, *A Statistical Method for Determining Authorship* (Göteborg, 1962) are representative titles.

present paper, there is only space to make a few additional suggestions. Though word frequency has been much used in identification of authors, the different kinds of frequency have been poorly exploited. Consider the following:

(i) *Frequency of particular words in the total corpus.* This is the normal method of assessment.

(ii) *Frequency in different defined semantic contexts.* As pointed out previously, the frequencies of words vary between different topics discussed by the same person.

(iii) *Frequency in circumstances of defined formality.* This has an effect on frequency. It is particularly important for words which are not dependent on topic, such as conjunctions.

(iv) *Frequency in particular collocations.* Noun-adjective combinations and other associations provide distinctive features. It is the collocation of each choice which is significant. Lexical items like 'internal combustion engine' are a single choice.

(v) *Frequency after first occurrence.* (*a*) on each separate occasion; (*b*) for intervals such as 100, 500, 1,000 text words. The tendency to repeat oneself varies between individuals.

(vi) *Frequency of first words of sentences.* It is necessary to find the first lexical word in these cases. First concept words are remembered better than later ones. They, therefore, help to show what was uppermost in the author's mind.

(vii) *Frequency of solecisms.* In societies where spelling mistakes, clichés and other undesirable features are rare, they provide statistically valuable aids to identification. Manuscripts (or authors' typescripts) are naturally better sources than published versions.

(viii) *Frequency with specified degree of spontaneity.* Most of the above factors will be influenced by whether the work has been revised or not.

This list could be extended indefinitely. Furthermore, combinations of the different frequency measurements can be made. For example, one could specify word frequency in writing on a given topic, in formal circumstances after careful revision, per 500 text words after each occurrence. In all measurements, monologue and participation in dialogue should be considered separately. The former is the product of long-term memory and the latter is influenced by short-term memory. In the long term, influence is also likely to provide clues to identity, to date and to knowledge. A person who has recently read a book or report of events may show this by extensions to his former expression vocabulary and by a shift in frequencies.

Apart from frequencies, the size and coverage of a person's vocabulary are both distinguishing features. Size is not necessarily an indication of intellectual ability and, indeed, some outstanding scientists use small vocabularies. The circumstances in which the measurement is made also require definition. Besides those mentioned above, the type of explanation is also significant. Exchanges between colleagues tend to use small vocabularies and these increase in size when explanations have to be made to less well-informed people. This is illustrated by scientific papers which have smaller vocabularies than text-books on the same subjects.

The means of definition are limitless and the merits of any form of definition require to be established with texts of known origin. When circumstances are specified, the individual's mean performance and likelihood of variation have to be ascertained and this data must then be compared to that of other individuals and to groups.

Much work is involved in all this. In order to achieve the maximum progress and to make the most of limited resources, standardization and cooperation are needed. With some care, the machine-readable texts produced by individual researchers could be widely used. If dictionary and other file formats are kept simple, exchange will be greatly facilitated. Programs can be made available to all with compatible machines. It is not enough to discuss and publish findings: future success depends to a large extent on technological cooperation.

Sorting the French vocabulary according to word endings

C. DUDRAP and G. EMERY*

Some twelve months ago, a systematic survey of French nominal genders was undertaken, the outcome of which was to be a short manual for the use of students of French in grammar schools and universities. The aim was to review, complete and rationalize the old gender-by-ending rules,[1] and the approach was to be limited to the study of spelling, as reference to etymology would have considerably increased the difficulty of the task, while at the same time making the proposed manual more complex than was intended.

To carry out this survey, for which the use of a computer was not originally envisaged, we turned first to three recent publications listing the French vocabulary in reverse alphabetical order, but printed in the normal form:

Dictionnaire des rimes françaises, by Ph. Martinon, Larousse (Paris, 1962)

Dictionnaire complet des mots croisés, Larousse (Paris, 1964)

Dictionnaire inverse de la langue française, by A. Juilland, Mouton (The Hague, 1965).

None of these dictionaries proved really suitable: the first classifies its material phonetically, thus rendering an investigation into orthographic endings somewhat difficult and time-consuming; it also fails to give the gender of nouns with any consistency; The second classifies its material according to word-length (thus yielding 27 separate lists), and above all omits all reference to grammatical categories (and therefore gender); the third, which like the first classifies its material phonetically, seemed to be

---

* Royal Holloway College, University of London.
[1] See, for example, L. S. R. Byrne and E. L. Churchill, *A Comprehensive French Grammar with Classified Vocabularies* (Oxford, 1950), pp. 32–8, 261–4, 323–57 and 477–98.

the most suitable list to work on, giving both grammatical category and nominal gender. Unfortunately this seemingly very scholarly work is totally unreliable, both in its inclusion and exclusion of items (no reference to the origin of the lexical material is given) and, more disturbingly, in its often mistaken attribution of genders.

It was therefore decided to base the investigation on the contents of the *Nouveau Petit Larousse* (1969 edition) and to make use of the computer facilities of the University of London.[1]

Data preparation

The data (initially limited to French nouns but later extended to include all of the *Nouveau Petit Larousse*, with the obvious exception of the historical section) was punched on data-cards (average content: four lexical items per card), using a space-delimited free format. For ease of handling it was decided not to continue any word from one card to the next, so that the cards did not have to be kept in a given order. It was not felt necessary to transcribe all accents. Only acute-accented *e* in final position has a direct bearing on the problem of genders: this was punched as E/.

The following numerical code was appended direct to each dictionary word:

(a) Nouns

1   Masculine nouns (with the exception of those listed under 3, 4, 5 and 6), e.g. *manteau1*

9   Feminine nouns (with the exception of those listed under 3, 4, 5 and 6), e.g. *chaise9*

3   Masculine and feminine 'noms d'agent', e.g. *machiniste3* (= *le +la machiniste*)

6   Masculine and feminine 'noms d'agent', where the feminine form is derived from the masculine by standard rules (the noun was punched in its masculine form), e.g. *chanteur6* (= *chanteur +chanteuse*), *magicien6* (= *magicien +magicienne*), etc.

4   Nouns having both genders, but different meanings according to the gender used, e.g. *voile4* (= *le voile +la voile*)

5   Nouns having both genders with the same meaning, e.g. *pamplemousse5* (= *le* or *la pamplemousse*).

---

[1] Similar work has been under way for some time at the *Centre de Linguistique appliquée* at Besançon, under the direction of Professor B. Quemada.

(*b*) *Other grammatical categories*

2 Verbs
7 Adverbs
8 Adjectives (punched in their masculine form)
0 Prepositions, conjunctions, pronouns, interjections, abbreviations, etc.

The use of up to two alphabetical characters after the numerical code enabled us to define further categories of particular interest:

C = compound nouns of the 'verb + direct object' type, e.g. *porte-monnaie1C*;

P = nouns with irregular plural forms, e.g. *ail1P* (= *ails*, *aulx*);

D = nouns with alternative spelling, e.g. *calife1*, *khalife1D*; and so on.

The numeral (whether or not followed by one or two alphabetical characters) was to serve a double purpose: to make possible the printing out of all nouns in six separate lists, i.e. groups 1, 9, 3, 6, 4 and 5; and to act as a validation mark during the preparation of the data: only items terminated by a numeral (with or without additional alphabetical coding) were accepted by the editing routine. Punching errors could thus be automatically eliminated as long as they were noticed in time and not validated by the addition of a final numeral. This made the punch operators' task much easier. The data had nevertheless to be checked subsequently by eye for correctness both of spelling and coding. As a result some 5% of all cards had to be repunched.

Environment and language

When the project was first proposed, we were making use of the London University Atlas to which we had access by slow paper-tape link or by courier. However, the University was expecting delivery of a CDC 6600 in a few months, and we were to have our own fast link to that a short time later. It would be on this machine that the work would be done, but we felt, nevertheless, that much of the program development could be carried out in the meantime on Atlas. The programming language had, therefore, to be transferable from one system to the other, and it was for this reason that FORTRAN IV was selected. It was also decided to use the courier rather than the direct link to Atlas, since in spite of the slow turn-round (no more than two runs per week) this would permit punched cards to be used throughout, both for data and for program.

It was decided to use a packed character representation and to ease the problem of compatibility between the two machines by providing a few simple character-handling subroutines at the assembly-code level. This approach largely obviates the need to use FORTRAN in a machine-dependent manner, and takes care of the differences in character code between the two machines. Indeed, compatibility apart, it is often better to provide a few assembly-code routines than to try doing character editing in 'raw' FORTRAN. The language was never intended for that kind of work, and is somewhat inefficient at it. Changing from the one machine to the other thus involved: (*a*) rewriting the assembly-code subroutines; (*b*) making changes to allow for the different word lengths (8 characters in Atlas, 10 in the 6600); and (*c*) correcting for minor differences in dialect.

Coding

Six assembly-code routines have been written. For Atlas these were separate segments; but for the 6600 it was easier to write them as a single segment with several entry points, saving some programming effort by making use of common code and using macro facilities. The two machines handle characters somewhat differently: in fact, Atlas provides a few extra-codes for character-handling, and it seemed reasonable to make use of these. Unfortunately, the extracodes are word-oriented, and the Atlas routines became word-oriented in consequence. Two parameters are necessary to define a character – an address and a positional index: in the Atlas version it was necessary to refer to a character by its position in the word that actually contained it, whereas in the 6600 version it would have been possible to refer to a character by its position relative to the beginning of any word earlier in the string. Consequently, the final program for the 6600 was more complicated than it need have been.

Four of the assembly-code routines are predicate functions:

ALPHA, which is true if the designated character is alphabetic,

NUMERAL, which is true if the designated character is a numeral,

SPACE, which is true if the designated character is a blank,

SYMBOL, which is true if the designated character matches a character given as a third parameter in the call.

This character must be specified, literally or through an identifier, as the left-hand character of a word with zero fill – though, in fact, in the Atlas version it was more convenient to specify it as the right-hand character.

A further function GET, returns the designated character as its value. The character is returned at the left-hand end of a word with zero fill, though in the Atlas version again, it was more convenient to leave it at the right-hand end. The last routine, PUT, inserts a character given as the third parameter into the designated character position. In a sense, PUT is the inverse of GET, so a loop of the form

```
        DO 99 I = 1, N
          J = I + J0
          K = I + K0
99      CALL PUT (J, THERE, GET (K, HERE))
```

can be used to transfer a string of N characters from HERE to THERE in the store.

The program

The easiest way to sort words according to their endings is to invert them and then carry out a conventional sort, leaving the user to decide just how many letters constitute the ending. The 6600 has a powerful and versatile sort package, and it was this, no less than the direct link, that made us decide that it would be worth while to change from Atlas to the 6600. A useful feature of the sort package is that the user can specify the collating sequence. Thus, it was possible to have the solidus, representing the terminal acute accent, sorted between E and F.

The complete job consisted of three runs: an editing run, in which items with detectable errors were eliminated, and the remainder inverted and written to disc; a disc sort using the package provided; and an output run, re-inverting the items and printing them four to a line.

During editing the items are first unpacked from the cards into buffers of three (computer) words. This means that there is a limit of 24 characters for Atlas (30 characters for the 6600) on item length. Only one adverb – *anticonstitutionnellement* – actually exceeded the Atlas limit. It was therefore punched in an abridged form. All items deleted during the editing process, for whatever reason, were printed out as a cross-check.

Research and teaching applications

The first production run was used to print the whole vocabulary, sorted in the desired manner. Subsequent runs have separated the output into categories according to the terminating numeral. What happens is that the output program has been modified to read a parameter card giving the number of the category to be output, and to select from the sorted file according to this category. Several categories can be output as a single job run, by arranging to rewind the file and enter the output program as many times as necessary, providing further parameter cards as required. Thus we have so far two inverse classified lists:

(*a*) of all validated data (i.e. groups coded 0 to 9)

(*b*) of all validated nominal data (i.e. groups 1, 9, 3, 6, 4 and 5, printed separately).

While on the one hand considerably simplifying the preparation of the intended manual on French genders (rules can now be better formulated, all exceptions listed and various percentages determined), these lists have been of undoubted value during the last few months in writing a course of lectures on French phonetics. The combined information from direct and inverse classifications of the same material has proved a valuable aid to teaching.

Further developments

The next stage in the project is to make counts of suffixes. What we actually count are terminal groups of X to Y letters occurring at least Z times, where X, Y and Z can be adjusted to screen out the items of greatest interest at a particular stage of the investigation. Some results have already been obtained, but unfortunately a change in the operating system has altered the output of the sort package and will necessitate some changes to the program.

A point of interest is that we are now programming in ALGOL. ALGOL on the CDC 6600 implements the full input–output proposals of the Knuth sub-committee and has the two additional procedures INCHARACTER and OUTCHARACTER, which make it very suitable for handling text.

It is intended to extend the project by writing programs to scan the data for given consonant, vowel, or consonant–vowel clusters in initial and medial as well as final positions. In fact the scope for morphological analysis seems very wide indeed.

Dr J. H. Cable, former Lecturer in French at Royal Holloway College, took a major part in the elaboration of the project and the preparation of the data. Dr G. F. Kingston piloted the project through the production stage.

The role of the computer in selecting contemporary German prose for a beginners' (second stage) course

STEPHEN KANOCZ and AL WOLFF*

1. Background

In 1966 the British Broadcasting Corporation was asked by the School Broadcasting Council to provide an audio-visual beginners' course in German for secondary schools. As the Nuffield Foundation was, at that time, already fairly advanced with a similar course for eleven-year-old beginners, and as the average age at which German is started in secondary schools is still somewhere between thirteen and fourteen, the School Broadcasting Council and the BBC thought that the latter age group would be the most appropriate target audience for the course.

An experimental version of the course 'Frisch begonnen . . .' was written, produced and tested in 1967, and the final version was broadcast in 1968/9. A revised, second edition was broadcast in 1969/70.

The course takes pupils more than half-way towards O-level. (The Ordinary Level examination of the 'General Certificate of Education' in England concludes the study of a language before specialization. In German the average time spent in a school on an O-level course is three years. Two years after the Ordinary Level examinations pupils take a few subjects for their Advanced Level examination. The basic requirement for admission to university is usually two A-level plus five O-level passes, but increasing competition has resulted in recent years in a stiffening of conditions.) It contains a vocabulary of approximately 1,300 words. While the course was being written, it was found impossible to keep track of the vocabulary, and some mistakes occurred in the vocabulary list published in the Teachers' Notes. (This list contains all the words used in the course with the number of the programme in which they are introduced. However, about twenty words were left out altogether. In some instances an incorrect programme reference was given, and some words were included in the

* Schools (Radio) Department, BBC.

list which, through cuts made during the production, did not actually appear in the texts.) It was estimated that about two years of human labour would be needed to work out an accurate and detailed vocabulary reference list for the course. That was the first reason why the help of a computer was envisaged. With the help of an adaptation of programs already existing at the Literary and Linguistic Computing Centre and used by Roy Wisbey and Benedict Heal for the examination of Middle High German texts, it was possible to evaluate the vocabulary of 'Frisch begonnen . . .' very accurately.

Not only was the total frequency of the words occurring in the course indicated, but the course was subdivided into something like 200 subunits. First of all, it was subdivided into the twenty broadcasts of which the course consists. The course was further subdivided into functional units according to the way in which a word was introduced.

Functional unit 1 contains words which the pupils both hear and see in print.

Functional unit 2 contains words which the pupils hear but do not see in print.

Functional unit 3 contains the material of the language laboratory drills.

Functional unit 4 contains the exercises printed in the Teachers' Notes which the teacher may use at his discretion – he may abbreviate or expand them.

A special category was established for words that were to be introduced by the teacher as suggested in the Teachers' Notes, and these words were listed in *functional unit 6*.

Finally, *functional unit 7* contains the texts of songs, and *functional unit 8* the texts of dictations suggested in the Teachers' Notes.

The break-down of the 80,000 word course was completed by the computer with an accuracy which no human mind could ever achieve. Well before experimental results with classes using the course were available, the count gave a fairly good indication of the consolidation of knowledge and vocabulary by an average pupil in an average class. Thus the count will serve as a basis for the continuation of the course, an O-level course to be broadcast by the BBC in 1971/2.

2. Linguistic treatment of the text

The computer as programmed for this exercise cannot distinguish grammatical categories. It was therefore very important to link up words which in the German language appear split up in two different parts of a sentence. These are the verbs with separable prefixes. They were typed in the following way: The sentence *Vater kommt zum Flughafen mit* was changed into *Vater kommtmit zum Flughafen mit*.

As the Cambridge computer provides us with a reverse alphabetical index, all the words ending with *mit* appear together. Some of these are not necessarily verbs with separable prefixes, for example *womit*, but these can easily be eliminated. Therefore, one can look up, with the help of the reverse index for the detailed count, all the words ending with *mit* which are, in fact, verbs with separable prefixes. By deducting their total from the total occurrence of *mit* one obtains, as a useful by-product, the frequency of the preposition *mit* used in the course in its true prepositional function.

3. Introduction of post-war literary texts in the pupils' reader

It was decided that the continuation of the 'Frisch begonnen . . .' course (called 'Halb gewonnen!'), which should lead pupils up to O-level, should contain some samples of German literature. An arbitrary decision was made that all texts would have to be post-1945 publications as it did not seem appropriate, at this level, to burden children with older linguistic forms.

Within this immense range of literary material some arbitrary choice had to be made, and whatever the means of choice, it would have been open to criticism because of its arbitrariness. We therefore decided to leave the first selection to one single expert who is recognized as an authority on post-war German prose and who has had considerable experience in selecting prose passages for English-speaking children in the early stages of their study of German. Our choice fell upon Professor H. M. Waidson of the University College of Swansea, who kindly agreed to cooperate in the venture and supplied us with a list of short stories and extracts from longer prose works.

4. Second stage of selection

The texts proposed by Professor Waidson are being typed on to 8-hole punched tape. The linguistic treatment given to the texts is the same as indicated under 2 above, with two further refinements: reflexive verbs (which were relatively rare in 'Frisch begonnen . . .') are specially marked (with a capital R), and where forms derived from the verb of *werden* leave some doubt as to whether they are derived from the auxiliary verb of the future tense, the auxiliary verb of the passive voice or from the main verb (*werden* meaning 'to become') they are specially marked: F = Future; P = Passive; H = Main verb.

These texts are being submitted to a vocabulary count by the Cambridge Titan (Atlas II) computer, first individually, then as a corpus.

The first count is giving an indication of the suitability of each text for the course as we shall be able to compare its vocabulary with that of 'Frisch begonnen . . .'. (Incidentally, as work on 'Halb gewonnen!' proceeds, cumulative counts of the vocabulary covered will be made at certain stages.)

Far more important than this individual examination of texts will be the total count obtained from the texts arbitrarily selected by one single universally recognized expert. This total count will, for the first time, indicate which words occur most frequently in post-war German literary texts considered to be 'good' literature and 'easy to comprehend'. The teaching of vocabulary via 'Halb gewonnen!' will be geared to cover the most frequently occurring words.

5. Comparison of vocabularies

Although no computational aid was available when 'Frisch begonnen . . .' was written, the course achieved a surprisingly high congruence of vocabulary with the only two oral frequency lists of German vocabulary at present available: J. Alan Pfeffer, *Grunddeutsch, Basic (Spoken) German Word List*, 1964; Hans-Heinrich Wängler, *Rangwörterbuch hochdeutscher Umgangssprache*, 1963. We do not consider Oehler's vocabulary list (*Grundwortschatz Deutsch*, 1966) as relevant as it has neither a methodological basis made known to the reader, nor does it give any frequency counts. The same reservations have to be made about René Michéa's *Vocabulaire allemand progressif*, 1959. (In spite of this, both books are outstandingly successful as intuitive compilations of basic German vocabulary.) Kaeding's count is one of syllables not of words and is by now well out of date. The vocabulary count of the Mannheim corpus has not yet been published. (This corpus of more than one million words is being used for an extensive study of contemporary written German by the Institut für deutsche Sprache.)

It was found that 'Frisch begonnen . . .' contains and consolidates to a large extent all the words, with a dozen or so exceptions, that have a frequency count of 100 or more in either Pfeffer's or Wängler's works.

'Halb gewonnen!' now aims, amongst other things, to introduce in its early stages the most important of such words omitted from 'Frisch begonnen . . .'.

6. Spoken, literary and journalistic vocabulary

Both Pfeffer's and Wängler's counts are largely based on spoken German, although Wängler has also counted the vocabulary of periodicals. One of the tasks which we are at present undertaking is to compare this spoken vocabulary with the intuitively achieved vocabulary of 'Frisch begonnen . . .' and to compare both with such counts as are available of German newspaper-language. Two projects deserve special consideration in this respect. One is the count of the *Frankfurter Allgemeine Zeitung* undertaken by Professor Hans Eggers and his assistants in Saarbrücken. They kindly supplied us with the first 500 words of their frequency list. The other possibly even more important research project is being undertaken by Dr Manfred Hellmann, an assistant of Professor Hugo Moser in Bonn. Manfred Hellmann's main aim is to compare the language of *Neues Deutschland* and *Die Welt*, the two leading newspapers of East and West Germany respectively. So far we have only obtained from him the beginning of the frequency list of *Neues Deutschland* for 1964, but we are promised similar counts for *Die Welt* of 1964 and for both newspapers of 1968.

As everybody concerned with such counts knows, frequency lists are sometimes depressingly similar. It takes some time to discover differences which are due to the specific nature of the texts. But it is a well-known fact that whereas in most counts of the German language *die* is the most frequent word, Wängler's count, based entirely on spoken material, starts with *ich*.

A surprising finding when studying the vocabulary of *Neues Deutschland* was that the first *zeitungsspezifisches Wort*, i.e. the most frequently used word that occurred in that list but which had a very low frequency in other lists, was *Regierung*. We cannot but pay a compliment to the author of one of the best, if not *the* best of the 'old school' language text-books, Walter E. Anderson, who introduces this word in the second sentence of *Das schöne Deutschland*.

7. First results

The first instalment of texts selected by Professor H. M. Waidson, 25

'Kurzgeschichten', was fed into the computer both individually and as one single corpus. (German 'Kurzgeschichten' are 'short short stories'. Short stories of more than, say, 3,000 words are called 'Novellen', while the equivalent of an English 'novel' is a 'Roman'.) The corpus amounted to 12,250 words. (Because of certain built-in inaccuracies of the program, figures higher than 100 were rounded up to the next 10.) In the corpus the computer counted a total of 3,130 graphic forms. The most frequently occurring word is – contrary to all presently available word counts – *und* with a frequency of 420 (3.4%), followed by *die* occurring 390 times (3.1%) and by *er* with a frequency of 270 (2.2%). *Ich* comes fourth with a count of 260 (2.1%).

In counts based on written texts, *die* invariably takes first place (being the nominative and accusative feminine and plural definite article and relative pronoun), and it appears to be a sign of the 'flow of narration' in short stories that it is displaced by the eminently narrative *und*. Unfortunately, the resources at our disposal do not allow us to engage in a more detailed comparison of various lists and we have to confine ourselves to the extraction of results which are of importance to the writing of 'Halb gewonnen!'.

The 97 most frequently used graphic forms (less than 3% of the items) occur 17 times or more and constitute just over half (50%) of the corpus. This is a most encouraging finding as it means in rough terms that a reader with an initial knowledge of only 97 words of German will understand every second word of the 25 short stories. Of these 97 items, 91 were introduced in 'Frisch begonnen . . .' and 6 were not. The latter were in fact left out deliberately as 5 of them were imperfect forms of 'main' (i.e. not auxiliary) verbs, and these verbs were only taught in the present, future and perfect tenses. (For the justification of this selection of tenses, see a letter to the editor of *Visual Education* (October 1969), page 3, and the first report of the Institut für deutsche Sprache (January 1968, page 10) quoted in the letter.) The sixth item is *sei* (subjunctive). The percentage of the corpus taken up by the items in this group introduced in 'Frisch begonnen . . .' is just under 49% and by those not introduced 1.2%.

However, these arithmetical results must be approached with caution. To take only one example: the form *seiner* is well established in 'Frisch begonnen . . .' and has a high frequency in the literature count. But *seiner* is polyvalent. It is introduced in 'Frisch begonnen . . .' as the feminine dative of the possessive adjective *sein* but not as the corresponding genitive feminine or plural, not as the genitive of *er* (with prepositions or verbs) or the nominative masculine of the (emphatic) possessive pronoun *seiner*, *seine, seines*. On the basis of quite valid analogies we are justified in believing that these secondary meanings ('secondary to what?' would be a legitimate question) do not occur very often. But we simply do not know how often they do occur. Thus we do not know how often readers whose knowledge of *seiner* is confined to one meaning only will be misled by the other meanings.

92 forms occur between 8 and 16 times. They constitute 3% of the items and make up 10% of the texts. In this second group the performance of 'Frisch begonnen . . .' is much less impressive: 68 of the items were introduced in the course and 24 were not. However, a look at the individual graphic forms makes it clear that this second group already contains a high proportion of words conditioned by the story-line of the 'Kurzgeschichte' in which they appear. This is why the group also contains a relatively high number of first names. (Proper names were counted by the computer but disregarded for the purposes of this summary.) Another important component of the 24 items in this group which do not occur in 'Frisch begonnen . . .' is, as in the case of the 6 items in the first group, grammatical forms which had deliberately been avoided.

450 graphic forms (14% of the items) occur between 3 and 7 times and constitute 15% of the corpus. 2,490 forms (80%) occur once or twice and take up 25% of the text.

The comparison of these figures shows how the 'law of diminishing returns' works in the build-up of useful vocabulary. Something like a hundred words enable the reader to understand half of the 'easy' stories, the second hundred increase his understanding by a further 10%. More than twice the amount needed to get a 60% understanding increases his range to 75%. In other words: Even with 'easy' texts there seems to be no alternative but to use a dictionary or guess the meaning from the context for something like 10–20% of the words encountered. (Many of the rare graphic forms will be recognized as derivatives, compounds or constituent parts of words known.)

8. Use of the count

When producing 'Halb gewonnen!' the results of the computer count will be used in three ways:

(*a*) When selecting the 'Kurzgeschichten' (and extracts from 'Novellen' and 'Romane'), those with a great deviation from the vocabulary of 'Frisch begonnen . . .', from general spoken, written and newspaper vocabulary, and also from the general vocabulary of 'easy' post-war narrative literature (the latter is emerging from our own count) will be discarded irrespective of their literary merits.

(*b*) The emerging ranking-list of the vocabulary of 'easy' post-war narrative literary texts will be taken into account when planning the vocabulary progression, so as to fill gaps left by 'Frisch begonnen . . .'.

(*c*) At present it looks, however, as if there are virtually no gaps to be filled as far as the knowledge of very frequent words or morphemes is concerned. Our main task will, therefore, consist of identifying items already introduced which have frequently occurring meanings different from those with which our pupils are already familiar. This will have to be done either by (one hopes 'inspired') guessing or computer analysis. The latter would require a considerable refinement and extension of our existing program, for which extension we have no funds.

9. Summary

(*a*) A detailed computer count of the vocabulary of a multi-media language course ('Frisch begonnen . . .') has been made, as far as we know, for the first time (although see the paper by D. G. Burnett-Hall and P. Stupples in this volume). On the basis of this, the further progress of instruction can be planned with an accuracy that could not be equalled if human labour alone were to be used. It would also be possible to draft an achievement test without reference to the actual achievement of pupils learning from the course. Such an achievement test could go a long way towards a more scientific and less intuitive definition and administration of language examinations. At present no funds are available for the latter work.

(*b*) A computer count is being made of texts of contemporary German literature, which are subjectively judged to be 'easy'. A comparison of this count with the count of 'Frisch begonnen . . .' and with published and unpublished frequency counts of words in written and spoken texts, will serve as the basis for:

  (i) selecting suitable prose reading-passages for pupils following an 'O'-level course;
  (ii) gearing the build-up of the vocabulary of the above-mentioned pupils so as to enable them to read contemporary German narrative literature.

(*c*) It appears that the graphic forms introduced in 'Frisch begonnen . . .' have been well selected for the purpose of teaching the pupils basic vocabulary needed for the reading of contemporary German narrative literature.

(*d*) To achieve even better results a more refined examination of the vocabularies would be required – based on a program that can differentiate between various meanings of forms, from the context in which they stand. Research in this direction would have the greatest general value for the future teaching of German (i.e. far beyond the needs of the course 'Halb gewonnen!'). We have no funds for such an extension of our research.

10. Literary texts

(*a*) *Self-contained pieces of less than 1,000 words each*
Ilse Aichinger: (From *Eliza, Eliza*, Fischer Verlag, Frankfurt, 1965)
 'Mein grüner Esel'
Johannes Bobrowski: (From *Mäusefest*, Wagenbach, Berlin, 1965)
 'Interieur'
Wolfgang Borchert: (From *Das Gesamtwerk*, Rowohlt, Hamburg, 1949)
 'Die Katze war im Schnee erfroren' 'Die drei dunklen Könige'
 'Die Küchenuhr'
Bertolt Brecht: (From *Kalendergeschichten*, Verlag Neues Leben, Berlin,
 1949)
 'Geschichten vom Herrn Keuner'
Wolfgang Hildesheimer: (From *Deutsche Erzähler der Gegenwart*, ed.
 W. Fehse, Reclam, Stuttgart, 1959)
 'Eine größere Anschaffung'.

(*b*) *Short stories and sketches, excerpts from*
Ilse Aichinger: (From *Auf den Spuren der Zeit*, ed. Rolf Schroers, Munich,
 1959)
 'Wo ich wohne'
Johannes Bobrowski: (From *Mäusefest*, Wagenbach, Berlin, 1965)
 'Mäusefest'
Heinrich Böll: (From *Erzählungen, Hörspiele, Aufsätze*, Kiepenheuer and
 Witsch, Cologne and Berlin, 1961)
 'Mein Onkel Fred' 'Unberechenbare Gäste'
 'Schicksal einer henkellosen Tasse' 'Hier ist Tibten'
Wolfgang Borchert: (From *Das Gesamtwerk*, Rowohlt, Hamburg, 1949)
 'Die Elbe. Blick von Blankenese'
Gerd Gaiser: From *Am Paß Nascondo*, Hanser, Munich, 1960

Siegfried Lenz: (From *Stimmungen der See*, Reclam, Stuttgart, 1962)
'Die Festung' 'Der seelische Ratgeber'
Wolfdietrich Schnurre: (From *Eine Rechnung, die nicht aufgeht*, Walter,
Olten and Freiburg, 1958)
'Die Tat'
(From *Als Vaters Bart noch rot war*, Zürich, 1958;
Ullstein, Berlin, 1964)
'Die Leihgabe' 'Jenö war mein Freund'
'Der Verrat'.

11. References

(a) Language courses

'Frisch begonnen. . . .', an audiovisual course in German for beginners by Stephen Kanocz, broadcast and published in 1968/9, second edition 1969/70. The complete second edition is on sale (BBC Publications).

It contains 4 tapes of programmes, 2 exercise tapes for language laboratory use, 20 filmstrips. 2 volumes of teachers' notes, 2 volumes of pupils' readers, and 30 flashcards.

'Halb gewonnen', an audiolingual course of German (follow-on to 'Frisch begonnen. . .'), first broadcast in 1971/2. Twenty programmes of 30 minutes. Publications: 2 pupils' readers, 2 volumes of teachers' notes, and 4 filmstrips. Exercise tapes are planned for the second edition.

'Vorwärts', an audiovisual course of German published by the Nuffield Foundation and the Schools Council (Leeds, 1968ff.).

Walter E. Anderson, 'Das schöne Deutschland', Erster Teil (London, 1955).

(b) Linguistic works

Forschungsberichte, vols 1–5 (Institut für deutsche Sprache, Mannheim, 1968–70).

René Michéa, *Vocabulaire allemand progressif* (Paris, 1959).

Heinz Oehler, *Grundwortschatz Deutsch* (Stuttgart, 1966).

J. Alan Pfeffer, *Grunddeutsch, Basic (Spoken) German Idiom List* (New Jersey, 1968).

Hans-Heinrich Wängler, *Rangwörterbuch hochdeutscher Umgangssprache* (Marburg, 1963).

The use of word frequency in language course writing

D. G. BURNETT-HALL and P. STUPPLES*

1. The Project

The Schools Council Modern Languages Project is preparing language teaching and learning materials for secondary school pupils aged thirteen to sixteen. The materials are to follow on from the Nuffield Foreign Language Teaching Materials for pupils aged eleven to thirteen (in the case of French from 8 to 13 years old). Each section of the project is responsible for preparing the materials in one foreign language and has considerable autonomy in the type of methodology it employs.

The Russian Section of the Schools Council Project consists primarily of a team of writers made up of three English specialists in secondary education who have also taught the Russian language in schools, and two native speakers from the University of Moscow who are specialists in the preparation of teaching materials in Russian as a foreign language.

2. Aims

The aims adopted by the Russian Section of the Project are to teach a pupil:

(a) to comprehend the Russian speech used in everyday situations;

(b) to be able to take part in limited verbal exchanges related to those same everyday situations;

(c) to develop an ability to take part in more extended speech, that is, to extend limited dialogue into more open discussion;

(d) to be able to read and understand those public notices and other printed matter associated with everyday situations;

(e) to be able to read and understand short stories and magazine articles written for their age group in modern Russian;

* Department of Computation and Schools Council Modern Languages Project, University of York.

(*f*) to be able to read and understand captions and chapter headings in non-fiction articles;

(*g*) to be able to write letters within the linguistic limits of the preceding programme;

(*h*) to have an understanding of the basic cultural and social mores of the Soviet people.

The pupils will be expected, at the end of the five-year course, to have an active vocabulary of approximately 2,000 words and a passive vocabulary of a further 3,000 words.

The writing team considers that these aims divide themselves into two parts, those associated with the development of speech patterns and those enabling the pupils to read texts for pleasure and information. The ability to write letters, within the limits imposed, is felt to be an extension of dialogue into monologue, rather than a development of the skills taught in learning to read. On the other hand these two parts are interrelated to the extent that speech patterns are also absorbed through reading texts, though the linguistic conventions peculiar to literature have less influence on speech patterns. (This interrelation is, of course, much more complex in reality. For example, the lecture, whilst spoken, is often very close to written language. For the purposes of the writing team, however, the simple distinctions made above are probably valid.)

3. Methodology

The authors are also concerned with the learning processes employed by pupils trying to master the skills developed in the course. The authors' basic methodological premise is that the materials should consist of a series of small advances in knowledge of the language in a matrix of what is already familiar. Linguistically these advances would be in the fields of grammar, syntax and lexis. This premise takes into account the insight that pupils learn faster and with greater confidence if they are presented with easily assimilated small learning steps in a linear progression through the language, and that there should be a constant repetition of what has been learned previously, especially in new linguistic situations (overlearning).

Adherence to these principles indicates the need for a very careful control of the introduction of new matter as well as regular repetition on the lines stated. Earlier course writers, often aware of these learning problems, have been hampered by the enormous amount of clerical work involved to ensure a methodical handling of their teaching materials. This has often meant the abandonment of systematic control, to the detriment of the effectiveness of their material. Also aware of the problem, the Russian Section of the project has made use of the services of the Computation Department at the University of York.

4. Design objectives

The Russian Section required a computer program which would sort a linguistic corpus, that is, analyse material that has already been written and analyse draft material in the light of what has already been used and in the light of future needs. The print-out had to be as simple as possible to enable the team of writers to make a rapid interpretation of the information.

The basis of the analysis is lexical as this is simple to notate and interpret. It also enables the team to use a very flexible system of introducing and removing material from the computer bank. The computer produces an alphabetical list of all the lexical items in a text. Each morphological form of a word is sorted as a separate lexical item. This is not only to maintain the simple system of notation but also to enable the writers to follow the progress of the morphological forms (case, number, tense or aspect) of every word. As morphological changes in Russian, for the most part, occur at the end of words, the various forms of a word naturally group themselves together in an alphabetical list. For each lexical item the print-out also lists the number of times the item has occurred in the current text and the number of times in all previous texts, the number of texts in which it has previously appeared, and the code-number of the last text in which it was used. On all cumulative lists another column gives each lexical item an index number, which is obtained by multiplying together the number of occurrences of the item and the number of texts in which it appeared. The index number is thus a rough guide to the thoroughness or otherwise of the team's adherence to the principle of repetition.

The occurrences of morphological forms as a grammatical group may easily be checked by sorting the words after reversing the order of the letters in each word. Words with the same ending will then be grouped, and a list can be printed with the words restored to their natural letter-order.

5. Computer programs

A suite of computer programs was developed to process the texts and produce the cumulative lists:

(i) *Load Text*. Read the unit of text from cards and record it on magnetic tape as a sequence of 20-character words.

(ii) *Sort*. Take the output of the previous program and produce a magnetic tape on which the words of the unit appear in alphabetical order.

(iii) *Summarize*. If a word is repeated four times in a unit, four successive copies of the word will appear in the output of the Sort program. The Summarize program produces a summarized text in which the words appear in alphabetical order, each with the number of occurrences in this unit.

(iv) *Merge*. This program, which merges two tapes produced by the Summarize program for the same unit, is used to make corrections to a text at the summary stage. The format of the magnetic tape produced by this program is identical with that of a tape generated by the Summarize program.

(v) *Word-Lists*. This program reads from two magnetic tapes, one containing the summarized text of a unit (produced by the Summarize or Merge programs), the other the cumulative list of all words used before the current unit (produced on the previous run of this program). The cumulative list contains all the words in alphabetical order: with each word is held the total number of occurrences, the number of different texts in which it appeared, and a code number for the last text in which it appeared. (The latter item indicates how recently the word last occurred: it also allows all previous occurrences to be found by tracing back through the print-outs for the relevant texts.)

The Word-Lists program writes the updated cumulative list to magnetic tape for use in the next run. It also prints out in alphabetical order all the words which occurred in the current text, divided into 'new words' (those not on the old cumulative list) and 'old words' (which appeared on the old cumulative list as well as the current text). With each old word there is printed the additional information specified in the previous section.

(vi) *Print Cumulative List*. This program is used only occasionally (not after every unit of text) to print out the complete cumulative list to date. This information is not provided by the Word-Lists program, which does not print any word which did not appear in the current text.

Further details of the computer programs are given in Appendix 1.

6. Concordance

A limited field of concordance is obtained by grouping together each preposition and each noun governed by it, in its appropriate form, as one lexical item. The nouns governed by the prepositions themselves appear separately with the other forms of that word in the alphabetical list.

This is made possible by employing a system of secondary spaces. To take an example in English, the phrase 'in time' would be marked IN* TIME in the manuscript and would be punched in this way. The Load Text program would write both the 'word' IN*TIME and also TIME on to its output text, and these would be treated as independent words by all subsequent programs. The preposition IN will not appear by itself in any list but, since the asterisk is regarded as a character following the last letter of the alphabet, all IN* . . . expressions will appear consecutively in alphabetical lists.

This system enables the writing team to observe the frequency of other limited concordances which they consider significant, such as adverbial expressions, emphatic, specific and non-specific particles, and some common expressions consisting of more than one word. A list of these limited concordances may be found in Appendix 2.

Often the writers need to know the frequency of the use of expressions rather than words. This can usually be obtained swiftly by checking for the keywords of the expression. This solution is not ideal, however. The remedy is a much more complex system of notation which would perhaps defeat the object of using a computer for speed and simplicity. For example, the University of Essex, in its analysis of modern Russian, has spent a very long time establishing a system of notation. Our purposes are not so complex and we have not the time for such elaborate preparation.

7. Banks of materials

The Nuffield Course, intended primarily to develop basic speech patterns, was fed into the computer first of all. This material (Bank 1) acts as a basis for the Schools Council course.

The draft Schools Council texts are then fed into the computer in the order in which they will be presented to the pupil. On an analysis of the print-outs of these texts the materials are rewritten, ensuring that the learning steps are minimal and that there is adequate repetition of new and previously learned material.

As the course is divided linguistically into two parts, the corpus is fed into two interrelated banks. The Reading Material Bank is further subdivided in order to differentiate between basic reading meant for all pupils and additional reading for pupils who can work faster than others in their group.

The Schools Council materials are, therefore, arranged in three banks:

Bank 2: Presentation Materials Bank (speech patterns)
Bank 3: Basic Reading Material Bank
Bank 4: Additional Reading Material Bank.

Bank 3 includes the material of Bank 2. Bank 4 includes Bank 3. The presentation materials are divided into units, which the pupils normally take at the rate of ten units a year. Each set of reading materials is divided into layers, which consist of two to four texts: there are six layers for each year of the course. Before a particular layer of basic reading can be studied it is necessary to have taken a certain number of presentation units, but the converse is not true – one of the aims has been to give the teacher considerable flexibility in choosing the order in which he uses the materials.

8. Revision of materials

These three banks could be developed in a straightforward manner, using only the programs described in section 5, if the work were done when the materials had reached their final forms: the operation becomes more complex when rewritten sections replace earlier drafts on the bank chain. It is fundamental to our plans that the writers should have the latest information available, both when preparing drafts and when they are being rewritten, at which stage future needs can be taken into account. This complexity is increased by the different writing rates of the different parts of the course and of individual writers.

At a particular moment the chains might have the following forms:

Draft Bank 2   Bank 1 +rewritten presentation units 1–3
                       +draft presentation units 4–6
Draft Bank 3   Bank 1 +rewritten presentation units 1–2
                       +rewritten basic reading units 1–4
                       +rewritten presentation unit 3
                       +draft presentation unit 4
                       +draft basic reading units 5–8
                       +draft presentation units 5–6
Draft Bank 4   Bank 1 +rewritten presentation units 1–2
                       +rewritten basic reading units 1–4
                       +rewritten additional reading units 1–4

+rewritten presentation unit 3
+draft presentation unit 4
+draft basic reading units 5–8
+draft additional reading units 5–8
+draft presentation units 5–6

In addition there will be three corresponding 'Rewritten Banks', containing only the rewritten materials shown in the draft banks.

Presentation unit 4 may now be rewritten in the light of information in both Rewritten Bank 2 (up to unit 3) and Draft Bank 2 (up to unit 6). It must then be added to the three Rewritten Banks, and it must also replace draft presentation unit 4 in the three Draft Banks. The latter operation requires an extra computer program to prepare a difference tape which itemizes the differences between the draft and rewritten versions.

Thus the banks are constantly updated and all subsequent analyses will reflect the rewritten versions, so that the writers have as accurate a picture as possible of the current content of the materials.

9. Other advantages

Besides the writing of presentation and reading materials the team is also preparing grammar explanation sections to accompany the course. These include exercises, commentaries on word formation, word root development and word recognition. All of these processes are helped by the computer print-outs and the degree of language redundancy in the materials is reduced to a minimum. The task of preparing vocabularies and indices is of course greatly speeded up. Cumulative frequency lists at various stages give the writers a regular review of their materials as a whole.

10. External linguistic checks

Further linguistic checks are made by ensuring that all the materials in their draft forms are written by native speakers or adapted by native speakers from scripts written by native speakers. The checking of rewritten versions is also done by native speakers. The new lexical items on the print-outs of the draft materials are also checked against existing word frequency counts of the language.

The authors would like to acknowledge the invaluable assistance given by Mrs Sinikka Wyatt, who wrote all the ALGOL programs and supervised the processing of the texts on the computer.

APPENDIX I

Practical problems

This appendix describes some of the practical problems which were encountered in processing the texts on a computer and the methods used to overcome them.

Alphabets

The fact that the Russian language uses the Cyrillic and not the Roman alphabet presents considerable problems in preparing the texts for input to the computer and also in the form of the print-outs. Inside the computer the letters of the Cyrillic alphabet must be held in numerical form, with values ranging from 1 to 33 so that the Sort program will produce the words in the order of the Cyrillic alphabet. The choice of the value 34 for the asterisk symbol ensures that all expressions of the form preposition*noun using the same preposition (and similar concordance items, see section 6) will be adjacent in alphabetically ordered lists.

It is therefore necessary to transliterate both on input to the computer and on the output of printed lists. The two transliterations, which were affected by table look-up, are distinct processes, so different transliterations of Cyrillic were chosen for input and output purposes.

The input alphabet is used by a punch operator with no previous experience of Cyrillic, working on standard card punches and verifiers. The symbols of the input alphabet were therefore chosen to be as close as possible in shape to the Cyrillic characters. The output alphabet, on the other hand, occurs in the print-outs which the writers use in preparing and revising units of text. In its choice, therefore, more weight was given to the sounds than the shapes of the Cyrillic characters. The details of the alphabets are given in Appendix 3.

While this problem arises in acute form where the Cyrillic alphabet is used, it can also occur in languages which use the Roman alphabet. As the characters are transliterated on input and again on output, the accented vowels in French presented no problems when the same programs were used to analyse Schools Council texts for this language.

Data preparation

In a project of this size, the preparation of the text in a form which can be read by the computer is a major task. When all the texts have been punched and verified it is probable that this will have required the equivalent of nine months' full-time work for a punch operator.

A punch operator is employed part-time to punch cards on a standard IBM 029 punch from the original texts – these are already printed (for the basic Nuffield course) or in typescript (for the draft and revised Schools Council units). The cards are then verified, i.e. the text is typed again on a verifier machine which checks that the information on the cards is identical with that typed; in this way the great majority of punching errors are discovered and can be corrected.

The verification was carried out by the same operator. A single operator can make the same mistake on the punch and verifier; this is particularly likely when she is typing a language which she does not understand. It would be preferable to have all material verified by a different operator, but the cost of familiarizing two operators in the Cyrillic alphabet prevented this.

Each text has to be typed twice (for punching and verifying) in the course of preparing the cards, but it will already have been typed from manuscript. An obvious economy on labour would be to type the original texts from manuscript on a machine which punched a paper tape as well as producing the typescript. Unfortunately time did not allow us to investigate the possibility of obtaining a paper-tape machine incorporating a Cyrillic typewriter, but this might have proved viable if the problem could have been foreseen sufficiently early in the project.

Corrections

In any computing project the data must be completely accurate if the results are to be of any value. It was therefore considered most important to provide opportunities for inserting corrections.

If verification detects errors in the original cards, the standard procedure is to re-punch the erroneous cards. However, an alternative method can be provided: since only the frequency with which words occur is being analysed and not their context, corrections can be added at the end of the text if they are marked to indicate insertions or deletions. If errors are found before the cards have been read by the Load Text program such correction cards can be added to the end of the pack.

The Load Text program produces a listing of the text on the lineprinter for proofreading. This is not as accurate a check as verification (particularly when the listing is in a pseudo-Cyrillic alphabet), but it may detect some errors. If so, correction cards are punched and fed to a separate run of the Load Text program, which adds them at the end of the original text on magnetic tape.

If errors are not detected until after the text has been sorted and summarized, the correction cards must be put separately through the loading, sorting and summarizing processes. The summary tapes of the original text and the corrections are then merged using a special program (see section 5(iv)), and the resulting tape is used to produce the various word-lists. The possibility of making corrections at this stage was found to be valuable, since most punching errors result in mis-spelt words which are easy to detect if they appear only once in an alphabetical list.

Number of programs

Every text has to be processed by at least four programs before the word-lists are printed, and it may be objected that fewer programs should be required. The number of programs is determined largely by the need to allow corrections both before the text is sorted and summarized and also before the cumulative list is updated and the word-lists printed. While it would be possible to write a single program combining all the processes, corrections could then be made only by re-running the complete program with the corrected text.

Sorting the 20-character words into alphabetical order is the most complex operation in programming terms. It was decided that a commercial sorting program should be used in order to save time on the writing and testing of programs: the NCR 4100 Sort Generator is the only such program readily available on 4100 computers. While this program sorts the words very efficiently, it has certain limitations for the present application. In particular, if a word appears several times in a text, the output from the Sort program contains the appropriate number of copies of the word in succession, and the Summarize program had to be written to reduce this to a single copy of the word with the total number of the occurrences in the text. Had the sorting program been written from scratch this reduction would, of course, have been included within it.

Programming language

All the programs were written in ALGOL, with the single exception just noted. While in theory they can be run on any computer with an ALGOL compiler, they call extensively on the set of 4100 ALGOL procedures for handling magnetic tapes and in practice a considerable amount of re-programming would be required. Indeed it is probable that any job using backing storage extensively would need to be substantially modified if it were to be run efficiently on a different computer.

APPENDIX 2

Explanation of limited concordance

A. All prepositions will be found printed out with the nouns they govern.
B. The following other concordances are also printed out.

А то	В следующий раз
Автомат (2) (machine gun)	В советском союзе
	В те годы
Боже мой	В то же время
Было бы	В чём дело
— бы	В эти годы
В конце концов	В эти дни
В котором часу	В эти же годы
В одно время	В это время
В одно и то же	В этом году
В — час (а) (ов)	В этот день
В том же году	В этот же день
В тот же день	В этот момент

В этот раз
В эту минуту
Во время
Во время —
Всё в порядке
Всё время
Всё равно
Всё это время

До нашей эры
До свидания
До сих пор
До скорой встречи
Доброе утро
Добрый день
Дорогой (2) (nom. masc. sing. adj.)
Друг друга и т.д.
— же

За это время

И так далее
И т.д.
И то
И тому подобнее
И т.п.
История (2) (story)

К тому же
Как же
Как будто
Как дела
Как жаль
Кто-то

Может быть

На! (2)
На другой день
На здоровье

На следующий день
На Советский Союз
На этот раз
Не за что
Недалеко от —
Некоторое время

Повести (2) (nom. pl.)
Потому что
Похож (а/и) на
Почему же
Прежде чем
Предмет (2) (object)
Представить себе и т.д.

Рядом с —

С днем рождения
С тех пор
Совет (2) (advice)
Спокойной ночи
Счастливого пути

Там ж
Только что
То есть
Тут (at this moment)

У меня (2) (chez)
Уже (2)
Узнать (2) (to recognize)

Что-то
Что ж (е)
Что это такое
Что с —
Что такое
Чувствовать себя и т.д.
Чуть не
Чёрт возьми

c. All future imperfectives are to be found together with the part of быть with
which they were used.

E

APPENDIX 3

Alphabets

Internal value	Input character	Cyrillic character	Output character
0	space	space	space
1	A	А	A
2	-	Б	B
3	B	В	V
4	L	Г	G
5	D	Д	D
6	E	Е	E
7	%	Ё	E
8	S	Ж	Q
9	Z	З	Z
10	N	И	I
11	V	Й	J
12	K	К	K
13	@	Л	L
14	M	М	M
15	H	Н	N
16	O	О	O
17	<	П	P
18	P	Р	R
19	C	С	S
20	T	Т	T
21	Y	У	U
22	F	Ф	F
23	X	Х	X
24	U	Ц	H
25	G	Ч	C
26	W	Ш	W
27	Q	Щ	$
28	.	Ь	'
29	,	Ъ	,
30	I	Ы	Y
31	/	Э	&
32	J	Ю	£
33	R	Я	@
34	*	*	*

Example: When the punch operator sees the Cyrillic character B, she types B (the input character); this will be stored as the number 3 and subsequently printed as V (the output character).

Punctuation: One space (or more) is punched between words. The punch operator is instructed not to punch any punctuation marks other than the space and the asterisk (concordance symbol).

IV

Stylistic analysis and poetry generation

Mathematical modelling in stylistics: its extent and general limitations

D. R. TALLENTIRE*

It may be readily seen from a recent survey such as *An Annotated Biblio-graphy of Statistical Stylistics*[1] that the conclusions reached about style via computational methodologies, far from being 'definitive' by virtue of their objectivity, are mutually contradictory. Discouraging reports abound, for example:

[Moritz] examines the claim of Sherman, Hildreth and Gerwig . . . [and] shows that [their chosen parameter] is extremely variable (p. 71).
Kroeber argues that the usual subjects of statistical measurement are insufficient to delineate the nuances of style (p. 7).
In reply to Williams' assertion that sentence-length is distributed logarithmic-ally and is distinctive of a given author, Buch shows that sentence-length distributions vary through time (p. 17).
See article . . . for a criticism of this claim. (This phrase is appended to entries throughout the bibliography.)

Why are 'objective' stylistic studies frequently inconclusive? Why do tests of proven value in other disciplines frequently yield conflicting results when applied to stylistic analysis? Two basic possibilities exist: either literary style must not be susceptible to quantification, or the mathematical models upon which recent stylistic studies depend are inappropriate, or have been misapplied. A few isolated but convincing projects[2] refute the first conjecture, but it is increasingly evident that the second is true. It is the intention of this paper, therefore, to indicate the diversity of mathematical modelling in stylistics (six representative approaches to style will be discussed, each dependent on a different branch of mathematics), and to suggest some of the reasons why contradictions arise in applications of these analogues to literature.

* Literary and Linguistic Computing Centre, University of Cambridge.
1 Compiled and edited by Richard W. Bailey and Lubomír Doležel (Ann Arbor, 1968).
2 See, for example, Frederick Mosteller and David L. Wallace, *Inference and Disputed Authorship: 'The Federalist'* (Reading, Mass., 1964).

It may be useful to precede an assessment of stylistic theories employing mathematical techniques with a diagrammatic representation of the possible approaches. That provided by H. P. Edmundson[1] will serve (see Fig. 1), with the reservation that the categories he lists are not as disjoint

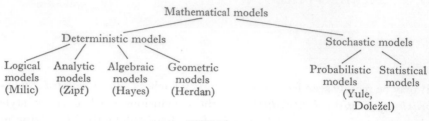

FIGURE I

as his diagram suggests. Logic and analysis, for example, are basic to probabilistic and statistical models, and the latter two are often considered to be a single branch of mathematics. Until recently, as Gustav Herdan pointed out, it was felt 'that language was all deterministic and had nothing to do with chance'.[2] Such a simplistic view is no longer tenable. In fact, the bulk of mathematical frameworks used in stylistics are now stochastic, though deterministic models (for example Chomsky's algebraic generation of syntactic structures[3]) are potentially highly relevant. Each type has its uses in stylistics, since literature involves both choice and chance, and the selection of model depends on the aspect of literature one wishes to study. The futility of searching for a 'best' model of literature will be shown, but a listing of desirable features may enable the reader to appreciate the problems faced by seekers after models of any real computational worth. A recent study categorizes the features a theoretician must consider in constructing a mathematical model of language behaviour. These include empirical properties essential in a working model, and comprise:

fidelity . . . the capacity of a . . . theory to reflect the reality of a language . . . closely linked to reliability and verifiability,
generality . . . the capacity of a . . . theory to be applicable to a variety of [natural] languages [and]
adequacy . . . the capacity of a theory to lend itself to practical applications [or

[1] 'Mathematical Models in Linguistics and Language Processing', *Automated Language Processing*, ed. Harold Borko (New York, 1967), p. 37 [hereafter 'Mathematical Models'].
[2] *Quantitative Linguistics* (London, 1964), p. 9.
[3] *Syntactic Structures* (The Hague, 1957).

under Chomsky's restraints, to account for all observed and potential behaviour of the data set for which a model is created].[1]

The fundamental criterion of course is the first. A model must have fidelity, or it is useless. In practice this requirement is often fulfilled by keeping one's model sufficiently flexible to evolve into a new form when new data cannot be consistently accounted for in terms of the original analogue. If the model were sufficiently 'predictive' to account consistently for all future observations it would, of course, be perfect, and comprise a closed system, represented in Fig. 2.[2]

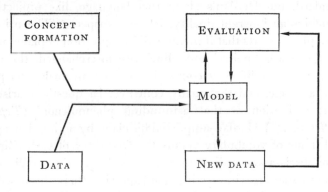

FIGURE 2

However, the fact that a model is an organized representation of reality ensures that such an ideal is short lived, since sooner or later new data (perhaps the result of random occurrences of which there is no shortage in the real world) will contradict the predictions of the model. It is precisely for this reason that stochastic models have been more frequently employed in stylistics than deterministic ones since the 'entity' to be modelled (literature) is known to be at least partially a random 'process', and hence a deterministic model is less likely to describe, explain, or predict stylistic features.

Each of the six terminal branches of mathematics shown in Fig. 1 has provided specific models for stylistic studies. Of course, combinations of these basic approaches are possible and successful work has been accomplished with 'mixed' models. For our purposes, however, it will be sufficient to consider only basic model applications.

---

[1] *A Syntactic Analyzer Study: Final Report.* Bunker-Ramo Corporation Study under contract AF30(602)–3506, dated 31 July 1965, pp. 6–7.

[2] This representation was suggested by Edmundson's open-ended model system, 'Mathematical Models', p. 40.

Of deterministic models, the geometrical one is seemingly the least likely to be of relevance to stylistics. This, however, did not deter Herdan, who posited that though 'geometrical methods have been used in structural linguistics so far only tentatively . . . a more fundamental approach is needed'.[1] Herdan went so far as to claim that 'the law of [geometrical] duality is the fundamental law of language' and likened the concepts 'type' and 'token', to 'point' and 'line', respectively. In so far as virtually all stochastic approaches to style need to delineate 'word' from 'word plus context' (phrase, sentence, or even entire text) this terminology has become standard, but Herdan's claim that language, like projective geometry, contains an inherent duality, is more suspect:[2] 'The principle of duality in a plane asserts that if in any valid proposition of plane projective geometry the words "point" and "line" are interchanged, the resulting proposition is also valid. My contention is that an analogous principle applies to language, and that many controversial questions arise out of insufficient realisation of that astounding phenomenon' (*Type-Token Mathematics*, p. 232). Herdan supported his claim by noting that a graph of individual items of vocabulary versus the frequency of each (Zipf's law) could have abscissa and ordinate reversed without substantially affecting the data summation. It is interesting that Zipf's law (to be discussed later as an application of analytic modelling) is thus chosen to illustrate the central theorem of Herdan's work, since this same law is elsewhere denigrated by Herdan as 'not, to the writer's knowledge, of much practical use to the linguist, and mathematically a triviality' (p. 33). This is not apt to inspire much confidence in 'duality', based as it is upon a relationship repeatedly deflated by Herdan in each of his linguistic studies. Similarly, when the 'law of duality' was applied as 'a methodological tool of research' (p. 239), which Herdan claimed it to be, the law was accorded a privileged status that transcended mere contradiction by results: 'In linguistic research if a relation between type and token is established we may try the reciprocation of these two concepts and see whether the new statement makes sense. If it does, it means enlargement of our knowledge; if not, this may point to the original statement requiring alteration in such a way that its dual is also true' (*ibid.*).

Whether or not linguistic duality actually exists has yet to be proved, since Herdan did not go beyond the phase in modelling known as parameter

[1] *Type-Token Mathematics* (The Hague, 1960), p. 230.
[2] M. F. Bott has, for example, disputed Herdan's 'duality' concept in reviewing *The Advanced Theory of Language as Choice and Chance: Modern Language Review*, LXIII (1968), 659–60.

determination. Nor is it likely to be proved, since his evidence that the geometrical properties of point, line, plane and solid were mirrored in language, as type, token, text and 'content of the text as reconstructed from the words in our imagination' (p. 257) was less than convincing.[1] However, Herdan's brief excursion into '4-dimensional space', which led him to suggest that *content is the permanence of the group wave composed of the fleeting waves of individual words* (p. 260), might prove to be of more significance than is immediately apparent. Since the periodicity of 'types' (individual words) in a unified text is now mathematically determinable by various frequency measures, the next logical step is to examine the recurrency of 'tokens' – of phrase, or sentence – and ultimately even of thematically related whole texts, and then to borrow physical formulae for these measurements. Herdan suggested that of de Broglie as one obvious choice (p. 259). Since de Broglie's concept is, like 'duality', largely geometrical (dependent as it is on patterns of reinforcement and opposition of individual waves), perhaps the geometrical model will yet prove relevant to stylistics.

Algebraic paradigms of style, unlike the geometric, are well established and far beyond the stage of being 'theoretically viable'. In fact, algebraic models (usually applied at the syntactic level) are the most numerous of deterministic approaches to style. This may be attributed largely to the legacy of syntactic generators available from machine translation work of the last decade, but the use of algebraic models of syntax also stems from the reasonable supposition that syntactic preferences are more likely indicators of style than lexical choices. In particular, the use of generative grammars in stylistic analysis is growing and most utilize the algebra of semi-groups and monoids.

The implications of this algebra are of considerable practical significance to stylistics, since an English grammar based on it must generate only the grammatical sequences of English (under the property of closure) and concatenated strings can be readily 'transformed' (under the property of association) into valid alternative structures, enabling a representation of most syntactic features. It is important to note that grammatical validity can be assured in such a system, if the process of parameter determination is rigorously defined. It is for this reason that so much effort has been spent in improving the various generative grammars, in an attempt to evolve an algebra-based grammar capable of producing sequences acceptable to a

[1] *Ibid.* pp. 263–6. The 'evidence' consists of a more impassioned than reasoned listing of examples of Nazi double-think.

native speaker (or under more rigorous conditions, capable of producing each possible sequence, and only such sequences).

It might not at first sight be obvious that algebra-based grammars have relevance to stylistic studies, but on reflection, certain of their facets must be seen to permit a precision in stylistic studies which was hitherto unattainable. First, the possibility of precisely describing characteristic, but peculiar syntactic features of a writer's work, is undeniably an advance over the use of vague descriptive epithets. Then too, if a feature can be structurally described, its presence, absence or existence in modified form, can be enumerated and comparative studies much facilitated. For example, Curtis W. Hayes observes that Edward Gibbon made 'characteristic, habitual, and recurrent'[1] use of sentences containing either (in transformational terminology) '3 and 4 embedded structures', or '4 conjoined S slot expansions' (p. 88). A Hemingway sample exhibited neither of these features, but was found to have twice as many 'doublet verb phrase expansions' as the Gibbon sample. Thus, rather than calling Hemingway 'simple' or 'linear' and Gibbon 'grand' or 'majestic' (terms which are both imprecise and misleading), analysts can objectively describe observed syntactic preferences, and allot facets of the two styles to discrete grammatical categories. It would seem, then, that algebraic models have a more immediate relevance to stylistics than the geometric ones proposed by Herdan.

Other deterministic models which seem to have little relevance to stylistic analysis at present are those based on logic, although their general utility is defended by Y. Bar-Hillel and others (see the bibliography appended to 'Mathematical Models in Linguistics and Language Processing'). Edmundson concludes, however, that propositional logics are 'far too primitive to provide interesting models of sentences',[2] although Louis T. Milic has recently suggested that this is far from true. Milic advocates a process of propositional reduction in which a 'simplified form of each sentence . . . stripped of all its recognizable stylistic adornment'[3] is compared with the actual sentence. This approach assumes that if a kernel sentence can be derived from the original this must bring certain advantages to the analyst of style. Specifically, a statement will be generated which is 'shorter, more direct and easier to understand' (p. 19), unless the original is itself a kernel. More interesting to the analyst is the difference between original and kernel,

[1] 'A Study in Prose Styles: Edward Gibbon and Ernest Hemingway', *Statistics and Style*, ed. Lubomír Doležel and Richard W. Bailey (New York, 1969), p. 81.
[2] 'Mathematical Models', p. 49.
[3] *Stylists on Style* (New York, 1969), p. 18.

since here will be (Milic feels) the 'affective' component of the writing, 'the means for producing different effects on the reader' (p. 2), in essence, the author's style divorced from substance. Milic is careful to concede that 'theoretically, of course, the complete dichotomy between [substance and style] . . . should not be insisted on' (p. 3). He continues, however, by stating that 'the claim that style and substance are separate entities which can be kept apart for the purpose of analysis seems fully consistent with intuition and experience'. Since other recent studies have, by contrast, concluded that style is inextricably linked to substance (context),[1] one wishes that Milic had at least elaborated upon the terms 'intuition and experience'. His method is eminently sensible, however, and provides the analyst of style with a heuristic task to replace traditional, but slovenly impressionistic labelling. In Milic's words, 'the value of the reductive procedure is the necessity it puts the analyst of style under to observe the actual detailed mechanism of the style at work'.[2]

The final deterministic model to be discussed is that based on 'analysis', and this has been left until last for several reasons, not the least of them being, as Edmundson observes, that 'in the nontechnical sense analysis refers in the process of analyzing or investigating, and hence, can be applied in all branches of mathematics'.[3] Therefore a smooth progression can be made from analysis to stochastic models, since the latter are as 'analytical' as any. In the technical sense, moreover, analytic models are the most comprehensive. They incorporate many divergent approaches to computational stylistics, and therefore perhaps deserve consideration after the other deterministic models, since analytical methods must of necessity involve the other approaches.

Specifically, analysis deals with functions, either of points or of sets. The latter category includes algebraic equations (linear functions) differential equations (those 'that express the functional relations of several variables in terms of their *derivatives*'[4]), and transformations (the 'rewriting' process used by Chomsky and others). Each of these functions have provided stylistic models, and will be briefly discussed in turn.

The simplest possible analytic model is a point function of one 'argument', that is, a relationship with one variable. Zipf's 'law', an established if suspect[5] notion, illustrates its use in stylistics. G. K. Zipf arranged the

1 See, for example, the articles by G. M. Landon and K. Kroeber in Doležel and Bailey, *Statistics and Style*.   2 *Stylists on Style*, pp. 20–1.
3 'Mathematical Models', p. 49.
4 *Ibid*. p. 52.
5 Herdan attacks Zipf's hypothesis in *Type-Token Mathematics*, pp. 33–6.

words in various samples by frequency in descending order, and awarded the word with the highest frequency the lowest rank. He found that a logarithmic plot of frequency versus rank approached a straight line relationship, leading him to postulate that the frequency of a word multiplied by its rank is a constant ($f_r r = c$; $c = 0.1$ for English). The actual hypothesis accorded the name Zipf's law could also be considered a stochastic one, since Zipf equated the probability of a word having rank r with the frequency for that rank: ($p_r = f_r = \frac{c}{r}$).

A step up from the point function model is that involving linear algebraic equations. Several approaches are possible but that proposed by Edmundson is especially interesting, since it promises to be compatible to some extent with Milic's method of propositional reduction. Edmundson suggests we could 'select sentences . . . by means of various linguistic factors, and combine [the latter]. . . to form a single factor. Suppose that each s_i denotes a factor such as semantic, syntactic, locational or editorial. To each s_i associate a weight w_i and form the *linear combination* $t = \Sigma_i w_i s_i$ of the s_i.'[1] Just as Milic's sentence model provides a means of explicit stylistic description, so too might Edmundson's yield a close approximation to the actual 'weighted significance value' of the sentence, mathematically the sum of $w_1 s_1 + w_2 s_2 + \ldots + w_n s_n$.

Differential equations have as yet played little part in stylistics, but because of a rather convenient feature of their calculi, they have attracted some notice. Herdan, for example, observed that while, in general, the ratio of the vocabulary in a given text, or a sample from it, to the total number of words comprised in the text or the sample, changes with the size of the piece of the literary work, the logarithm of this ratio (the bilogarithmic type/token ratio as Herdan called it) does not change, and therefore is a more suitable descriptor of style. It is not immediately obvious what this has to do with differential equations, but it happens that this bilogarithmic ratio is the solution to the simultaneous differential equations which Herdan advanced to pattern the rate of growth of literary vocabulary.[2]

The last analytic model of interest to stylistics employs transformations, which provide a means of deriving from a particular sentence a 'kernel', plus residue. The implications for analysts of style are many and Milic's propositional reduction earlier alluded to is a non-mathematical attempt to use this concept, to strip off the 'style' that encrusts a kernel statement. Surprisingly, little work has been done in using transformational frame-

---

[1] 'Mathematical Models', p. 52.
[2] *Type-Token Mathematics*, pp. 27–8.

works to facilitate stylistic (rather than merely syntactic) analysis, but since transformations provide a mathematically rigorous method of producing syntactically 'equivalent'[1] statements, their future in stylistics is promising. Much as a Hinman collator can pinpoint textual variants by a process of optical superimposition, so too would this mathematical tool more readily illuminate stylistic aberrations from the kernel 'norm', by superimposing a transformed sentence upon its kernel.

Turning now to stochastic models that have facilitated computational analysis of style, one notes that at the present moment probabilistic stylistics is somewhat more advanced than deterministic approaches. On the other hand, while stochastic methods have yielded impressive results, statistical tools have frequently been misapplied. In addition, the fact that probabilistic techniques are incapable (by definition) of proving conjectures has led some to neglect their obvious advantages in literary work. In assessing stochastic models, the reader should note that a distinction exists between the theories of probability and statistics,[2] but since stylistic studies invariably draw upon both theories, and usually in conjunction, the distinction is unimportant for our purposes.

All approaches that represent literature as a stochastic model make one of two assumptions. The first is that any natural language is a process at least partially analogous to physical systems for which well-established laws exist. For example, the redundancy inherent in any language permits some prediction of syntactical or lexical forms, making concepts like probability and entropy as relevant to literature as to physics. The second assumption, less presumptive, merely treats a language and its written manifestations as a data set, obtained by an operation that can be regarded as repetitive,[3] and therefore susceptible to statistical techniques. The two assumptions may be treated as one for practical purposes. Both theories view language as essentially a sequence of symbols (generated from a finite symbol-set) and being a partly random, partly predictable process. Neither assumption admits any quantitative difference between literature and any other form of written language, yet, paradoxically, methodologies born of these assumptions are expected to delineate stylistic nuances. One suspects that literary works are most distinguishable from the more pedestrian written examples of a language at the semantic level, but since language, as described by

---

[1] Chomsky, *Syntactic Structures*, p. 28.

[2] Basically, probability involves 'chance' and statistics 'decision', but more formal distinctions are discussed in 'Mathematical Models'.

[3] Certain 'non-repetitive' sets of data can be regarded as repetitive, as Paul G. Hoel explains in *Introduction to Mathematical Statistics*, 3rd ed. (New York, 1962), p. 1.

statistical and physical models, is treated merely as symbols in combination, the semantic component is largely neglected.

Herdan has argued, however, that probabilistic tools are capable of measuring both 'linguistic diversity', and 'stylistic diversity', and that Yule's 'characteristic K' is in fact a measure of the latter.[1] His claim rests on the observation that Yule's measure is 'of the nature of a repeat rate', closely linked to that estimated by I. J. Good as the probability that two words selected at random from a given text will be the same. Thus, to the extent that the repetitiveness of an author's vocabulary is a valid characteristic of style the 'characteristic K' is a truly stylistic measure, suggesting that probabilistic models can discriminate beyond the level of mere 'linguistic diversity', the level at which J. H. Greenberg applied probabilistic measures.[2]

The rationale for stochastic approaches to style in general, as expressed by Lubomír Doležel, is that style is manifested 'not as a fixed habit, but rather as a preference for one or another mode of expression. The overall character of a style is called forth by the *degree* of presence (or absence) of a certain mode of expression, rather than by its exclusive use (or complete suppression).'[3] That an author is variable rather than absolute in his stylistic characteristics is probably true, but it is ironic that the most lauded statistical study of style to date (see note 2, p. 117) owes its deservedly high reputation to the discovery that, in admittedly limited samples from two authors, certain linguistic preferences were absolutely fixed. Frederick Mosteller and David L. Wallace resolved the disputed authorship of *The Federalist* papers by showing that function words (those that occur very frequently and are generally independent of context) exhibit a surprising power to discriminate among authors. In fact, certain words were *never* found in samples known to be by one of the two candidates, while these words frequently occurred in the work of the other and vice versa. This evidence, suggesting that certain habits of authors are immutable, does not, however, invalidate the probabilistic approach to style. In fact, stochastic approaches have a particular advantage over other models in that they are time-dependent. It is now generally accepted (with computational support)[4] that an author's style changes as he matures,

---

[1] *Type-Token Mathematics*, p. 94.
[2] *Loc. cit.*
[3] 'A Framework for the Statistical Analysis of Style', Doležel and Bailey, *Statistics and Style*, pp. 10–11.
[4] 'A Note on Sentence-Length as Random Variable', Doležel and Bailey, *Statistics and Style*, pp. 76–9.

hence a model which comprises 'a family of random variables that are functions of time'[1] admits the possibility of establishing a style matrix for an author at various discrete phases in his evolution as a writer. For this and other reasons, Doležel has committed himself deeply to a probabilistic approach to style, insisting that 'the probabilistic conception is to be considered *an adequate theory of style*, rather than a secondary aspect of stylistic theory or a mere descriptive technique'.[2] However, his credo: 'that the breaking down of style into a limited number of specified, exactly measurable style components represents the most important contribution of the statistical conception to the theory of style' (p. 21) is perhaps based on a misconception, since his view of the statistical method contradicts the generally accepted one: '[where complexity] . . . is too great for us to attempt to describe it in terms of cause and effect for every single event, we take refuge in statistical or probability concepts [which focus] . . . not upon the individual event, but upon the cumulative or integral aspect of the process.'[3] If the latter explanation of the role of statistics is correct (and it is a conventional one confirmed by many statisticians), there is little hope that Doležel will isolate 'specified, exactly measurable style components' using statistical techniques. What is more important, subsequent studies, attracted by Doležel's apparently sophisticated and mathematically rigorous '*specified text-style formula*',[4] could perpetuate his fundamental misconception that statistical methods can both describe a probabilistic trend, and determine the specific determinants of that trend. It should be evident that these demands are mutually contradictory.

Two observations might be made here. First, it has been shown that analysts of style have now fashioned or adopted models based on each of the possible mathematical approaches. Secondly, it is fair to say that the prevailing atmosphere in computational stylistics is less optimistic than a decade ago, since few of these mathematical frameworks have produced consistent stylistic tests. It would seem worth-while then, since analysts of style are increasingly committed to diverse mathematical approaches, often with indifferent success, to ask what is the justification for the use of mathematics in stylistics at all?

The defence may be stated thus. By methods of successive approximation, formulae can come to resemble actual linguistic behaviour more and

[1] H. P. Edmundson, 'A Statistician's View of Linguistic Methods and Language-Data Processing', *Natural Language and the Computer*, ed. P. L. Garvin (New York, 1963), p. 161. [2] 'A Framework', p. 11.
[3] Gustav Herdan, *Language as Choice and Chance* (Groningen, 1956), p. 43.
[4] 'A Framework', p. 21.

more closely and thus provide a predictive apparatus of general stylistic utility. However, it is often forgotten that mathematics can at best provide *analogues* of literary style, just as the fact is neglected that statistics can at best suggest probabilistic tendencies in literature (not proofs). Analysts of style are beginning to regard mathematical techniques as indigenous to language studies, and in doing so they often ascribe a potency to mathematics that it lacks. This can be seen in the many attempts to 'refine' Zipf's law, which, as Herdan has shown,[1] is basically flawed. Each new supporter assumes that only slight adjustment is necessary to make the Zipf relationship fit his data, instead of questioning the fundamental hypothesis.

Certainly it is true to say that, despite the ever increasing use of mathematics in stylistics, these odd bedfellows will never lie completely harmoniously together. Stochastic approaches must ensure statistical 'homogeneity' in order to perform valid operations, yet stylistic nuances in literature are nothing if not heterogeneous, since our ability to distinguish between styles depends on perceiving differences. In addition, all models, deterministic and stochastic, must pre-select their parameters for study and in doing so often obscure the details that delineate the style they seek.

Many popular methods of reducing data (for example, the method of 'least squares') ensure satisfying straight-line graphs of literary features, but this 'adjusting' process, like most mathematical operations, necessitates the neglect of slight departures from the dominant trends, and such departures very probably constitute the subtleties comprising style. In addition, as A. G. Oettinger has correctly observed,

the only verification offered to date of the validity [of mathematical models of language] . . . is the agreement between the model formula and observed data. The degree of agreement must not be over-emphasised. For one thing, the shape of the observed curve is, to some extent, an artifact . . . Furthermore, the agreement is subject to the adjustment of at least one parameter . . . Whether or not these model elements can ultimately be placed in significant correspondence with observable data remains an open question.[2]

It is evident that mathematical paradigms of style are becoming more diverse and sophisticated, but it is fair to say that their practical applications have been only moderately successful. Therefore, for the present at least, the most potent tool for stylistic evaluation remains the most basic, that of intuition. In the foreseeable future it is likely to remain the scholar's most valuable aid in stylistic research.

[1] *Type-Token Mathematics*, p. 36.
[2] 'Linguistics and Mathematics', *Studies presented to Joshua Whatmough* (The Hague, 1957), pp. 182–3.

Computer stylistics: Swift and some contemporaries

PATRICIA KÖSTER*

' . . . great Genius's are not easily traced by their manner of writing . . .'
—Mrs Manley, *Memoirs of Europe* (London, 1710), II, 103.

The present study has grown from a long-continued interest in Swift and
his associates of the Tory propaganda machine, and more immediately
from a desire to discover the author(s) of *The Story of the St Alb–ns Ghost*,
one of the better products of that machine.[1] The interest continues, but the
question of authorship remains unsolved; my results are inconclusive, and
my conclusions therefore largely negative. The only positive conclusion
from over a year of effort and the coding of over 40,000 words is that a
great deal of further study will be needed to unlock the secrets of style in
Swift and his companions before we can use the computer for settling
cases of disputed attribution.

Various approaches have been made to computer stylistics; the most
relevant book for the present problem is of course Professor Louis T.
Milic, *A Quantitative Approach to the Style of Jonathan Swift* (The Hague,
1967), whose methodology I have adopted. Although Professor Milic's
work is already well known, a brief recapitulation here may help to clarify
what follows. Professor Milic assumes 'that [syntactical] consistency is
characteristic of all [Swift's] work, regardless of subject matter' (p. 80). He
selects prose samples approximately 3,500 words in length, in full sentences.
Using a grammatical scheme modified from the word-classes of Charles

---

* Department of English, University of Victoria, Canada.

[1] In addition to being read in abbreviated form at the Cambridge Symposium of March
1970, this study has already been published by *Computers and the Humanities*, IV (1970),
289–304. I would like to thank Dr Joseph Raben, Editor of *CHum*, for permitting the
republication. Professor Louis T. Milic generously sent me advice during the original
research, chaired the session at which I read the paper, and wrote a 'Comment' which
has been appended to the version in *CHum*. Several changes in the present republication
are owing to Professor Milic's 'Comment'. Dr Roy Wisbey has also suggested some
changes here incorporated; the errors of course remain my own responsibility.

All references to 'Milic' in the following pages denote sections in Professor Milic's
book, *A Quantitative Approach to the Style of Jonathan Swift* (The Hague, 1967), the
study which first inspired and provided the methodology for the present piece of
research.

C. Fries, he assigns a code number of two digits to each word in a sample according to grammatical function. Thus he codes nouns as 01, main verbs as 02, auxiliary verbs as 21 and so forth to a total of 24 grammatical classes (Milic, pp. 143–53). Punching these coded words continuously on the first 72 columns of IBM computer cards, with intervening end-of-record marks between sentences, he has approximately 100 cards for each sample. After running a number of different tests on ten samples of Swift's work, and on eight control samples (two each from Addison, Johnson, Gibbon and Macaulay), Professor Milic has selected three tests as the most reliable discriminators, and on these he bases his 'Swift Profile' (pp. 230–6). The three profile discriminators are high scores for the use of *Verbals* (VB), of *Introductory Connectives* (IC), and of *Different* three-word patterns (D). In other respects Swift does not differ significantly from the four controls, but in the three 'Discriminators' scores consistently higher, through various genres and over a number of years. As a result Professor Milic concludes: 'If it should be desired to test the attribution of a work to Swift, the matter may be quickly verified by reference to the three points of the profile' (pp. 235–6). I have summarized Professor Milic's results in the first two sections of my Appendix C, and very impressive results they are.

The first problem which this research set me was to reproduce Professor Milic's coding system; unless I could duplicate his coding of the Swift samples, I could not with any show of validity compare my figures for an 'unknown' with his figures for Swift. As a test case I selected his sample *Examiner* I as being closest in time and intention to my 'unknown'. Unfortunately this problem turned out to be one of formidable dimensions; after a matter of months and a series of letters to and from Professor Milic I had learned the rudiments of the system and embodied them in a second test case, his sample *Examiner* II; some finer points I have never learned at all. The finer points and the '*ad hoc* decision' (Milic, p. 151) do not make much difference to the percentages under Parts of Speech (see Appendix A, below), but have rendered my total for *Examiner* II slightly lower than Professor Milic's under Verbals, and sufficiently higher under Different patterns to require scaling of all other results (see p. 132). Part of the problem is simple human error: not only have I made careless errors, but even Professor Milic has omitted an end-of-record mark somewhere in his coding of *Examiner* I – he lists (p. 229) one sentence less than a manual count reveals as actually present. Apart from error, there seems to remain a small but persistent bias due to individual ideas about parsing, increased by the fact that Professor Milic has used highly personal definitions for certain parts of speech. Although this obviously does not alter the validity of *his* work, since he has coded all his samples by the same method, it does create difficulties for any other scholar who like myself wishes to use Professor Milic's tables. Even the word *page* turns out to have a variable definition which depends on the amount of material in the sample already coded: each *page* listed in his Appendix (Milic, p. 285) needs separate definition, available only by writing to Professor Milic himself. While admitting my own deficiencies, I suspect that somebody else might also find it less than easy to duplicate Professor Milic's coding.

Compared to the problem of coding, the problem of devising programs was relatively simple. With a good deal of friendly advice from Mr Philip Rhynas, Operations Manager of the University of Victoria Computing Centre, I wrote a FORTRAN program which counted the number of occurrences of each word-type and also the total number of words and total number of sentences. The program then manipulated these numbers to calculate the percentage of each word-type and of certain combinations: VA (02 and 21: finite verbs and auxiliaries), VB (05, 06 and 07: infinitives, participles and gerunds), M (31, 32, 33 and 34: determining adjectives, post-verb particles, 'intensifiers' and 'function adverbs'), C (41, 42, 43, 44, 45: coordinating conjunctions, subordinating conjunctions, relatives, interrogatives and correlatives). Finally, the program printed out these percentages in a column, together with the total number of words and of sentences. Of all the tests performed by the first program, only the result under VB is a 'reliable discriminator' for Swift (see Milic, pp. 247–63). Since, however, the other tests add something to our knowledge of the sample, I have in Appendix A given the full results for word-frequency distribution in all samples, together with Professor Milic's figures for the common sample *Examiner* II as well as his means for Swift and for controls.

The second FORTRAN program is even simpler than the first. It finds each end-of-record mark, and adds the following word (i.e. the first word of the next sentence) to a counter for its word-type. It then makes one combination, IC (41, 42, 91: coordinating and subordinating conjunctions, and conjunctive adverbs), and calculates what percentage of sentences begin with each word-type and with the combination. Only the result for the Introductory Connectives is considered 'reliable', but as before I have given all results below in Appendix B. The test IC has the advantage of being easily checked by a manual count; with sentences of a Swiftian length, there are fewer than one hundred sentence-openers in a sample, and these can quickly be coded without coding the rest of the sample. The test has, however, the corresponding defect that the samples are too small to make the results entirely satisfactory. If this were the sole test, we should not need a computer at all.

The third program on the other hand, to find and classify the three-word groups, is extremely complex. The computer must first pick out each group of three words in the sample (a total of between 3,300 and 3,400 patterns, depending on sentence length) and then compare the patterns and classify them. For example the first sentence of this paragraph would be coded: 31 81 01 51 31 03 01 61 05 41 05 31 81 01 01 21 33 03. These eighteen words give sixteen three-word groups, beginning 31 81 01; 81 01 51; 01 51 31; 51 31 03 and so forth until one reaches 21 33 03. The patterns are not taken across a sentence break; the program must then move forward to take the first three words of the next sentence. The program eventually produces as its most important result the figure D: number of Different patterns used. (In the sentence coded above, the pattern 31 81 01 is repeated; of the total sixteen patterns there are therefore fifteen Different patterns and D is 15.) I was unable to write a program of this complexity, and unable to borrow Professor Milic's SNOBOL program as the computer to which I have access has no facility for that language. Mr Ian McCririck of the University of Victoria Computing Centre wrote a FORTRAN program for me. Unfortunately this test reveals that the small coding differences caused by error, by my misunderstanding of Professor Milic's 'determiners' and perhaps by some variations in *ad hoc* decisions can add up to a large difference: whereas Professor Milic obtains the D value 844 for the sample *Examiner* 11, I obtain 895. I have checked the program by running a small sample of two cards only, and find that every pattern present has been entered, and no others. The fault lies then with the coding, not with the program. Since, however, the bias due to my coding must presumably be fairly constant in all my samples, I have ventured to give the raw results for D together with scaled results. To obtain the figure D (scaled) in the final column of Appendix C I multiplied D (raw) by the constant scaling factor 844/895.

After the two *Examiner* samples had been run on these programs, and the programs if not the coding rendered satisfactory, came my 'unknown' pamphlet, *The Story of the St Alb–ns Ghost, or the Apparition of Mother Haggy. Collected from the best Manuscripts* (London, 1712). This pamphlet, whose title is here abbreviated to *SAG*, is only slightly longer than a standard sample, coming to a total of 3,549 words. I therefore coded the entire pamphlet on 102 IBM cards, and ran them with my programs. Professor Milic has kindly examined the results for *SAG* of the first two programs, and observes 'considerable similarity between [the] unknown and Swift in the parts of speech frequency distribution. Only one of the classes is more than one percent away (02)' (unpublished letter, 11 February 1969). Furthermore, the D result, 823 after scaling, is remarkably close to the Swift mean D score of 833 – closer in fact than are any of the Swift results listed by Professor Milic. Even without scaling, the D result for my coding of *SAG* is closer to the Swift range than is the D result for my coding of *Examiner* 11. Under Verbals on the other hand *SAG* receives 2.5, significantly lower than any of the Swift scores and even a little below the mean of Professor Milic's controls. The score for Introductory Connectives, 6.9, is proportionately lower still, below all but one of Professor Milic's controls, and distant indeed from Swift. Thus the *Story of the St Alb–ns Ghost* has failed to resemble Swift in two out of the three 'profile' tests, and probably was not written by him. Who else then could have constructed it?

The satirists who have been named by scholars as possible authors of the *Story of the St Alb–ns Ghost* are Swift,[1] Swift in collaboration with Arbuthnot,[2] or else Dr William Wagstaffe.[3] Having by the use of Professor Milic's tables substantially eliminated the case that Swift wrote the pamphlet alone, I wished to test the probability of the other two cases. Unfortunately for the second case, there are no examples of Scriblerian collaboration in which the shares of Arbuthnot and Swift are already known; one could only attempt to construct an Arbuthnot profile and then extrapolate. Accepting Professor Milic's figures for Swift as given, I chose samples of Arbuthnot, of signed prose by Wagstaffe, and of the satiric works published with the *Story of the St Alb ns Ghost* in the so-called *Miscellaneous Works of Dr Wagstaffe* (London, 1726). This would provide a total of four stylistic profiles against which to check the figures for the 'unknown'

1 *The Works of Jonathan Swift*, ed. Thomas Roscoe (London, 1850), 1, 529.
2 Sir Walter Scott suggests the collaboration, 'judging from the style' in his edition of *The Works of Swift*, 2nd ed. (London, 1883), v, 414.
3 First (?) claimed by the unknown editor of *The Miscellaneous Works of Dr Wagstaffe* . . . (London, 1726), who included but did not discuss or justify the inclusion of the *Story*. Modern scholars generally prefer this third possibility; Vinton A. Dearing, 'Jonathan Swift or William Wagstaffe?', *Harvard Library Bulletin*, vii (1953), 121–30, gives a detailed survey of previous discussions, and concludes that since Swift was not responsible Wagstaffe wrote all the pieces in the *Miscellaneous Works*. See also Professor Herbert Davis, 'Introduction', *Prose Works of Swift*, viii, pp. xiv–xv (Professor Davis does not, however, specifically name the *Story*).

pamphlet. Professor Milic helpfully suggested that three examples of a single author would be enough to make a minimum stylistic profile (unpublished letter, 11 February 1969). As an outside control, I chose Mrs Manley, who wrote Tory pamphlets during the Harley ministry, some of them under the direct supervision of Swift,[1] but who has never been named in connection with any of the pseudo-Wagstaffe pamphlets. It seemed best to select a control author writing at the same time and in the same genre (political fiction) as those of the work under scrutiny.[2] It was not possible to control all factors in the choice of samples; other samples might then produce somewhat different results.

For Arbuthnot I chose first the *Art of Political Lying* (*APL*), a pamphlet of about the same length as the *Story of the St Alb–ns Ghost* but of rather a different genre, the mock proposal; secondly the John Bull pamphlets (*JB*), considerably longer, but having the advantage of genre similarity to the *Story*. I coded the whole of *APL* (105 cards), and made a stratified sample of *JB*. Both of these Arbuthnot items were written in 1712, the same year as the *Story*. Although this fact is naturally an advantage, it has a corresponding defect: 1712 was the peak year of Swift's term as propaganda minister without portfolio, and the pamphlets may already include an undiscoverable portion of Swift's own work. Indeed, Dr Herman Teerink has gone so far as to suggest that Swift wrote nearly all of *John Bull*.[3] The third Arbuthnot sample, to detect any difference between Arbuthnot as influenced by Swift and Arbuthnot working independently, is taken from *A Sermon Preach'd . . . at the Mercat Cross of Edinburgh . . .* (*SMC*), a propaganda piece written in late 1706, about four years before Arbuthnot met Swift.[4] I coded continuously from the beginning to a total of 100 punched cards (about 70% of the whole *Sermon*).

---

[1] Not only does Swift praise some of the pamphlets in his *Journal to Stella*, but Professor Davis includes two of them in appendices to his edition of the *Prose Works of Swift* (III, 260–72; VIII, 183–97). The *Memoirs of Europe* on the other hand has not been associated with Swift in any way. The first volume was written during the winter 1709/10 and published in May 1710, a time when Swift was in Ireland and had not yet joined the Tories. This volume seemed therefore a suitable outside control.

[2] This point has already been made, although without any testing, by Cynthia S. Matlack and William F. Matlack, 'A Statistical Approach to Problems of Attribution: *A Letter of Advice to a Young Poet*', *College English*, XXIX (1968), 629.

[3] *The History of John Bull for the first time faithfully re-issued from the Original Pamphlets, 1712, together with an investigation into its composition, publication and authorship* (Amsterdam, 1925). Dr Teerink later changed his mind however, and in the revised edition of his *Bibliography of the Writings of Jonathan Swift* (Philadelphia, 1963) returns the credits for the *History of John Bull* to Arbuthnot.

[4] Lester M. Beattie, *John Arbuthnot, Mathematician and Satirist* (New York, 1967), p. 4, places the meeting in the winter of 1710/11.

The results for these three samples of Arbuthnot are ambiguous in two ways. The results under Introductory Connectives do not show the consistency which one might expect from a test labelled by Professor Milic as 'reliable' and do not promise well for any further comparison with 'unknown' samples. The *Art of Political Lying* with 14.9%, the lowest of these scores, is already higher than all but one of the control samples used by Professor Milic; *John Bull* with 22.3% is closer to the Swift range than to the control range, and the *Sermon* with 29.7% is well within the Swift range. When normalized, using the mean 22.3 as 100, the figures spread 33% on either side (see Appendix D). The results under Verbals and Different Patterns are more consistent than those under Introductory Connectives: they all fall within the Swift range. Only in the least consistent of the three 'profile' tests is Arbuthnot different from Swift at all, and in only one of the three samples is he significantly different. We might almost want to reconsider Dr Teerink's theory, were it not for the unexpected ordering of the results. *The Art of Political Lying* follows the same propaganda line as the Swift pamphlets of the Harley period, and although written by Arbuthnot was seen through the press by Swift (*Journal to Stella*, 9 October 1712) – a weighty fact since Swift might well have adjusted the style while proof-reading.[1] The *Sermon* on the contrary was written by Arbuthnot before he knew Swift, and is dissociated from Swift by subject matter: it urges the Scots, whom Swift disliked, to accept the Union with England, a measure which Swift disliked. We might then reasonably expect the stylistic features of the *Sermon* to be correspondingly further from Swift's norms than are those of the Swift-influenced pieces. We find, however, that in the 'profile' tests the *Sermon* is not only within the Swift range but parallel to the pattern established by Professor Milic's *TALE* sample, whereas the *Art of Political Lying* has a pattern quite different from any of those produced by Swift. And *John Bull*, although a little lower in Introductory Connectives than either of the Swift narrative samples, is almost parallel to *GULL* II. These results differentiate Arbuthnot from the author of the 'unknown' pamphlet, but not from Swift.

Turning to the less reliable tests, we find that on the whole (as already in Introductory Connectives) Arbuthnot demonstrates little stylistic stability. In use of finite verbs (VA) he ranges from the rather low 13.38 of the *Art of*

---

[1] For a detailed analysis of the political slanting, see my article, 'Topical Allusions in *The Art of Political Lying*', *Transactions of the Samuel Johnson Society of the Northwest*, II (1968), 86–94. There is some evidence that Swift did not give Arbuthnot's work the same meticulous correction as he gave his own; an article now in preparation will discuss this.

Political Lying to the rather high 16.23 of *John Bull*. This may in part be a reflection of genre: the narrative *John Bull* requires more finite verbs, as indeed also more pronouns than do the other Arbuthnot samples. Similarly in the use of word-class 51 (prepositions), which Professor Milic finds relatively stable for Swift (Milic, p. 189), Arbuthnot fluctuates from the low 9.6 of *John Bull* to the high 12.5 of the *Art of Political Lying*. The M value (modifiers) is on the other hand fairly stable, and shows the characteristic of being rather low – lower than all of the Swift samples listed by Professor Milic (Milic, p. 174), and only just touching the two lowest control samples. The difference, however, is too small to establish a 'distinguishing' feature, and in the main reflects my difficulties with class 31 (determining adjectives) – as a glance at my figures and those of Professor Milic for *Examiner* II makes clear. In sentence openings too (see Appendix B below) Arbuthnot is irregular. Not only does he vary in his use of Introductory Connectives, but of most other word classes as well. In *John Bull* he uses seventeen different word classes to open sentences, in the *Art of Political Lying* only eleven. For use of 31 as first word, he touches an astonishingly low 8.7 in the *Sermon* and a high 30.8 in the *Art of Political Lying*; for 51, a low 5.3 in *John Bull* and a high 20.2 in *APL*.

I have found then no grammatical feature in which Arbuthnot is both consistent and clearly differentiated from Swift. The most consistent Arbuthnot figures are in fact those for VB and for D, which fall within the Swift range. The computer has mathematically justified Professor Saintsbury's highly trained ear: '. . . Arbuthnot, in this [i.e. rhythm] as in others, is almost inseparable from Swift',[1] and has thereby challenged stylists to devise some new tests sensitive enough to make that separation. For stylistic differences do exist: Arbuthnot not only employs a number of Scotticisms and the 'clipped' forms which Swift dislikes,[2] but uses in general more terms from the technical and the colloquial vocabularies than does Swift. Unfortunately none of these differences are measured by Professor Milic's system of analysis except the technical words (08), and Arbuthnot scores 0.0 for 08 (see Appendix A below) in the highly colloquial and informal narrative of *John Bull*. Without yet having attempted to enumerate, I suspect *a priori* that the other vocabulary items too may vary

---

[1] G. Saintsbury, *History of English Prose Rhythm* (London, 1912, repr. Bloom ington 1965), p. 252.

[2] See the unpubl. diss. (Cambridge, 1956) by Angus M. Ross, 'The Correspondence of Dr John Arbuthnot. First collected together and edited, with a Biographical Introduction, Notes, and a Dissertation', pp. 835–54, 894–7 and *passim*.

in proportion according to various matters of tone and intention, perhaps also of genre, and would therefore be shaky aids to attribution.

Wagstaffe unlike Arbuthnot causes no problem in selecting samples: apart from the items in the so-called *Miscellaneous Works of Dr Wagstaffe*, whose very doubtfulness is part of the problem, only three pieces are known to have been published with his name. The earliest is *Ramelies, a Poem* . . . (London, 1706)—but Professor Milic has deliberately excluded poetry from his samples, and applies his method only to prose. That leaves only the 'Preface' which Wagstaffe wrote to the second edition of Dr James Drake's *Anthropologia Nova* (London, 1722), and *A Letter to Dr Freind, shewing the Danger and Uncertainty of inoculating the Small Pox* (London, 1722). Unfortunately neither of these works is a satire, but the *Letter* uses some quasi-satiric devices in its attack on the 'artificial way of depopulating a Country' (p. 39). The *Letter* is about twice as long as a standard sample, and has been therefore divided into two sections, *LF* 1 (104 punched cards) and *LF* 2 (103 punched cards). The 'Preface' (*ANP*) is only about half the length of a standard sample, and in its entirety it fills 50 punched cards, with eight words over on a 51st. In addition to these genuine works, I tested three further pamphlets from the so-called *Miscellaneous Works of Dr Wagstaffe*, in order to see whether these seemed to be by the same author as the *Story of the St Alb–ns Ghost*, and whether their author(s) had any affinities with Wagstaffe. Of the three, *A Comment upon the History of Tom Thumb* (London, 1711), abbreviated in the Appendices to *CTT*, is the item which has been most confidently attributed to Wagstaffe, because some early owner endorsed his copy, 'By Mr Wagstaffe'.[1] A parody of Addison's praise for 'Chevy Chase', the *Comment* is written by somebody who much admired and apparently wished to emulate the *Tale of a Tub*. The whole pamphlet, omitting the quotations, fills slightly over 101 punched cards. *The Testimonies of the Citizens of Fickleborough, concerning the Life and Character of Robert Hush* . . . (London, 1713) bears some analogy to the *Art of Political Lying* as well as to the *Comment* in being a parody of a particular style, this time the legal. Omitting only the subheadings and the initials which are appended to each 'testimony' I coded the entire *TCF* on a little over 101 punched cards. The third Pseudo-Wagstaffe sample, *SCT*, is taken from *The State and Condi-*

---

1 James Crossley, who owned the endorsed copy, believed in the authenticity of the endorsement (*Notes and Queries*, 3rd ser., 11, 132); Dearing, in the article cited in note 3, p. 133, follows Crossley. William K. Wimsatt, Jr., states however in his 'Introduction' to *Parodies of Ballad Criticism*, Augustan Reprint no. 63 (Los Angeles, 1957), p. 14, that the attribution to Wagstaffe rests 'on somewhat uncertain authority'.

tion of our Taxes, Considered . . . (London, 1714). As this pamphlet attacks Oxford, and was in any case written after Swift returned to Ireland, it has long been dissociated from Swift. (Arbuthnot too was a friend of Oxford.) About three-quarters of *SCT* fills a standard sample, taken continuously from the beginning to ' . . . Good of the Publick' (p. 20, l. 5). Both *SCT* and *TCF* are attached to the name of Wagstaffe solely by inclusion in the so-called *Miscellaneous Works*, but have not been ascribed to anybody else except in the general ascription of Wagstaffe material to Swift by Dilke (*Notes and Queries*, 3rd ser., II, 253–4, 396).

In the signed works, Wagstaffe shows unlike Arbuthnot a fairly consistent patterning for the first two profile discriminators: results for Verbals are bunched about 2.58, lower than Arbuthnot and much lower than Swift; results for Introductory Connectives spread somewhat but are more consistent than those of either Swift or Arbuthnot, and reach from the upper part of Swift's range into a hitherto untapped region above that again. Perhaps Emerson was right about the 'foolish consistency', or perhaps argumentation requires more connection than narrative, as indeed Professor Milic's own results seem to hint. Wagstaffe's results for Different patterns are, however, less consistent than those of either Swift or Arbuthnot. Before scaling, the 'Preface' is within, and the two parts of the *Letter* are somewhat above the Swift range; after scaling, the 'Preface' below and the other two within that range. The 'Preface' is of course a rather special problem because it is a half sample, and has to be scaled twice. Professor Milic on his p. 217 gives the figure for the Different patterns of a Swift half-sample as 592, and the corresponding figure for a whole sample as 858. I multiplied by the scaling factor 858/592 to obtain a figure for a whole sample, and then scaled the result by the former factor 844/895. Appendix C below includes only the original score under 'D (raw)' and the final result under 'D (scaled)'. If the distinctive pattern of Wagstaffe's means for the three 'reliable' tests, a pattern unlike any of those which Professor Milic has established (except oddly the Swift Letter I), can be assumed a constant for Wagstaffe, then it will be easy indeed to evaluate the Pseudo-Wagstaffe pamphlets. In his use of class 51 Wagstaffe is more consistent than Arbuthnot but less consistent than Swift. Unfortunately his figures, although a little higher than Swift's, are not particularly distinctive. In the grouping VA, however, Wagstaffe is even less consistent than Arbuthnot, and in sentence openings aside from Introductory Connectives he is equally irregular.

In profile pattern, Pseudo-Wagstaffe turns out highly irregular indeed:

he produces a different pattern in each of the three samples, and achieves only a mild sort of parallelism at a considerable distance between the *Comment* and the *Story*. He shows the greatest variety yet seen in the use of Introductory Connectives, from a near-record low of 6.9 for the *Story* to a record high of 45.6 for the *Testimonies* (higher than Wagstaffe, the former champion). In making this extraordinary total in the *Testimonies*, he has completely reversed the usual proportions of subordinating to coordinating conjunctions. However, the majority of these apparently idiosyncratic subordinators occur in the second part, the actual 'Testimonies', where the vast majority of the sentences begin with *that* as part of the parody on legal style. In the first section, 'Some Memoirs . . .', Pseudo-Wagstaffe uses only 17.0% Introductory Connectives, fewer than in *SCT* and *CTT*. When these two sections were run as separate samples on the program for word-frequency analysis, they turned out similar results in all word-groups except VA: the first section has 14.65% finite verbs; the second, only 11.75%. Apparently the legal style requires less action than the historical. The results for Verbals, 3.39 and 3.99, seem as usual more stable than those for finite verbs, and in this case far more stable than those for Intro-ductory Connectives. Both 'profile' discriminators seem, however, to be affected by the generic difference of the two sections, and Introductory Connection in particular appears here as a consciously manipulated organ of style. Since the sections are of unequal length, results for Different patterns could not, unfortunately, be compared. (None of these compari-sons appear in the appendices.) Under Verbals Pseudo-Wagstaffe shows a reasonable uniformity in the *Story of the St Alb–ns Ghost*, the *Comment on Tom Thumb* and *The State and Condition of our Taxes*, but shoots up into Swift territory in *Testimonies of the Citizens of Fickleborough*. Only under Different patterns are his results consistent with the theory of single authorship, for although more widely spread than Arbuthnot's they are less so than those of Wagstaffe and Swift. The two lowest scores, those for *SCT* and *TCF*, are grouped about Wagstaffe's lowest; the highest, for *SAG*, is near his highest. In the 'less reliable' tests on the other hand, Pseudo-Wagstaffe is more consistent than either genuine Wagstaffe or Arbuthnot, and in VA he is even more consistent than Swift. His use of 51 is in Wagstaffe's range for *TCF*, at the lower limit of that range and into Swift's for *SCT*, and below either range for *CTT* and *SAG*.

It is then difficult to decide whether Pseudo-Wagstaffe is a single author or a group. If tests reliable for Swift *must* be reliable for other authors, then perhaps each of the four pamphlets here selected from the so-called

Miscellaneous Works of Dr Wagstaffe was written by a different author. Furthermore, Swift, Arbuthnot and Wagstaffe would not only all fail the paternity test with respect to the 'unknown' *Story of the St Alb–ns Ghost*, but would also seem not to have written any of the other Pseudo-Wagstaffe pamphlets here examined. If, however, tests reliable for Swift are not reliable for minor authors, then it will be almost impossible to assign the authorship of any pamphlets written by minor authors under the super-vision and perhaps the correction of Swift. The profile of the *Story*, our present 'unknown', is more like that of Addison or Macaulay than like that of the possible authors. . . .[1]

The last author to consider is the outside control, Mrs Manley. Since Mrs Manley seems to have no connection with the *Story of the St Alb–ns Ghost* (apart from the fact that she lived with the printer), she serves only to test the possibility that there existed a sort of Tory 'house style' or that genre and length influenced that style. I coded a sample from random pages of the *Memoirs of Europe, Towards the Close of the Eighth Century. Written by Eginardus, Secretary and Favourite to Charlemagne* . . . (London, 1710), later reissued as the third volume of the *New Atalantis*. This work resembles both the *Story* and the *John Bull* pamphlets in being a narrative with a secondary political level of meaning, but differs in the type of story told and in its greater length. The subject matter, mainly sexual in-trigue among high-ranking Whigs, is quite different from that of any of the other authors studied; the sprawling sentences and thickly sprinkled exclamation points give the style an apparent if superficial individuality.

When, however, we examine the results which Mrs Manley offers, we are doomed to disappointment: the profile pattern of *ME* is fairly similar to that of *JB* (taken from *John Bull*), the item among my samples most similar to *ME* in genre. And when we turn to Professor Milic's results, we dis-cover that *ME* is closer to the *Gulliver* samples than are the *Modest Proposal* or the selection *Examiner* 11. Although *ME* is low in word classes 31 and 51 and high in VA, these tests have been so unreliable before that they do not inspire confidence here. The *Memoirs of Europe* sets an apparent record for opening sentences with a finite verb, but is fairly close to *John Bull* in this as in some other features. Distinctive as Mrs Manley seems when we read her scandals, she uses the same grammatical patterns as do her greater

[1] For a more recent study showing that by one aspect of typographical usage certain Pseudo-Wagstaffe works do in fact form a cluster, see the Introduction to *Arbuthnotiana: The Story of the St Alb–ns Ghost* (1712) . . . , forthcoming from the Augustan Reprint Society.

rivals in long satiric narrative, and is as different as they from the patterns of the short satiric narrative *Story of the St Alb–ns Ghost.*

In order to bring out more sharply the relation of the *Story of the St Alb–ns Ghost* to each group of samples, Appendix D normalizes each author (including Pseudo-Wagstaffe, but excluding Mrs Manley as we have tested only one sample of her work) by his own mean. Each mean listed in Appendix C is taken as 100 for that author under that determiner, and the individual scores listed in Appendix C are multiplied by a scaling factor of 100/cm, where cm is the computed mean. Thus *John Bull* registers 100 under both Verbals and Introductory Connectives because it is nearly at Arbuthnot's mean for both, and it registers 97 under D as a result of multiplying either $829 \times 100/854$ or $780 \times 100/805$. *The Story of the St Alb–ns Ghost* is then tested against each norm in turn. The new grouping 'Extended Satiric Narrative' has been suggested by the results already examined, and shows that these narratives form a population more coherent under Introductory Connectives than the Arbuthnot population, and more coherent under Different patterns than the Wagstaffe. If we compare these figures with the ones given for Swift's norms (Milic, p. 235), we see that both *Gulliver* samples are closer to all three of the norms for Extended Satiric Narrative than they are to those for Swift. This grouping must remain tentative for the time, however, as the figures for *Gulliver* depend on Professor Milic's coding, and those for *John Bull* and *Memoirs of Europe* depend on mine. None the less it is curious that both *Gulliver* samples come closer to the Arbuthnot than to the Swift means. The 'unknown' *Story* on the other hand does not find any population where it fits under all three discriminators. With respect to the D discriminator, the *Story* is about equally close to every mean except oddly that of Pseudo-Wagstaffe. With respect to Introductory Connectives, it is about equally remote from all – and a little further still from Wagstaffe and Pseudo-Wagstaffe. The only discriminator which seems in this case to discriminate gives the *Story* to Wagstaffe. Because the Verbal score speaks clearly for Wagstaffe, we might perhaps attribute the pamphlet to him; because of the conflict between that and the score for Introductory Connectives we must do so with about the same degree of uncertainty as before the testing began.

What do all these results show, if anything? In the first place, we have about as far to seek as before for the author of the 'unknown' pamphlet on whose behalf the whole experiment was launched. Although reasonably discriminated from the Swift pattern, the *Story* is almost equally so from the Arbuthnot and the Manley patterns, and yet more clearly from the

Wagstaffe pattern of abnormally high scores for Introductory Connectives, while close to Wagstaffe's use of verbals.

In the second place, we may have dicovered some constants of the Queen Anne Tory style, but we have thereby removed the efficacy of the so-called 'reliable' discriminators. Professor Milic says: 'If [tests] do not show adequate consistency, if they are unduly sensitive to the type of writing tested, or if they fail to discriminate between greatly different authors, they are considered Not-reliable' (pp. 247–9). As a non-statistician, I do not understand the first criterion here specified: Professor Milic establishes a Swift range for Introductory Connectives from 26.1 to 41.8 (p. 231) and does not regard it as inconsistent, but feels that a further extension of 1.3 renders *Letter* 1 somewhat suspect (pp. 252–5). But if the Introductory Connectives are not inconsistent in Swift, they surely are in Arbuthnot, and are therefore Not-reliable for discriminating Arbuthnot from Swift or from anybody else. And Introductory Connectives also seem to be somewhat 'sensitive to the type of writing tested'; the long narrative *John Bull* is closer in this respect to Professor Milic's two *Gulliver* samples and to *Memoirs of Europe* than to the other Arbuthnot samples, just as the *Gulliver* samples are closer to the other Extended Narratives than to the Swift group. This may of course have another cause than undue genre sensitivity, but it does in any case fall under the condemnation of the third criterion: *Gulliver* is a far better connected book than either *John Bull* or the *Memoirs of Europe*.

The discriminator of Different patterns, although more consistent than the Introductory Connectives within each author's samples, has not discriminated one author very well from another in the eight samples with almost-certain authorship. When scaled, the D results for two of the genuine Wagstaffe samples, for the three Arbuthnot samples and for Mrs Manley *all* fall within the Swift range. Unscaled, one Arbuthnot sample, two Wagstaffe samples, the Manley sample and the Swift sample all belong together above the Swift range. While glad to give Arbuthnot a place near Swift, I cannot help feeling that any test which puts Mrs Manley and Dr Wagstaffe in a similar place is Not-reliable. The fact that Pseudo-Wagstaffe seems to have a range somewhat lower than Swift's is not much consolation.

The discriminator of Verbals turns out the best performance of the three; it is far more consistent for each author than is that of Introductory Connectives, and it discriminates more than that of Different patterns: at least it manages to discriminate Wagstaffe from Swift. None the less it still leaves Arbuthnot and Mrs Manley very close to each other and to the Swift mean, along with *Testimonies of the Citizens of Fickleborough*. Although the tests can naturally perform better together than singly, we must note that while only one sample, Arbuthnot's *Sermon*, falls wholly within the Swift range, only one, Wagstaffe's 'Preface' to *Anthropologia Nova*, falls wholly outside the Swift range. We shall find it difficult indeed to make further attributions of Tory pamphlets, when the authors already tested overlap in so many characteristics.

Professor Milic points out that he has tested his discriminators only 'against . . . a limited range of prose produced by writers of great distinction between 1700 and 1850' and adds, incontrovertibly, 'It seems highly likely that Swift would be easier to distinguish from a less homogeneous group . . .' (p. 182, n. 110). But the logical corollary suggests that Swift would be harder to distinguish from a more homogeneous group – as indeed he has proved to be. The discriminators which separate Swift from four prose masters have failed to separate him very far from those who worked with him for the Harley ministry during the last four years of Queen Anne's reign. The present samples are not exhaustive for Arbuthnot or for Pseudo-Wagstaffe, and they have obvious defects (though I hope consistent throughout) in coding. The samples do, however, tend to show more virtuosity in these minor writers than has been generally expected, and to imply that the mysteries of Swift's greatness are still hidden. If Wagstaffe can use as many or more Introductory Connectives, Mrs Manley and Arbuthnot as many Verbals, and all of them as many Different patterns as Swift, why does Swift obstinately remain a giant?

Word frequency

	Milic		Köster		Arbuthnot			Wagstaffe			Pseudo-Wagstaffe			Manley	Un-known
	Control mean	Swift mean	EX II	EX II	APL	JB	SMC	LF 1	LF 2	ANP	CTT	SCT	TCF	ME	SAG
01	23.4	20.3	19.2	19.2	21.6	21.6	20.7	18.9	18.0	20.0	20.7	20.6	22.3	20.0	20.8
02	7.9	7.2	7.4	7.6	6.7	9.4	6.7	7.3	7.8	5.7	6.9	6.7	6.7	8.2	8.9
03	7.1	6.0	5.2	6.8	8.3	6.6	7.5	8.2	7.4	6.7	6.2	5.7	6.5	7.1	6.3
04	.6	.8	.6	1.2	1.3	.9	1.0	.6	1.1	1.2	1.2	1.0	.8	1.1	.5
05	1.6	2.3	2.7	2.5	2.4	2.7	2.5	1.0	1.2	1.2	1.8	1.9	1.8	2.3	1.6
06	.6	1.0	.8	.7	.5	.7	.4	.5	.6	.3	.5	.2	.8	1.1	.5
07	.5	.7	.6	.6	.8	.3	.5	.9	.6	1.0	.5	.6	.8	.5	.3
08	.0	.1	.1	.1	.5	.0	.2	.2	.0	.3	.5	.1	.1	.0	.0
11	5.6	7.1	6.9	7.1	5.4	9.8	6.6	7.2	8.5	6.5	6.4	6.2	5.8	8.9	7.9
21	7.0	7.2	8.2	8.1	6.6	6.8	7.6	7.6	8.5	7.0	8.1	8.9	6.9	7.6	6.9
31	16.3	15.3	15.6	13.4	14.6	13.7	13.0	15.3	13.9	15.9	15.7	17.2	16.0	13.7	15.0
32	.4	.6	1.0	1.0	.6	.7	.3	.3	.4	.3	.5	.1	.3	.5	.9
33	1.9	2.4	2.6	2.1	2.2	2.2	3.2	2.6	1.9	2.7	2.8	1.4	1.7	2.8	2.1
34	1.5	2.0	2.1	1.5	1.1	1.1	1.4	2.1	1.9	1.0	.9	1.3	1.3	1.8	1.8
41	4.9	4.9	4.6	4.6	4.1	4.4	4.6	4.3	4.6	6.4	5.0	5.8	5.2	4.4	5.7
42	2.1	2.7	2.6	2.3	2.7	3.0	3.2	3.4	3.9	2.9	2.7	2.9	3.4	2.5	1.8
43	2.1	2.1	2.7	2.2	1.6	.5	1.4	1.7	1.2	1.1	1.6	1.4	3.1	1.7	1.5
44	.0	.1	.1	.3	.3	.3	.7	.3	.5	.5	.7	.4	.2	.6	.1
45	.3	.4	.5	.8	.2	.5	.4	.6	.6	1.0	.4	.4	.6	.1	1.2
51	13.8	12.6	12.4	12.4	12.5	9.6	11.9	13.2	12.4	14.6	12.2	12.4	13.5	10.8	11.7
61	2.0	2.7	3.0	2.9	3.4	3.0	3.4	1.5	2.0	2.0	2.6	2.9	2.5	2.6	2.7
71	.0	.0	.0	.0	.0	.0	.0	.2	.3	.0	.4	.5	.2	.0	.1
81	.4	.9	.7	1.0	1.1	.4	1.0	.6	.8	.1	.4	.5	.2	.1	.3
91	.2	.5	.3	.3	.2	.6	.8	.5	.8	.3	.4	.3	.4	.5	.2
VA	14.9	14.4	15.6	15.77	13.38	16.23	14.44	14.98	16.39	12.79	15.16	15.71	13.61	15.85	15.91
VB	2.6	4.1	4.2	3.87	3.94	3.75	3.52	2.54	2.56	2.64	2.95	2.89	3.60	4.03	2.50
M	20.1	20.4	21.3	18.24	18.66	17.93	18.08	20.49	18.24	20.06	20.09	20.17	19.49	18.99	20.00
C	9.5	10.2	10.6	10.57	9.17	9.06	10.49	10.54	10.98	12.17	10.56	11.01	10.62	9.52	10.53
Words	3,500	3,500	3,489	3,480	3,675	3,541	3,516	3,650	3,622	1,774	3,548	3,558	3,576	3,495	3,549
Sentences	118	79	87	87	94	94	91	81	80	34	77	59	79	78	87
Mean sentence length	29.9	43.3	40.1	40	39	37	38	45	45	52	46	60	45	44	40

APPENDIX B
Sentence openings (see p. 131)

	Swift		Arbuthnot			Wagstaffe			Pseudo-Wagstaffe			Manley	
	EX I (Milic)	EX II	APL	JB	SMC	LF 1	LF 2	ANP	CTT	SCT	TCF	ME	Un-known SAG
01	1.1	2.2	.0	10.6	2.1	.0	1.2	2.9	1.2	.0	5.0	7.6	12.6
02	.0	.0	.0	3.1	.0	.0	2.5	.0	.0	1.6	.0	3.8	.0
03	.0	.0	.0	1.0	.0	1.2	.0	2.9	.0	.0	.0	.0	5.7
04	.0	.0	.0	2.1	2.1	.0	.0	.0	.0	.0	.0	1.2	.0
05	.0	.0	.0	.0	.0	.0	.0	.0	.0	.0	.0	.0	.0
06	.0	.0	.0	1.0	.0	.0	.0	.0	.0	.0	.0	.0	.0
07	.0	.0	.0	.0	.0	.0	.0	.0	1.2	.0	.0	.0	.0
08	1.1	1.1	.0	.0	.0	.0	.0	.0	.0	.0	.0	.0	.0
11	19.5	19.5	25.5	21.2	12.0	19.7	27.5	5.8	20.7	11.8	21.5	14.1	33.3
21	4.6	3.4	1.0	1.0	13.1	1.2	3.7	.0	.0	3.3	3.7	3.8	1.1
31	16.1	14.9	30.8	15.9	8.7	18.5	5.0	20.5	28.5	33.8	12.6	24.3	13.7
32	.0	.0	.0	.0	.0	.0	.0	.0	.0	.0	.0	.0	.0
33	1.1	1.1	1.0	.0	.0	1.2	.0	.0	2.5	.0	1.2	5.1	1.1
34	1.1	2.2	2.1	2.1	.0	25.9	23.7	26.4	16.8	13.5	.0	8.9	8.0
41	26.4	26.4	1.0	4.2	13.1	8.6	7.5	14.7	2.5	11.8	1.2	6.4	3.4
42	10.3	10.3	9.5	7.4	6.5	1.2	.0	.0	.0	.0	37.9	.0	2.2
43	1.1	.0	.0	.0	.0	1.2	5.0	5.8	6.4	1.6	.0	6.4	.0
44	.0	.0	.0	1.0	7.6	1.2	10.0	.0	.0	.0	1.2	.0	1.1
45	1.1	1.1	.0	.0	.0	12.3	2.5	.0	5.1	3.3	.0	5.1	.0
51	6.8	6.8	20.2	5.3	8.7	3.7	.0	14.7	11.6	11.8	5.0	5.1	2.2
61	4.6	3.4	3.1	10.5	12.0	.0	.0	.0	.0	.0	3.7	1.2	13.7
71	.0	1.1	.0	1.0	.0	.0	.0	.0	.0	1.6	.0	.0	.0
81	.0	1.1	1.0	1.0	3.2	.0	.0	2.9	.0	.0	.0	.0	.0
91	4.6	4.5	4.2	10.6	9.8	3.7	11.2	2.9	2.5	5.0	6.3	6.4	1.1
IC	41.3	41.4	14.9	22.3	29.7	38.3	42.5	44.1	22.1	30.5	45.6	21.8	6.9

APPENDIX C
Three-discriminator profile

	VB	IC	D(raw)	D(scaled)[1]
Professor Milic's controls				
Highest score	3.7	17.8	769	
Lowest score	1.6	3.8	440	
Mean	2.6	11.6	652	
Professor Milic's Swift				
Highest score	4.4	41.8	868	
Lowest score	3.5	24.0	768	
Mean	4.1	33.1	833	
GULL I	3.5	24.0	789	
GULL II	3.8	26.1	768	
EX II	4.2	41.3	844	
My figures for EX II	3.87	41.4	895	844
Arbuthnot				
APL	3.94	14.9	844	795
JB	3.75	22.3	829	780
SMC	3.52	29.7	890	840
Mean	3.74	22.3	854	805
Wagstaffe				
LF 1	2.54	38.3	877	827
LF 2	2.56	42.5	914	861
ANP	2.64	44.1	549	740[2]
Mean	2.58	41.6		809
Pseudo-Wagstaffe				
CTT	2.95	22.1	842	794
SCT	2.89	30.5	782	737
TCF	3.60	45.6	803	756
Mean	3.15	32.7	809	762
Mrs Manley				
ME	4.03	21.8	916	863
The 'unknown'				
SAG	2.50	6.9	873	823

[1] See p. 132.
[2] See p. 138.

APPENDIX D

Three-discriminator profile, normalized (see p. 141)

	VB	IC	D
Professor Milic's Swift			
EX II	95	125	101
GULL I	86	73	95
GULL II	93	79	92
SAG	61	21	99
Arbuthnot			
APL	105	67	99
JB	100	100	97
SMC	94	133	104
SAG	67	31	102
Wagstaffe			
LF 1	99	92	102
LF 2	99	102	106
ANP	102	106	92
SAG	97	17	102
Pseudo-Wagstaffe			
CTT	94	68	104
SCT	92	93	97
TCF	114	139	99
SAG	79	21	108
Extended Satiric Narrative			
JB	100	95	98
ME	107	93	108
GULL I	93	102	99
GULL II	101	110	96
SAG	66	28	104

Note: The figures for 'Extended Satiric Narrative' cannot pretend to absolute validity, since the samples *JB* and *ME* depend on my coding, whereas *GULL* I and *GULL* II depend on the coding of Professor Milic.

Sonnets and computers: an experiment in stylistic analysis using an Elliott 503 computer

JOSEPH LEIGHTON*

What is described here are the first, tentative steps of a conventional, would-be literary historian into the baffling world of computer applications and if they do nothing else they may serve to demonstrate, indirectly, the difficulties of adjustment experienced by the non-scientist in the face of a new and sometimes impenetrable technical discipline.

The present project has its origins in a relatively conventional study of the German sonnet in the seventeenth century. For a variety of reasons it was decided to devote some attention to occasional sonnets, and not only to those of known authors but also to a selection of the many occasional sonnets by worthy German citizens whose literary pretensions were minimal. It is hoped that a kind of literary geography will emerge, with the main emphasis on the cities of Nürnberg, Strassburg, Breslau, Danzig, Hamburg, Leipzig and possibly also Dresden. One of the minor aims within the overall study is to try to determine whether certain towns, in effect certain groups of poets, are distinguishable from each other by a predilection for specific stylistic techniques. It is intended to carry out basic tests on the 'run-of-the-mill' material, and the results will then be tested against the work of 'genuine' poets. The problem, however, is firstly what kind of analysis to carry out, and secondly how to store and make use of the information provided by this analysis.

Work on the analysis of material already collected[1] quickly showed that the second of these problems was by far the more acute. There are so many ways of analysing a sonnet that a straightforward personal choice, provided that it is carried out consistently, can always be justified. It is less easy to record the information about any individual sonnet in such a way that, when the time comes to survey the several thousand sonnets to

---

* Department of German, University of Bristol.
[1] It is perhaps worth mentioning that the collection of material is almost more problematical than the processing of it.

be used for the study, it will be possible to extract readily the relevant and strictly comparable and ignore the irrelevant. It was this point that produced the first hazy notions about using a computer as a glorified card-index.

As this line of thought progressed, another monster reared its head quite independently, namely the problem of comparative stylistics. Traditionally description of style has been an attempt to rationalize subjective impressions on the basis of carefully preselected examples. Even if this had been considered adequate enough in itself as an approach to the problem of style, it seemed likely to prove extremely unreliable in the discussion of several thousand sonnets. The inevitable decision to use quantitative data as the basis of any description of style quickly reinforced the desire to explore computer techniques.[1]

The next stage was to decide what data to quantify. Aware that word-frequency counts had been used in relation to problems of authorship,[2] but sceptical of the claims made for such techniques, I felt nevertheless that, given the notably epigrammatic qualities of the seventeenth-century sonnet, Herdan's type/token ratio[3] could perhaps provide a useful measure of style, but it soon became obvious that, for a novice, this was very much the wrong end of the scale to begin at. The problem was shelved, but not lost from sight.

More important in my considerations of style, long before the word 'computer' entered my vocabulary, was the question of sonnet structure. In my earliest analyses of sonnets I had pursued in vain the elusive concept of 'structure of meaning', and while this concept never became any more tangible it none the less seemed to contain something of relevance to the particular problems of sonnet writing. What it reduced itself to was this: that the rigidity of the rhyme structure of the sonnet (and also, for a great deal of seventeenth-century German sonnetry, of the metrical structure) imposed certain limits on the type of statement possible within a sonnet. It seemed that most writers of sonnets put their rhyme schemes together first and then set about writing a sonnet to fit them, an observation which can be documented from contemporary poetic theory.[4] From this it

---

[1] Apart from discussions with colleagues in the Computer Unit at Bristol, which were both stimulating and extremely helpful, I found the following article a particularly useful introduction to the subject: Robert S. Wachal, 'On Using a Computer', in *The Computer and Literary Style*, ed. Jacob Leed (Kent State University Press, 1966).

[2] Among others G. U. Yule, *The Statistical Study of Literary Vocabulary* (Cambridge, 1944); F. Mosteller and D. L. Wallace, *Inference and Disputed Authorship. 'The Federalist'* (Reading, Massachusetts, 1964).

[3] G. Herdan, *Type-Token Mathematics* (The Hague, 1960).

[4] G. P. Harsdörffer, *Poetischer Trichter* (Nürnberg, 1650), pp. 35–6: '. . . und ist in den

followed that a poet's personal style or mannerism was perhaps most likely to show itself in the way he adapted his language to the requirements of the form, and in this respect it seemed that sentence structure might well be the most important indicator of personal style.

The description of sentence structure is, of course, a problem of linguistics and one which is by no means unambiguously resolved. In the case of the sonnet, however, it was not sentence structure alone that was important but rather its relationship to line structure. It was this latter point which put to an end, at least temporarily, to a brief flirtation with structural linguistics and transformational models *et al.*, which did not seem to help in dealing with the particular problems of the sonnet form. It was an article by Professor John Sinclair[1] that first suggested to me the possibility of conducting a fairly simple kind of analysis based on the distinction between main and subordinate clauses.

To demonstrate the technique I quote part of a table from Sinclair's analysis of the poem 'First Sight' by Philip Larkin, substituting italic characters in the code for Sinclair's Greek characters. Here *a* represents a main clause, and *b* a subordinate clause:

a	Lambs that learn to walk in snow
b	When their bleating clouds the air,
(-*a*)*a*-	Meet a vast unwelcome, know
(-*a*)	Nothing but a sunless glare.

'To account for interruptions the symbols *a*- and *b*- . . . indicate that a clause is interrupted by a line ending or another clause, and (-*a*) and (-*b*) indicate the conclusion of an interrupted clause.'[2]

In adopting this technique I found that certain additions and modifications were necessary. In order to cater for particularly important seventeenth-century rhetorical techniques it was necessary to include symbols for apostrophe and question and for figures of speech which affect sentence structure, such as anacoluthon and inversion, and to indicate incapsulated and elliptical clauses. Also certain types of phrase in apposition to a main or a subordinate clause, which could not readily be categorized, were placed under a general heading of 'extension phrases'. In preparing the data for analysis by computer one other important modification was made: since (-*a*) uses four characters and *a*- two characters for one piece of

Sonneten / oder Klingreimē sehr gebräuchlich / daß man alle Reimendungen zusammensuchet / und daraus vier anständige in Verfassung deß Gedichtes wehlet'.

1 J. McH. Sinclair, 'Taking a Poem to Pieces', in *Essays on Style and Language*, ed. Roger Fowler (London 1966), pp. 68–81.
2 *Ibid.* p. 71.

information, it was decided to reduce all the symbols to a simple alphabetic code which, when end of line and end of sentence characters are included, ranges from *a* to *s*. There follows a table of the characters used and their significance, and an example of the application of this system to a sonnet by John Donne.

KEY

a	main clause	*k*	completion of subordinate clause
b	interrupted main clause	*l*	incapsulated subordinate clause
c	completion of main clause	*m*	elliptical subordinate clause
d	elliptical main clause	*n*	end of sentence
e	extension phrase in apposition	*o*	inversion
f	apostrophe	*p*	anacoluthon
g	double apostrophe	*q*	question
h	incapsulated apostrophe	*r*	end of line
i	subordinate clause	*s*	end of line and sentence
j	interrupted subordinate clause		

CODE

ajr	1	Death be not proud, though some have called thee
kir	2	Mighty and dreadfull, for, thou art not soe,
jlmr	3	For, those, whom thou thinks't, thou dost overthrow,
kfir	4	Die not, poore death, nor yet canst thou kill mee;
bir	5	From rest and sleepe, which but thy pictures bee,
cr	6	Much pleasure, then from thee, much more must flow,
ar	7	And soonest our best men with thee doe goe,
ees	8	Rest of their bones, and soules deliverie.
ar	9	Thou art slave to Fate, chance, kings, and desperate men,
dr	10	And dost with poyson, warre, and sicknesse dwell,
ar	11	And poppie, or charmes can make us sleepe as well,
daqs	12	And better than thy stroake; why swell'st thou then?
mar	13	One short sleepe past, wee wake eternally,
aas	14	And death shall be no more, Death thou shall die.

DATA   (punched on a single card):
ajr kir jlmr kfir bir cr ar ees ar dr ar daqs mar aas;

It is clear that this system is far from perfect; it means inevitably that several arbitrary decisions have to be taken, some of which may well involve interpretation of the text and lose all claim to objectivity. For example, line 1 of the poem by Philip Larkin would be described as *bi* under my scheme, the phrase 'that learn to walk in snow' being considered as a subordinate clause. A more awkward question is the one posed by line 13 of the Donne sonnet: how does one categorize the phrase 'One short sleepe past'? In my scheme this is represented with *m* as an elliptical subordinate clause, i.e. implying 'When one short sleep is past', but clearly this is a matter of interpretation. A point which has considerable impact on any statistical analysis is found in line 8 of the sonnet: does one consider the line to consist of one phrase or two quite separate phrases? In this instance I have chosen the latter solution but where, as often happens in the seventeenth-century German sonnet, the so-called extension phrase or phrases are an asyndetic list of nouns, the decision is not an easy one. Some agreed standard must be found for decisions such as this if the statistics produced are to be taken seriously.

To return to the actual experiment and the problems of what to do with the code once it was worked out: with the Elliott 503 the choices open to me for the actual programming were to use the list-processing language WISP or to adopt ALGOL. It is this stage of the process which is perhaps most painful for the literary historian; even when one has 'learnt' a programming language one soon realizes that the ingenuity needed to exploit it can only come from wide experience. The argument for leaving all this to professional programmers, assuming they are available, would be overwhelming if it were not that it is precisely this part of the work which makes one aware of both the limits and the potentialities of the computer. Be that as it may, the attractions of using a list-processing language were considerable, and had it been possible to use list procedures within an ALGOL program,[1] then this would have been ideal. In practice, however, it soon became clear that WISP could not handle the statistical part of the analysis, and finally the flexibility and ease of handling (for the amateur) which ALGOL offered decided the issue.

The first objective was a simple program that would carry out basic counting and statistical operations. The material chosen for the initial experiments was 20 religious sonnets by Paul Fleming[2] and Andreas Gryphius's so-called Lissa sonnets[3] (31 in all). The choice of these poems was essentially arbitrary, though influenced by three quite important factors: firstly, all of these sonnets are written in alexandrines, which makes them readily comparable; secondly the Fleming sonnets are ordered chronologically in the Lappenberg edition; and thirdly the Gryphius sonnets are the first versions of sonnets which were later much revised, so providing a basis for further comparison. Also, since the two poets wrote in such

---

[1] As indicated in examples used by J. M. Foster in his book *List Processing* (London, 1967).
[2] Paul Fleming, *Deutsche Gedichte*, ed. J. M. Lappenberg (Stuttgart 1865), Erstes Buch der Sonnetten, pp. 443 ff.
[3] *Andreae Gryphii Sonnete*, in Andreas Gryphius, *Gesamtausgabe der deutschsprachigen Werke I*, ed. M. Szyrocki (Tübingen, 1963), pp. 5ff.

obviously different styles it was hoped (as it turned out, not entirely justifiably) that the statistics would indicate fairly clearly which types of measurement would prove most useful in the description of sonnet style. The counting was not only of the individual features listed, i.e. of main and subordinate clauses and the various figures of speech, but also of enjambments, given by a count of c and k, and of octet divisions, which were considered to exist where the patterns of the eighth lines ended with s. Table 1 gives a small selection of the kind of comparative statistics produced by the program.

TABLE 1. *Mean frequencies of standard features*

		Fleming	Gryphius
1.	Main clauses per sentence	1.65	2.62
2.	Sub clauses per sentence	0.88	3.57
3.	Main clauses per poem	13.45	7.25
4.	Sub clauses per poem	7.20	9.90
5.	Sentences per poem	8.15	2.77
6.	Coincidences	6.15	2.70
7.	Enjambments	1.95	2.80
8.	Apostrophes	2.40	1.10
9.	Extension phrases	2.40	1.93
10.	Percentage of octet divisions	80.00	32.26

The readings for items 1, 2, 5 and 6 must be treated with some reserve: the only objective test for the end of a sentence is the presence of a full stop and the singular lack of full stops in Gryphius's sonnets may not be entirely intentional.

While the information produced by the computer here is not particularly exciting – after all, one doesn't need a computer to point out that Gryphius uses more subordinate clauses than Fleming, or has fewer clear octet divisions – it must be remembered that the significance of these readings is likely to be greater when there are 'normal' frequencies against which to measure them. Similarly the measurement of correlation between individual stylistic features was in one sense little more than a programming exercise for its own sake, and yet, as Table 2 shows, some of the information is not entirely without interest.

The two most striking points here are perhaps the complete lack of significant relationship of enjambment to any other feature, and the remarkably positive correlation between the number of sentences and the coincidence of end of line and end of sentence in Gryphius.

The value of such statistics in the first instance is very limited, but they are capable of generating hypotheses which may merit further exploration. For instance, when the series of readings on the individual sonnets of

TABLE 2. *Correlations*

(a) Paul Fleming

	Main	Sub	Sentences	Coincidences
Main				
Sub	−0.5			
Sentences	0.68	−0.18		
Coincidences	0.62	−0.02	0.73	
Enjambments	−0.36	0.04	−0.05	−0.36

(b) Andreas Gryphius

	Main	Sub	Sentences	Coincidences
Main				
Sub	−0.44			
Sentences	0.51	−0.26		
Coincidences	0.53	−0.32	0.98	
Enjambments	−0.21	−0.1	0.06	0.09

Paul Fleming were represented graphically, it was striking that the second half (i.e. later sonnets) showed considerably less variation from the mean than the first. Immediately the question came to mind: is this an indication of greater maturity of style and of early experimentation? Implicit in the question is perhaps the truism that more mature style is less adventurous style; on the other hand, comparison with Gryphius at this point suggested that it might merely be the consolidation of a personal manner, since Gryphius's sonnets, his first and therefore those which one might be tempted to consider experimental, showed in general less variation from the mean than Fleming's. Again this seemed to be an indication of personal mannerism. A curious observation here, which I find interesting but to which I attach little objective significance, is that on the whole the better-known poems seem to show greater variation from the mean than the others.

The second stage of the experiment was to produce a program, now combined with the one already mentioned, to provide for any given group of sonnets a ranked frequency list of line patterns. This line of approach seems more likely to lead to interesting observations not only because it is closely linked with the important question of the relationship of line structure and sentence structure, but also because at the experimental stage it might help to refine the initial system of analysis. If we return to the example of the Donne sonnet it can be seen that the pattern *ar* occurs three times, in lines 7, 9 and 11, and in each occurrence the real structure of the line differs significantly. The prospect arises here that if individual patterns of high frequency can be studied on a basis of several examples, it might be possible to differentiate further (by identifying sub-groups) and to produce an altogether more sophisticated analysis. However, the implementation of such a plan must await the result of several further developments, most particularly the linking of the abstract scheme used here with the analysis of literary text. Techniques now being used and developed in Germany for automatic syntactic analysis of modern German give rise to considerable optimism that much refinement of the present data presentation could be achieved automatically.[1]

As expected, the frequency list of line patterns proved to be the most interesting part of the experiment so far, and while its significance cannot be fully assessed here an indication of its usefulness can perhaps be given in Table 3 and the relevant comments:

TABLE 3. *Most important line pattern frequencies*

Fleming (20 sonnets)		Gryphius (31 sonnets)	
as	19	ir	59
ar	18	ar	30
is	11	air	20
ir	10	as	19
ais	10	eir	15
air	6	is	13
aaqs	5	kr	12
aer	5	jr	10
		mr	10
		kjr	10
		iar	10
		ajr	10

Number of different patterns used:
  Fleming 151 in 20 sonnets
  Gryphius 128 in 31 sonnets

The most important point made by this frequency list is Fleming's relatively wide range of expression. The relatively few patterns of high frequency inevitably mean many more patterns of low frequency, and, of course, vice versa for Gryphius. Also of interest here is the fact that for both poets four 'simple' patterns (*ar, as, ir, is*), in which the line is a complete and uninterrupted clause, all come high in the frequency list; it could well be that this is already an indication of technical mastery, a hypothesis that will certainly merit further investigation. For Gryphius the suggestion of mannerism made by the extremely high frequency of the pattern *ir* is reinforced when one realizes that *mr* is often of a very similar form, involving simply the non-repetition of a subordinating conjunction in a parallel clause. A typical *ir mr* constellation would be the following lines:

Ehdeñ er Zeboim ließ in die asche legē
Und die erhitzte Lufft erklang von Donner-schlägen,[2]

[1] Hans Eggers and collaborators, *Elektronische Syntaxanalyse der deutschen Gegenwartssprache* (Tübingen, 1969).
[2] Andreas Gryphius, *Gesamtausgabe*, p. 7.

A further interesting point is the high frequency in Gryphius of several patterns involving enjambment, namely *kr*, *jr*, *kjr* and *ajr*. Although Gryphius uses considerably more enjambments than Fleming, it is worth pointing out that, while Fleming uses 49 different line patterns in 78 lines involving enjambments, Gryphius only uses a similar number in 174 lines. This is a further indication of Fleming's greater range and possibly also of his discreet use of enjambment.

I have already mentioned in passing the possibility of linking the abstract code system used here with machine-readable text, and it is the concern with line-pattern frequencies which makes the need for this acute. While one is dealing only with small groups of sonnets this is not a large problem; one can still refer back to the source very easily, and if specific references to sonnet numbers and lines are needed for particular patterns, they can be provided easily enough by adding a short extra section to the present program. When, as is the ultimate aim, these techniques are applied to the study of several thousand sonnets, it will clearly be necessary to have some kind of text print-out accompanying the pattern frequencies if their full value for descriptive and comparative stylistics is to be exploited. However, even without that, the exercise is not entirely without point. If some thousands of sonnets are to be examined, then clearly it should be possible to work out theoretical normal frequencies for all the individual patterns (and, for that matter, for all the other stylistic features analysed) against which to measure the work of individual poets; this would provide the groundwork for a more thorough statistical study, and could yield extremely useful information for the description of personal style.

Nothing in this experiment so far goes beyond the trivial, but it is not, after all, intended as an end in itself. Its purpose at this stage is simply to test techniques on a small body of material. Since the findings of these experiments will influence later decisions, and since any decisions will inevitably affect the form of data preparation, it is clear that the experimental stages of a project must be extremely thorough, and a wide range of tests must be used since it is impossible to decide in advance which readings will be most significant for any given group of sonnets. What is perhaps more important is that a really flexible system would allow the exploration of a host of small but pertinent points in a way which has not been possible before. Here, for instance, one such apparently insignificant point might be that of enjambment. Given the demands of a rigid rhyme structure it seems to me that, in German, it is easier to write a sonnet keeping the rhyming words in the middle of the clause or sentence than at the end, i.e.

enjambment is technically easier than coincidence of rhyme and end of clause. On the other hand, of course, a sonnet with no enjambment may well seem more wooden and less versatile. There would seem to be some crucial point at which the use of enjambment becomes an indication of lack of technical mastery rather than a sign of freedom and flexibility, and while I should be the last to claim, for example, that more than 2.257 enjambments per sonnet is bad, I nevertheless feel that, on a point like this, a wide-ranging statistical study might well illuminate the relative technical skills of a group of poets. Other problems which might be examined include the frequency of particular patterns at particular points in a given author's sonnets, structural differences between octet and sestet and perhaps, eventually, the extremely important question of rhyme.

Using the Elliott 503 it will not, in the first instance, be possible to analyse the sonnets in groups much larger than thirty until suitable routines using backing storage are developed – a step, incidentally, which is taken for granted by the computer professional and yet can seem terrifyingly large to the amateur, even if he knows what backing storage is! Alternatively it may be decided to adapt the present work for implementation on Bristol's recently acquired ICL 4-75, which may make it much easier to expand present procedures to cope with larger bodies of material. The most important development, however, will be the combining of sonnet texts with other information, a step which will widen the scope of the project considerably. As envisaged at present, each line of each sonnet will be punched separately and will be accompanied by a card containing, where appropriate, the coded stylistic analysis, word class information and also identification of author, work, sonnet number, date and place of publication. It would be a happy situation if some kind of automatic syntactic analysis could be devised which would reduce the need for pre-editing, but the remarkable work which Professor Hans Eggers and his team have done for the syntactic analysis of modern German[1] does not appear to be immediately applicable to seventeenth-century German. Here, the problem of dialect and of lack of standardization seem to be an insuperable barrier for the moment.

[1] See note 1, p. 156.

∗

Collocations as a measure of stylistic variety

PEGGY I. HASKEL*

This study was inspired by John Rupert Firth's work on collocations. In his essay 'Modes of Meaning'[1] he demonstrated the fact that a word of diverse meanings is defined by its co-occurrence with other words. His interest was not limited, however, to meaning as this is revealed by collocation. Especially in collocations that he discovered in poetry, he studied the formal and semantic characteristics of the co-occurring words. He noted the attraction for each other of words of the same derivation, of words expressing opposite meanings, of words beginning with the same consonant clusters. Beyond the word level, he was interested in the collocation of similar grammatical structures for the contribution these made not to definitional meanings but to larger meanings, perhaps stylistic. Unfortunately for any present study using the computer, Firth did not designate the linear limits of a collocation. For that matter, the clearest explicit definition of the term itself comes not from Firth but from Barbara M. H. Strang, who clarified it as 'a form consisting of two or more words in juxtaposition', thus having the meaning of 'phrase', plus the special sense, a 'collocation' of a head word and its adjuncts.[2]

Further work with collocations as an index of meaning has been done by several scholars. Professor M. A. K. Halliday has established what might be called a subdivision of a collocation – a lexical set – and has placed more emphasis upon that than upon the full collocation. As he describes it, 'The lexical set is identified by privilege of occurrence in collocation, just as the grammatical system is identified by privilege of occurrence in structure; the set is a grouping of items with similar tendencies of collocation.'[3] He is concerned principally with lexical cohesion, which, he says, 'is carried by

* Department of English, Nassau Community College, New York.
[1] John Rupert Firth, *Papers in Linguistics 1934–51* (London, 1957), pp. 190–215.
[2] Barbara M. H. Strang, *Modern English Structure* (London, 1962), p. 67.
[3] M. A. K. Halliday, 'The Linguistic Study of Literary Texts', *Proceedings of the Ninth International Congress of Linguists*, ed. Horace G. Lunt (The Hague, 1964), p. 304.

two or more occurrences, in close proximity, of the same lexical item, or of items paradigmatically related in the sense that they may belong to the same lexical set'. Thus in a collocation containing *peak, ascent, climb, mountain* and *summit*, he recognizes not one but two lexical sets: *ascent* and *climb* cohere, by his definition, as do *mountain, summit* and *peak*. He recognizes *ascent . . . peak* as a high frequency collocation, but he argues that frequency alone does not constitute cohesion. Though elsewhere in the paper Halliday said of style that 'the creative writer finds and exploits the irregularity that the patterns allow' (p. 305), the work that he has done on collocations suggests an interest that is primarily linguistic, not stylistic.

Another scholar who has studied collocations in order to learn more about lexical structure is J. McH. Sinclair.[1] Sinclair's sample, which was apparently rather small since the nodes or keywords appeared at most seven times, revealed a large number of *hapax legomena*. He noted in passing that these 'casual collocations' might 'include the magnificent images of some of our greatest poetry' (p. 418). But he did not pursue that possibility because he was trying to arrive at the lexical meaning of an item by measuring the way that it is predicted by other items.

Collocations can, however, do more than define the words of a language and reveal aspects of its structure. Sometimes, of course, they are little more than stereotyped word groups or clichés that are empty of thought, if not of meaning. Firth himself, writing in *Tongues of Men* of the irony of defining speech as the expression of thought, said that speech is often an effort not to reveal thought.[2] A mechanism for identifying this tendency to conceal thought and a formula for producing ready-made expressions might be provided by the stereotyped collocations in the language. No doubt it was just such collocations in 'modern writing at its worst' that George Orwell attacked in 'Politics and the English Language' as 'long strips of words' which have been 'tacked together like the sections of a pre-fabricated hen-house'.[3] If, as Coleridge claimed, the creative mind brings together disparate images and ideas,[4] perhaps the creative author brings together disparate words, forming unorthodox collocations. Louis T. Milic in *Stylists on Style* has pointed out Ernest Hemingway's alertness to 'the

---

[1] J. McH. Sinclair, 'Beginning the Study of Lexis'. *In Memory of J. R. Firth*, ed. C. E. Bazell and others (London, 1966), pp. 410–30.

[2] John Rupert Firth, *Tongues of Men* and *Speech*, Language and Language Learning Series (London, 1964), pp. 98–9.

[3] George Orwell, *Shooting an Elephant and Other Essays* (New York, 1945), pp. 79, 85.

[4] Samuel Taylor Coleridge, *Biographia Literaria*, Everyman's Library (New York, 1962), p. 174.

possibility of novelty available from the collocation of familiar words'.[1] If competent writers do, in fact, use unusual collocations and if, as is supposed, their chosen collocations are a part of their style, the computer should be invaluable in examining and measuring this variable.

Considering the possibilities for substitution of sentence, clause, and phrase patterns within a language, a writer has numerous stylistic choices he can make, though each choice of course limits the number of choices available to him at the next decision point. Studies of word predictability indicate that this is true of words as well. Some ready-made phrases are so well known that a writer's decision to replace one word with another will cause the whole phrase to come alive as a dead metaphor will when something causes attention to focus on its literal meaning. In word groups that are rather firmly established if a writer rebels against (and within) the expected pattern, he does something that is interpreted as stylistically significant. Whether this should be called 'foregrounding [, which] means the violation of a scheme',[2] deviation from a norm,[3] or choice – conscious or unconscious – [4] is of less importance in this study than is the determination of the degree of divergence from some established norm which reflects the collocational habits of the language of the period.

As Gustav Herdan said at the Ninth International Congress of Linguists, 'Stylostatistics leads to establishing the general laws for the use of language as a necessary preliminary of the determination of divergencies from these laws in individual style'.[5] At the same conference M. A. K. Halliday warned, 'if a linguist hopes to contribute to the analysis of English literature he must first have made a comprehensive description of the English of the period at all levels'.[6] Making specific reference to an author's style as revealed by his clause structures, Halliday observed that such a study would be meaningless unless one knew what the permitted clause structures in a language were. Yet without such a comprehensive statement as would justify the assertion, he said that some words were collocationally 'restricted'. He cited *caress* and *stagger* as lexically powerful but colloca-

---

[1] Louis T. Milic, *Stylists on Style* (New York, 1969), p. 483.

[2] Jan Mukařovský, 'Standard Language and Poetic Language', *A Prague School Reader on Esthetics, Literary Structure, and Style*, ed. Paul L. Garvin (Washington, 1964), p. 19.

[3] Michael Riffaterre, 'The Stylistic Function', *Proceedings of the Ninth International Congress of Linguistics*, ed. Horace G. Lunt (The Hague, 1964), p. 318.

[4] Louis T. Milic, 'Against the Typology of Styles', *Contemporary Essays on Style*, ed. Glen A. Love and Michael Payne (Glenview, Illinois, 1969), p. 289.

[5] Horace G. Lunt (ed.), *Proceedings of the Ninth International Congress of Linguists* (The Hague, 1964), p. 323.

[6] Halliday, 'The Linguistic Study of Literary Texts', p. 302.

tionally restricted as opposed to *hold* and *push*, which he described as lexically weak and collocationally unrestricted (p. 305). If for the purpose of a test a collocating word may be defined as a word[1] appearing no more than four words away from a focus word, then it is true that *caress* and *stagger* collocate with smaller numbers of different words. Because it occurs only once, *caress* could have no more than eight collocates in the million-word Brown Corpus; *stagger*, which appears twice, could have only sixteen. On the other hand, *hold* (frequency: 169) and *push* (frequency: 37) could have 1,432 and 296 respectively. The degree to which a word seems to be collocationally restricted may be nothing more than a condition of its frequency – that is, it may reflect nothing more than a characteristic of the language to use some words more than others.[2]

It may of course be true that some words of the language are collocationally restricted, but to be certain of that it is necessary to control the frequency variable in order not to be misled. What seems to be necessary, then, is a dictionary of collocations which will contain for each keyword or dictionary entry not only the complete list of collocating words but the percentage of the time that each collocating word appears with the keyword in question. Such a dictionary, based upon a large sample of written English, could serve as a standard against which to measure the works of an individual writer. Even though the sample used for an individual author might be small,[3] the results of a comparison should be valid because there would be no attempt to indicate how many words were used, only the percentage of the time that particular collocates occurred with certain keywords.

The dictionary itself will not be based upon a small sample. The million-word Brown University Standard Corpus of Present-Day Edited American English will serve as the Corpus. Consisting of 500 different prose selections, each approximately 2,000 words long, it includes material chosen by

[1] A word is here defined as any number of characters with a space or punctuation on either side. This follows the definition provided for the Brown University Corpus. W. N. Francis, *Manual of Information to accompany a Standard Sample of Present-Day Edited American English, for use with Digital Computers* (Providence, Rhode Island, 1964), p. 5.

[2] Elsewhere it seems that by 'collocationally restricted' Halliday does not mean that few words collocate with *caress* and *stagger* but that these two words do not collocate (as part of a span) with many other words. In either case, the low frequency of the words would account for the degree of apparent restriction. M. A. K. Halliday, 'Lexis as a Linguistic Level', *In Memory of J. R. Firth*, ed. C. E. Bazell and others (London, 1966), p. 155.

[3] Gustav Herdan has observed that if sample length is not constant, a study of richness of vocabulary, which is dependent on sample length if the samples are small, can be quite misleading. It should be possible to avoid this problem if the collocating words in both the standard dictionary and in the individual author's works show percentages. Gustav Herdan, *The Advanced Theory of Language as Choice and Chance* (Berlin, 1966), p. 77.

random methods from fifteen categories of prose – everything from press reportage to sermons, science fiction to *belles lettres*. The genres are well marked, making it possible to discover whether collocations vary from one genre to another. If we may expect to find differences among individual authors, we cannot ignore the possibility of gross differences among genres as well, but only to the extent that the categories actually correspond to genres.

All of the selections in the Corpus were first published in 1961. As Kučera and Francis indicate, some of the works may have been written prior to 1961, but nothing was included which was known to have been published earlier.[1] Since the Corpus satisfies the requirement that it describe the language of the period, a dictionary based on it can serve for a synchronic study of present-day authors.

As Sinclair wrote in 1966, a study of lexical form requires a very large computer.[2] Even with such a computer, the IBM 360/91, storage space becomes short if one seeks to gather collocates for very many keywords or dictionary entries. Thus it has been essential to limit this preliminary list. The proposed standard dictionary will include 100 keywords. This study began with a list of 28, though only 10 of these occurred often enough to show any patterns worthy of analysis.

It would have been tempting to use such words as *summit, peak, mountain, hold, stagger, caress, charm,* and numerous other unrelated words which various scholars have cited as examples of units that are lexically weak or strong, collocationally limited or free. But the rationale for such a list could hardly be considered respectable. Professor Milic pointed to Carl Darling Buck's *A Dictionary of Selected Synonyms in the Principal Indo-European Languages.*[3] This dictionary includes over a thousand sets of synonyms arranged in 22 'semantically congeneric groups', such as Parts of the Body, Food and Drink, Clothing, Dwelling, etc. For each of the principal Indo-European languages information is provided on 'the most usual expressions of a given notion' (p. xii). Since this dictionary presents words which can be considered keywords in any language, it offers an especially good source from which to select the entries for a dictionary of standard collocations. The words on Buck's list which occurred very infrequently in the Brown Corpus had to be eliminated in order to gain a

[1] Henry Kučera and W. Nelson Francis, *Computational Analysis of Present-Day American English* (Providence, Rhode Island, 1967), p. xviii.
[2] Sinclair, 'Beginning The Study of Lexis', p. 410.
[3] Carl Darling Buck, *A Dictionary of Selected Synonyms in the Principal Indo-European Languages* (Chicago, 1949).

base wide enough for collocations which might be considered standard. The words of highest frequency were also eliminated. Most of these were words like *will* and *can*, the high frequency of which is probably accounted for by the fact that they can serve in several capacities, one of which is that of function or structure word. It was determined that function words would be excluded from the list of collocating words as well as from the list of keywords. Function words can, of course, reveal a great deal about the structure of a language. Here, however, the emphasis is on lexical word selection as an independent parameter of style.

Despite the fact that words of the highest frequency were omitted for this study, which would use only a sample of the total Corpus, it was necessary to choose words of rather high frequency to be certain that they would appear in the sample. Once the words in Buck's dictionary had been marked with the frequency of occurrence in the Brown Corpus – information provided by the study of the Corpus made by Kučera and Francis – it appeared that it would be possible to select words appearing two hundred or more times. With function words deleted, 157 words remained on the list. The final list will be chosen by random methods, but since this list was to be limited to 28 words for reasons of economy of computer time, it seemed justifiable to check the words for their formal and semantic characteristics. The original intention was to see whether words beginning with a certain consonant cluster actually attracted words with the same cluster, whether words of two or three syllables attracted words with the same syllable count. It was not difficult to find some of the more popular clusters like *ch*, *pl*, and *str*, the popularity of which is suggested by any dictionary of English and borne out by the frequency counts in Kučera and Francis. The difficulty came in finding words of two and three syllables. This should not have been and was not particularly surprising considering the studies that have already been made of word length. Herdan discovered that in four English authors: Carlyle, Macaulay, Johnson, and Gibbon, average word length in syllables ranged from a low of 1.48 for Carlyle to a high of 1.63 for Gibbon.[1] His report on word length in number of phonemes, which he considered more useful than word length in number of letters, showed a mean of 2.85 phonemes per word. The mean number of letters was 3.5 (p. 300). The words of the Brown Corpus have not been subjected to syllable or phoneme counts, but the mean word length in characters is reported as 4.74.[2] These studies, however, included function words, which

[1] Herdan, *The Advanced Theory of Language*, p. 25.
[2] Kuˇera and Francis, *Computational Analysis*, p. 366.

had been removed from the tentative list based on Buck's dictionary. The assumption that the deletion of function words would leave two- and three-syllable words in abundant supply over the middle frequency range was erroneous. Of the 157 words from the Buck list which occurred 200 or more times in the Corpus only 33 had more than one syllable; 31 of these had no more than two. Further it was noted that more than a third of the 157 words could fall into two or more part of speech categories. So long as the words still carried related meanings it seemed useful to include them on the list. But other words like *hard* and *close*, which have multiple diverse meanings, seemed questionable. The Brown Corpus defines a word as 'a continuous string of letters, numerals, punctuation marks, and other symbols . . . uninterrupted by space' (p. xxi). Thus the spelling c-l-o-s-e, whether it would be pronounced /klous/ or /klouz/, represents a single word. Since, as Firth long ago pointed out, the meaning of a word is determined by collocation, it might be possible by computer to purify the type-token count available for the Corpus by programming to see which meaning, which word, is intended. Since no such study has been done, most words of multiple diverse meanings were removed from the list. When these had been deleted it was clear that at least 6 of Buck's 22 word categories would have no representatives. Thus the decision was made to include the one or two words in each division falling nearest to the 200 frequency mark. This would provide the 28 words to test in the preliminary project.

The computer used in this study is the IBM 360/91. The language is SNOBOL4, Version 3,[1] a string manipulation language developed by Bell Telephone Laboratories, Inc. This language has several primitive functions which serve to find and delete rapidly whole classes of words which have been identified in advance or to find and keep certain other words which have also been indicated. To retain a specified number of words which precede a keyword it is necessary to maintain a string of words which is always in flux – that is, as soon as a word is added on the right, one is subtracted on the left. The language itself is prodigal of computer time and this is particularly true of the constant pattern matching required to retain the specified number of words (and no more) in reserve; nevertheless, for people in the humanities who want to write their own programs, SNOBOL4 is excellent because it is thrifty of the programmer's time. It will ignore all except gross syntactic errors and it will operate on clean text, a very important feature for computer studies of literature.

The program for this study operates in three stages. In the first stage the

1 R. E. Griswold, 'Version 3 of SNOBOL4' (Holmdel, New Jersey, 1970).

computer scans the categories separately, deleting function words and focusing on keywords. Whenever a keyword occurs, the entire sentence in which it appears (including function words) is printed. For this preliminary project I have kept the text sentences for the help they might provide in setting the arbitrary limits of a collocation. In his study Sinclair used a span of three words.[1] In my program I have used a span of four words on either side of a keyword. A study of the text sentences indicates that a span of two is adequate in many sentences to collect the words that have a direct structural or semantic relationship; in other cases a span of eight may be required to get all the related words. The span length remains arbitrary, with a span of three or four serving about 75% of the time. In this same stage of the program all collocating words within the span of plus and minus four are placed into an array (a particular kind of data object in SNOBOL4) with the appropriate keyword. Finally the words in each array are counted, the words and the counts are printed as well as punched with the keyword and its count.

A second stage of the program collects all of the collocating words from the punched cards for the various samples into one alphabetized dictionary complete with counts for keywords and counts for collocates. Raw counts rather than percentages have been used in this preliminary study since the percentages keep changing as more material is scanned. So far I have sampled only 7% of the million-word Corpus.

In the third projected stage all collocating words will be placed into a list which shows the percentage of the time that the word appears with each of the several keywords that it may on occasion accompany. The percentage will use as denominator not the number of appearances noted in these selected spans, but the total number of occurrences of the word in the Corpus.

Since the sample so far tested amounts to only 7% of the Corpus, any conclusions at this point must be tentative. Only 5 of the 28 test words appear 15 or more times, and the words do not appear with equal frequency in the samples for the different genres. Nevertheless, for ten of the test words there are noticeable patterns now which could be indicative of final results.

The words which appeared most frequently fulfilled the expectation that the greater the frequency the less would be the occurrence of *hapax legomena. Tax*, which occurs 31 times in the sample from press reportage and 43 times in the sample from government documents, has 12 different words which appear in both samples. These 12 (considering their frequency

---

[1] Sinclair, 'Beginning the Study of Lexis', p. 417.

of occurrence) account for 64 of the total number of collocates. Sixty-one additional collocates are accounted for by duplicate occurrences in a single sample. The second most frequently appearing word, *town*, has 28 words accounting for 76 of the collocates. Twenty-six of these (9 words) are found in at least two of the three samples.

Court and *peace*, which occurred 25 and 15 times respectively, are different in that they show practically no overlap in the different samples; but the duplications within a single sample do indicate an emerging pattern. Fourteen words in the press sample accounted for 37 collocates. For *peace* 10 words account for 26 collocates. This leaves a great number of collocates which appear a single time, but the significance of the single occurrence must be judged later, when the third stage of the program shows each collocate in ratio to its total occurrence.

A much more interesting subject for speculation at this point is a difference between press reportage and government documents on one hand and fiction on the other in the literal and figurative use of words. Though I had expected just the opposite, government documents and press tend more often to use words figuratively. In fiction *cut* means literally to cut as with a knife. Its collocates are *open, belly, concussion, boy*. In press reportage its meaning of 'decrease' is shown by its collocation with *inflate, modest, expenses*, and *estimates*. The word *dead* reveals this same tendency. In press reportage issues are dead and republicanism is dead; but in fiction *dead* collocates with *fight, mourned*, and *wounded*. The same holds true for *top* and *red*. In fiction *top* is used to indicate literal elevation; it collocates with *steeple, head, stairs, wall*. In press reportage and government documents *top* appears with *officials, personnel*, and *executive*. Finally, *red* apparently represents a colour to a fiction writer, a creed to a reporter. The collocations for all of these words in press reportage and in government documents suggest that they are used at best in a very low-level metaphorical way. As Professor Buck observed, 'such use is . . . not a rhetorical or poetic device . . . but a feature of ordinary speech anywhere'.[1] It is interesting, nevertheless, that it occurs in press reportage and in government documents but not in fiction. Whether this tendency will continue to develop as the sample size increases is impossible to say, but this observation seems to justify the decision to compile counts for the samples separately before combining them for a standard dictionary.

The general hypothesis for this study is that originality is represented by numerous different collocates for a given word or, better, by unusual

[1] Buck, *A Dictionary of Selected Synonyms*, p. vi.

collocates; lack of originality is represented by stereotyped word groups or clichés. Thus far this study fails to show any difference between categories in the use of recognized clichés. They appear about equally in all samples.

The tendencies of greatest importance to this project were revealed by collocations for two words which appeared almost exclusively in the fiction sample: *road* and *black*. The word *road* occurred 18 times in the fiction sample: only once elsewhere. Among the collocates there was less evidence of *hapax legomena* than for any other keyword of approximately the same frequency. Eight words appeared twice; 2 occurred 3 times; 1 appeared 5 times. Since this was unusual, I returned to the text sentences to see what the sentences were for *road*. Even with some sentences (those without keywords) missing, the text ran smoothly enough to show that all 18 occurrences appeared in a single selection in the fiction sample. In time I intend to measure the collocations of individual authors against the standard to see whether there is a significant difference. Since all of these occurrences appeared in the work of a single author, it seemed useful and meaningful even at this early stage to compare his collocations to those for other words which appeared with approximately the same frequency. Whether the conclusion will be borne out or not, it seems thus far that this author likes to make repeated use of a single word – much more than the standard tendencies of repetition would indicate at this point.

The word *black* showed some evidence of duplication among collocates, but it had something else of greater interest. In 12 occurrences it collocated with 8 different words beginning with the bilabial voiced plosive sound: *back*, *bastard*, *bit*, *board*, *bottom*, *brushed*, *buggy* and *boy*. These 8 words (counting multiple occurrences) accounted for 13 words beginning with /b/ – more words than those with any other initial sound and more than the customary use of initial /b/ would predict. Once again the text sentences revealed that 7 of the 12 occurrences came from the same author. All 8 of the words beginning with /b/ appeared in those sentences and the count would have been still higher if the words *be*, *by* and *beyond* had not been deleted as function words. It would seem that the collocations for this particular author reveal a weakness for alliteration.

Originally I had hoped only to establish a standard dictionary in order to see whether competent authors select unusual collocations. I had assumed that the lower the frequency of the collocates the greater would be the indication of stylistic individuality. It now appears that the study may indicate other stylistic characteristics as well.

The possible usefulness of poetry generation

LOUIS T. MILIC*

One interesting result of my activity in computer poetry generation is a new definition of poetry. In an important sense, strings of words are interpreted as poetry if they violate two of the usual constraints of prose, logical sequence and semantic distribution categories. Such a sentence as 'The pond under my rocker saw the sunrise so the porch post planted carefully' exhibits both of these violations. Because ponds cannot see and porch posts cannot plant, the semantic constraints of English would normally prohibit their being used as subjects of verbs displaying human (or animate) action. And because even if a pond could see the sunrise that would provide no satisfactory justification, as indicated by the conjunction *so*, for the activity of the porch post, we conclude that the usual logical requirements of discursive prose have also been violated. In short, since the sentence is obviously well-formed syntactically but does not 'make sense', it is interpreted as poetry, as part at least of a larger poetic structure. This conclusion does not seem whimsical. Rather it seems to shed some light both on how we read poetry of our own time and on how poets operate. It might not be excessive to say that such a conclusion justifies what many consider a rather foolish pastime, computer poetry generation.

It might be pointed out, of course, that in the Western world, the writing of poetry has always been considered a wasteful thing for an able-bodied man to do, when he could be earning a living in a more serious way. The purpose of computer poetry generation differs, however, from the normal activity of the poet in that the usual poetic intention (prophecy, self-expression, aesthetic creation) is replaced by a heuristic one. The possible usefulness of computer poetry is concerned with what the doer can learn about language, about poetry and about poets from this sort of simulation. If his product has poetic interest so much the better but he has no illusions that he will be set beside Pope, Shelley and the other inhabitants of the Par-

* Department of English, Cleveland State University.

nassus. In this, his aim is more modest than that of the computer musicians, who have some respectable compositions to their credit, and the producers of computer graphics, whose beautiful arrangements of lines adorn a number of walls in good artistic company. Apparently, music, art and poetry, whatever they may have in common, are significantly differentiated both in their elements and in our expectations of how these combine into aesthetic structures.

The random generation of sentences is a fairly simple procedure, especially when programmed in a high-level computer language like SNOBOL4.[1] A formula for a sentence is established, say the following:

Article / Noun(1) / Verb / Preposition / Article / Noun(2).

A list is provided for each word-class. For example, the list in Noun(1) is: *boy, girl, shirt, cat, table, book, house, knife, box.* The program instructs the computer to select the first word in each appropriate list, to reconstitute the list placing the word just used at the end, and to print the resultant sentence. Provided the lists are of different lengths, the program will generate by this means a great number of different sentences of the following type:

    3. A girl picked about a script
   67. A shirt thought with a dog
   78. The table thought of the window
   88. The book sat around the dog
   93. A girl learned about a man
  104. The cat learned in the hair
  107. A house imitated to a man
  335. A boy learned to a hair
  341. A house sat to a picture
  392. The cat studied in the curtain.

Syntactically, these sentences are well-formed in that the order of the word-classes is consistent with English grammar and the inflection is properly managed. Many of the sentences would obviously be considered perfectly good English by a native speaker (e.g. 93). Many others, however, though syntactically adequate would be considered in some way defective. Some of those cited above (67, 78, 107), for example, have inanimate subjects with verbs that require human or animate ones. Other defects result from the tendency of certain collocations to acquire idiomatic meaning: 'to a man' (107), 'sat to' (341), 'to a hair' (335). These unpredictable results

---

[1] It should be noted that SNOBOL4 is quite inefficient compared with FORTRAN and requires a good deal more computer time as well as approximately 200k bytes of core, but it is easy to learn and less critical of errors than more efficient languages.

suggest that a grammar for generating sentences should be linked to a dictionary, so as to prevent the occurrence of aberrant sentences. Several sentences, however, are not clearly well-formed or defective. In sentences 88 and 392, a little licence at the interpretative level permits us to accept the notion of a book sitting around or a cat studying. In the proper context such sentences would go completely unquestioned. By context is meant not only the verbal environment (i.e. the sentences before and after) but the situational context (i.e. whether the sentence is identified as poetry). What this suggests is the difficulty of producing a grammar of poetical sentences: if the grammar produces only well-formed sentences it inhibits certain metaphorical possibilities [6, *passim*].

The number of different sentences which can be generated with a short vocabulary, though not infinite, is quite astronomical if a recursive feature is introduced. If the sentences are not built to a simple pattern like the one shown above but permitted to be short or long according to some device built into the program the results can be extremely varied. A linguist took the first 10 sentences of a children's story and derived from it 77 rules which recursively could produce 10^{20} different sentences, of which these are a selection:

Engineer Small is polished
When he is polished, he is proud of smokestacks and fire-box
Steam is shiny
The water under the wheels in oiled whistles and its polished, shiny, big and
    big trains is black [14].

Because of the necessary repetition, most of the sentences would not be very interesting.

A more stimulating sentence produced by Victor Yngve of MIT is 'What does she put four whistles beside heated rugs for?' [8]. For some obscure reason this sentence has a great deal of interest, for I have seen it quoted often since I first mentioned it in a talk at IBM in 1964. In fact, one poet felt obliged to write a poem in reply, incorporating the line. Despite this unusual response, these utterances are not presented as poetry, merely as randomly generated sentences.

Whatever rules are established for the production of sentences, the rules for producing poetry are generally more complicated because they involve the selection of the sentences according to more stringent rules. Obviously, poetry does not usually consist merely of stringing together any sentences that may happen to occur. In the production of poetry, sentences are produced in conformity with further constraints, such as metre, rhyme, logic, diction, subject-matter, imagery . . . Pope's line, 'The hungry judges soon the sentence sign', is followed by another line to the effect that the accused are denied justice because of the impatience of the officials of the court. Let us rewrite the couplet:

> The hungry judges soon the sentence sign
> And the accused are railroaded as usual.

Obviously this formulation falls short of being a perfect Augustan couplet. After the application of a series of further constraints, we might get something like Pope's second line,

> And wretches hang that jurymen may dine.

As everyone knows, poetry is more difficult to write than prose.

But there is one sense in which poetry is freer than prose and that is due to the willingness of the reader to interpret a poet, no matter how obscure, until he has achieved a satisfactory understanding. Modern poets have exploited this willingness. An instance is Dylan Thomas. A cursory glance at his poetry reveals lines such as these, which are not immediately grasped by the average reader:

> Because the pleasure-bird whistles after the hot wires,
> Shall the blind horse sing sweeter?

According to one of his childhood friends, Thomas constructed some of his poems in what is surely an unorthodox way. Thomas's aim

was to create pure word-patterns, poems depending upon the sounds of the words and the effect made by words in unusual juxtaposition. . . . he would draft the general scheme of a stanza, leaving some of the words to be filled in later. He carried with him a small notebook containing a medley of quite ordinary words, most of them very short — tree, bough, hive, gold, numb, and so on. When he wanted to fill in a blank he read in his dictionary, as he called it, and tried one word after another, so that he would obtain (let us say) *tree of night*, *bough of night*, and *hive of night*. An unusable arrangement often suggested other possibilities; thus, the rejected *hive of night* might be replaced by *starry hive*.

If nothing in his dictionary satisfied him, he would sit with his mouth partly open, hoping to pick up a promising word from someone's conversation. As a last resort he might open a book at random and experiment with any likely word in the top line of each successive page [7].

This procedure is plainly reminiscent of a sentence-generating program. It is interesting to reconstitute the poet's private dictionary and to derive from it poetical fragments which he never got around to trying, or perhaps rejected. The creation of new Dylan Thomas poems on this basis is not terribly difficult and is very instructive. Here is a poem which I have selected for this experiment. It is entitled 'In the Beginning', and consists of five stanzas of six lines, each one beginning with the title phrase. Here is the first stanza:

> In the beginning was the three-pointed star,
> One smile of light across the empty face;
> One bough of bone across the rooting air,
> The substance forked that narrowed the first sun;
> And, burning ciphers on the round of space,
> Heaven and hell mixed as they spun.

Careful reading of this and the succeeding stanzas will show the traces of the method described by Thomas's friend: 'bough of bone', 'minted face', 'blunt flower'

My procedure consists very simply of taking out all the nouns in the poem, alphabetizing them and re-inserting them in the poem in this new order. The resultant form adds the element of alliteration to the other poetic devices of the poem. Here is the result:

> In the beginning was the three-pointed air
> One bough of bone across the empty blood
> One basis of bases across the rooting breath
> The birth forked that narrowed the first brain
> And burning brain on the blood of ciphers
> Crosstree and cloud mixed as they spun.

In the second stage, the verbs are rearranged in the same way and the new version now reads as follows:

> In the beginning was the three-pointed air
> One bough of bone across the empty blood
> One basis of bases across the rooting breath
> The birth forked that abstracted the first brain
> And burning brain on the blood of ciphers
> Crosstree and cloud mixed as they burst.

The final permutation includes the adjectives, as well as the nouns and verbs. The result reads:

> In the beginning was the blunt air
> One bough of bone across the cloudy blood
> One basis of bases across the empty breath
> The birth forked that abstracted the first brain
> And burning brain on the blood of ciphers
> Crosstree and cloud first as they burst.

I do not claim that this effort to place words in even more unusual juxtaposition than Thomas managed has any poetical value, though some of the lines are not without poetic interest. With some refinement of the procedure, the result could be made much more attractive and consistent, perhaps sufficiently so to pass for a genuine example of the poet's work.

A more ambitious effort involved the creation of a set of quatrains distantly modelled on the first stanza of Blake's 'A Poison Tree':

> I was angry with my friend:
> I told my wrath, my wrath did end.
> I was angry with my foe:
> I told it not, my wrath did grow.

As compared with the Dylan Thomas experiment, which simply adopts the form of the original poem, the pseudo-Blake is of a different kind. It has a static form, in that every stanza has the same number of words as every other. Its peculiar features are the rhymes and the attempt to achieve consistency of internal reference. The following example is typical:

> 1. You were happy with your foe
> And your puny joy did glow
> Your foe relived your joy
> And you renewed the foolish ploy.

I will not claim a great deal of poetic merit for this quatrain but it is possible to point out that it rhymes, it scans in an approximate way and, most difficult of all, it has a certain consistency. The rhyming is achieved by arranging the line-ending words in separate lists. Whichever list is randomly selected for the first line-ending word, the next line-ending word must come from the same list. The same occurs for the second pair of lines. Because the lists are arranged in fixed arrays the same number of rhyming words must occur in each list. In English this can be a considerable problem, especially for words like *gaiety*. *Ploy* (in line 4) represents the exhaustion of my resources for words to rhyme with *joy*. The scansion is controlled by establishing a formula which scans, and by using words in each position of the same syllabic length and status pattern. The internal consistency is maintained by relating all pronouns and pronominal adjectives to the first word in line 2. Similarly the choice of the adjective *happy* in line 1 determines the noun *joy* in lines 2 and 3, whereas the noun ending line 1 appears as the first noun in line 3. Unfortunately, the constraints severely limit the possible variety of the output. As soon as the first adjective is selected for line 1, the rhyme-scheme of the second couplet is determined. By means of a relatively simple system of pre-determined relationships of this type, something approximating sense can be produced over a span of four lines consisting of two sentences. Over a larger span, the problem of maintaining sense without falling into tautology would be progressively greater unless one used a highly sophisticated semantic compatibility procedure.

On the semantic level an interesting by-product of this set of permutations is the finding (also observed by Yngve [14], p. 71) that words change meaning drastically in contexts which may be only slightly different. Such words as *gay*, *bride*, *puny* in collocation with each other develop unexpected possibilities:

> 143. You were gay with your bride
> But your great gaiety did hide.
> Your bride renewed your gaiety
> And you reviewed the foolish satiety.

> 34. He was grieved at his bride
> But his puny grief did chide.
> His bride relieved his grief
> And he renewed the silly belief.

Syntactically, it is also notable that line 2 can be regularly read as an inversion (i.e. the object before the verb).

In a static format of the type just described a number of ingenious solutions to the problem of variety are possible. An initial subordinate clause arrangement was tried by some experimenters at the RCA laboratories [5] in Lancaster, Pennsylvania, who produced the following stanza among a thousand:

> 27. While life reached evilly through empty faces
> While space flowed slowly o'er idle bodies
> And stars flowed evilly upon vast men
> No passion smiled.

Randomness was achieved by manual intervention, the operator depressing an interrupt button to select a word for each position. At Michigan State University, John Morris produced a number of haiku-type poems, using a vocabulary derived from an anthology of Japanese haiku [10]. The basic constraint, apart from a plausible syntax, consisted of the requirement that seventeen syllables be distributed over three lines. There were no semantic constraints. The results are like these, apparently the best of four thousand produced by the Michigan computer:

> Still midnight, silent,
> Still waters, still frozen,
> Battle dusk, and far.
>
> The savage, savage
> Scarecrow, down in silent dusk,
> Frozen, well frozen.
>
> Distance, I listen:
> Far weird savage frozen spring,
> Old song, echo still.
>
> Glittering midnight:
> Our hollow well, glittering,
> Silent, savage, weird.

Mr Morris sent a group of these to the student literary magazine at his University, but they were not printed. Apparently, they smelled of the machine. Or perhaps the lack of quality was plainly perceptible to a student poetry editor.

The preceding examples illustrate the difficulties of computer poetry generation on the technical level of versification (rhyme, metre). These difficulties, however, can be dealt with by means of suitable correction routines applied after the sentences have been generated. Moreover, they are not fundamental to the problem in that neither rhyme nor metre is an essential constituent of poetry. The problems of imagery (e.g. metaphorical consistency) raised by this process are in a different class. Unlike versification features, which are linguistic at the phonological level, imagery features are linguistic at the semantic level, or are extra-linguistic, in that they cannot be detected without reference to the world of things. Only linguistic features, those which can be specified by rules applicable to the world of symbols, can be taken into account in algorithms for poetry generation. Consequently, such imagery problems are of minor interest for poetry generation at the present stage in the development of semantic theory.

More interesting, both from a theoretical and a practical viewpoint, is the question of randomness or uncertainty: how to produce well-formed sentence strings whose syntactic pattern has not been previously determined by the algorithm. The basic difficulty consists in introducing enough uncertainty to ensure variety in the resultant output without violating the constraints that govern well-formed sentences. Though this is primarily a practical problem, it touches on theoretical considerations of syntax primarily in the taxonomy of word-classes and the placement of constructions. When, for example, a simple (static) sentence pattern is established and generation merely consists of inserting vocabulary items from various lists into syntactical slots (as in the example on p. 170, above), the resulting sentences are likely to be well-formed, if care has been taken to confine the membership of each list to items with distributional parity. When, on the other hand, the principle of true recursion is given free play, when, that is, any word may be replaced by a larger construction (adverb by adverbial clause, adjective by relative clause), the possibility of producing ill-formed sentences exists. Between these extremes there is a middle ground involving the use of iteration and option which I have exploited in my current work.

The basis of my RETURNER programs is a poem entitled 'Return' by Mrs Alberta Turner ([12], and see Appendix). This poem has served as the source of vocabulary items, both individual words and some phrases, in the preparation of the programs. Of the five versions of this program that have been developed, the first was merely a trial and the fourth and fifth have been abandoned as unpromising. Consideration is therefore limited to Versions Two and Three.

RETURNER TWO is based on a pattern consisting of subject and verb, with optional modifiers and complements, and an optional conjunction at the end which provides the opportunity of iteration. Options are decided by drawing a random digit (1 is success, 0 is failure). The subject having been selected, the first option is for a post-modifier. Then the verb is selected and followed by an optional complement, which may be a direct object or an adverbial. The third and final option is for a coordinating conjunction, in which case the process begins again. The following selections from the output illustrate the possibilities from the simplest to the most elaborate (oblique strokes show the boundaries between constructions):

61. Deer / planted (subject–verb)
87. Hemlocks / saw / a thin curd (subject–verb–object)
12. The snow / planted / again (subject–verb–adverbial)
117. Tracks / around it / shelled (subject–modifier–verb)
125. Apple twigs / from salad to salad / saw / the sheep (subject–modifier–verb–object)
50. The pond / through the willows / planted / yesterday (subject–modifier–verb–adverbial)
93. Deer / shelled / yet / my dog / wouldn't take (subject–verb–conjunction–subject–verb)
109. The pond / shelled / yet / the porch post / wouldn't take / and / the snow / saw / the sheep (subject–verb–conjunction–subject–verb–conjunction–subject–verb–object).

G

The attractive unpredictability of the output of this program suggested that a more elaborate design would yield more interesting results. The consequence, RETURNER THREE, is based on a tagmemic matrix of six slots: a front adverbial, the subject, a middle adverbial, the verb system (including complement), an end adverbial, and a terminal conjunction (in the case that iteration is selected). Each slot leads to the selection of a construction. The subject, for example, may be a pronoun, a noun, or a complex nominal. The adverbials and the conjunction include a zero option. The choice of construction then leads to a list from which the particular lexical unit is chosen. To illustrate the process, the following list of steps is involved in the generation of the verb system:

(1) The 'V' slot is selected from the tagmemic matrix.

(2) A choice is made among copulative, transitive and intransitive verbs.

(3) (a) If the copulative verb option has been selected, a verb is chosen from the appropriate list and the route leads to the selection of a noun or adjective complement, the choice being decided by an odd/even test of the number of words in the string.

(i) The adjective is chosen from an adjective list.

(ii) The noun complement is chosen from the noun list, one of three lists available for the choice of subject.

(b) If an intransitive verb is selected, a verb is chosen from the appropriate list and an optional adverbial complement is added.

(c) If a transitive verb is selected, a verb is chosen from the list and a direct object is added, either

(i) a nominal construction or

(ii) a pronoun in objective case.

(4) The routing then proceeds to the next slot in the matrix.

After the string has been generated but before the iteration (if any) occurs, the string is subjected to a set of adjustment routines to ensure grammatical agreement and concord:

(1) In the case of the verb *be*, suitable forms are substituted in accordance with the person of the subject.

(2) If the presence of a leading adverbial (*yesterday*) signals a past tense, a test is made for verb regularity:

(a) if the verb is irregular, the suitable past form is substituted from a list;

(b) if the verb is regular, the past morpheme is attached, subject to the necessity of orthographic adjustment (e.g. doubled final consonant).

(3) If the leading adverbial has a future sense, the auxiliary *will* is added before the base form, except that in the case of *be* the base form is substituted for the inflected form already in place.

(4) If neither tense adjustment is required and the verb is not *be*, a test is made for the possibility that the person of the subject requires the singular verb morpheme (-*s*) and this is added as needed, subject to phonological rules.

The final option is rhetorical. If the odd/even test so dictates, a subject–verb inversion is applied, or a verb–object/complement inversion, except that the collision of pronouns in inverted position is avoided as unidiomatic. After iteration is complete and a clean-up routine is performed which removes signals, markers, diacritics, and other symbols internal to the program, the generated string is then set out as a stanza by a function that makes each line as long in words as the first word of each line has letters.

The following stanzas have been generated by this program, RETURNER THREE-C:

2. In the
   Morning melons often fall and tomorrow separate
   Blankets will bring me through the willows.

7. They turn locusts today
   Yet at home
   Crowbars never stagger in the morning.

9. Tomorrow a thin curd often will shell her
   In the
   Morning.

16. Often was he nearly gray
    Yesterday.

19. We again
    Will appear nearly round
    Tomorrow.

27. Yesterday hemlocks planted all the apples at home yet
    They often turn crowbars
    Today.

48. Turn the crowbars today
    So through
    The willows my

> Dog again staggers
> At home
> And carefully separate
> Blankets knead me in the morning.

Despite a tiresome lack of variety, both in syntax and in vocabulary, these synthetic stanzas have an unmistakable 'poetic' quality and a family relation to the source poem. It would be too simple to ascribe this effect merely to the presence of the same words in 'Return' as in RETURNER. Nor do we believe any longer in such a thing as a poetic diction, unless a diction is poetic which collocates crowbars with kittens, dogs and staggering. The unexpected collocations of poets like Dylan Thomas have perhaps oriented us towards a different conception of poetic texture or a different sound of the poet's voice.

The unquestionably primitive output of RETURNER can be brought closer to the source poem by adding linguistic refinements to the program design. The next version will include more of the vocabulary of the original, will attempt to incorporate syntactic algorithms for subordination, possibly a question transformation and a less random stanzaic formula. With enough refinements, RETURNER should be able to generate 'Return', not only in its original form but in the alternative forms which Mrs Turner presumably wrote and discarded. But this is not an easy task. The difficulties so far overcome (for instance, the priority of decisions applied in the adjustment routines) suggest that one can more easily write poetry with pencil and paper than with a computer. But my experience with this humbling process has persuaded me that it is a good way to learn about the design of poetry and the reading of it.

A consideration of the problems involved in generating computer poetry alerts us to the curious behaviour of familiar words in unfamiliar combinations or contexts. We perceive how readily we accept metaphor as an alternative to calling a sentence nonsensical. We always tend, that is, to try to interpret an utterance by making whatever concessions are necessary on the assumption that the writer had something in mind of which the utterance is the sign. Of course, this is inappropriate when the speaker is a computer. The consequence seems to be the demolition of the critical axiom that the poem is sufficient. If we are not to waste our time in vain interpretation we must now ask a new question before beginning an exegesis: Who or what wrote this poem? The problem, however, will not arise in a serious form until computer poetry becomes somewhat better than it has been up to now.

APPENDIX

Hemlocks are nearly round,
Deer paw the pond,
My dog squirts the porch post.

Last night the snow wouldn't take tracks,
But apple twigs are cut
Higher than porcupines.

Yesterday I saw the weathercock
Through the willow;
Today the cock is gone.

Holding my bowl,
I step carefully
From salad to salad.

The swamp has shores again
And the quicksand grass.

Have I planted crowbars under my porch
And chisels under my rocker?

No crumbs fall from the agate pebble,
But around it acres of sand are also red.

Melons crack,
Locusts have shelled my sisters on the porch,
The collie's tongue sticks.

The kittens hiss, at the milk pan,
And knead separate blankets.

This morning all the apples ringed the tree
So close the boy turned his ankle
And rabbits staggered.

The jack o'lantern's soft now
And nearly gray.

Mica silvers the sheep.
When my child brings his paper star,
Will it glitter? It's not silver paper.

Hemlocks are nearly round,
Mice run under the snow,
Sunrise reddens a thin curd.

BIBLIOGRAPHY

1 Richard W. Bailey, 'Automating Poetry', *Computers and Automation*, XIX (April 1970), 10, 13.

2 Jean A. Baudot, *La machine à écrire* (Montreal, 1964).

3 'Computer Poems and Texts', *Cybernetic Serendipity* (London, 1968), pp. 53–62 [articles by Marc Adrian; Robin McKinnon Wood and Margaret Masterman; Nanni Palestrini; Alison Knowles and James Tenney; Edwin Morgan; Jean A. Baudot; and E. Mendoza].

4 Wilbur Cross, 'Machine Miltons', *The New York Times Magazine*, 4 December 1966, pp. 59, 62, 64.

5 'Electronic Poetry', *Electronic Age*, XXII, no. 3 (Summer 1963), 30–1.

6 Samuel R. Levin, 'On Automatic Production of Poetic Sequences', *Texas Studies in Literature and Language*, V, no. 1 (Spring 1963), 138–46.

7 J. H. Martin, Correspondence in *Times Literary Supplement*, 19 March 1964, p. 235.

8 Margaret Masterman, 'The Use of Computers to Make Semantic Toy Models of Language', *Times Literary Supplement*, 6 August 1964, pp. 690–1.

9 Louis T. Milic, 'Computer Programs and the Heroic Couplet', *Think*, May–June 1968, pp. 28–31.

10 John Morris, 'How to Write Poems with a Computer', *Michigan Quarterly Review*, VI (January 1967), 17–20.

11 'Poetry, Prose and the Machine', *Freeing the Mind* (London, 1962), pp. 45–9.

12 Alberta T. Turner, 'Return', *The Midwest Quarterly*, IX, no. 2 (Winter 1968), 168–9.

13 Jon Wheatley, 'The Computer as Poet', *Queen's Quarterly*, LXXII (Spring 1965), 105–20.

14 Victor H. Yngve, 'Random Generation of English Sentences', *1961 International Conference of Machine Translation and Applied Language Analysis* (London, 1962), 1, 66–80.

V

Computer applications to oriental studies

Automatic alphabetization of Arabic words
A problem of graphic morphology and combinatorial logic

R. D. BATHURST*

For the student of Arabic there is a dearth of good graded vocabularies, general lexicographical aids and bilingual dictionaries of a satisfactory standard. Only recently have some of the latter been provided by the publication of Wehr's Arabic/German and Arabic/English dictionary and al-Ba'albaki's English/Arabic dictionary. Ideally, there would also be available for the student and user of modern Arabic not only a large bilingual general dictionary of the quality of Harrap's Standard French–English dictionary, but also lexicons for all specialized fields in which new words, or new meanings, that have gained general acceptance, would be given. There would also be dictionaries of regional dialects supplemented by colloquial glossaries. In practice, such a situation is incapable of achievement and is quite beyond the scope of scholars available to undertake the work. The most glaring deficiencies can be tackled but it is unlikely that they will be overcome unless the considerable work of assembling references is accomplished with the aid of a computer.

In April 1968 a research project was commenced in the Middle East Centre in Cambridge with the object of devising and preparing a computer program capable of alphabetizing Arabic words by the etymological method. The solution obtained was then to be tested by a large word frequency count of modern non-scientific Arabic prose.

Unfortunately, Arabic is not amenable to being processed by a computer. It is an agglutinative language and the abundance of prefixed and infixed letters make it impractical to alphabetize Arabic words by taking the letters sequentially. There can be up to 2,300 different combinatory prefixes preceding the first letter of a verb stem and more than 1,600 preceding a substantive stem. The stems themselves are subject to infixion and there are more than 500 patterns for them. Varieties of combinatory suffix are almost as numerous as those of the prefix. In order to write a program for

* Middle East Centre, University of Cambridge.

the computer to recognize Arabic word-roots (stems without their infixes) non-intuitively, and without a knowledge of the grammatical significance of the patterns, it is necessary to determine the complete range of morphological phenomena occurring in the language.

The stem in an Arabic word is customarily a triliteral consonantal root. From the consonantal root the basic unit of the vocabulary, the verb, has developed within a rigid system. For this reason there is a finite variety of vowel schemes and, therefore, of word patterns. In normal printed Arabic the short vowels are not shown, and the reader is required to interpret the words rather than read them. This absence of short vowels, together with the abundance of prefixed and infixed letters, makes the location of the lexeme for an Arabic word a matter of intuition – guided by a knowledge of the grammatical bases for the word patterns – rather than a matter of systematic matching of stems. For example, the meaning of the Arabic word *bactxrajoa* has to be sought primarily under its root lexeme *xrj* and then determined precisely by considering its derived form and its grammatical affixes. *In toto* these provide the meaning 'with its removal', in which 'with' is provided by *b* and 'its' by *oa*. For readers ignorant of Arabic the apparent difficulty in pronouncing this example is caused by the absence of short vowels. The reader of Arabic will provide these intuitively by recognizing, or trying to recognize, the word pattern.

In view of this, the first step was to determine the complete range of patterns represented by the corpus of verbs and substantives in Arabic. Because of the omission of short vowels in printed Arabic this had to be done by considering the varieties of graphic morphological patterns only, and not their phonemic counterparts. Moreover, in the case of weak roots the visible (i.e. the printed) changes brought about by the effect of the notional vowelling had to be taken into account also. This was effected by compiling complete conjugation tables for the sound, doubled and singly weak root types as well as for quadriliteral roots. For the substantives, tables were prepared to show variations in the patterns for the various root types, covering the complete range of substantives as identified by customary function, i.e. nouns of instrument, etc. Within these substantive tables consideration was given to any modifications the patterns might suffer by reason of gender, number, definition, declension, elision and grammatical affixation. The verbs, similarly, were considered for the effect of affixation. The resulting corpus of graphic morphological patterns was listed in a pattern register from which the combinatorial logic for the sort algorithm (identification of roots) was developed.

The sort algorithm takes the premise that the great majority of patterns encountered in Arabic texts comprise a combination of root letters (radicals) and a finite variety of augmentory items, and that the key to identification of the radicals, non-intuitively, lies in recognition of the augmentory items and, where necessary, of the changes effected on weak radicals. The remainder of patterns encountered, generally grammatical words of high frequency, are dealt with separately by a look-up list. The success of the sort algorithm is dependent upon the complete role of individual letters acting as radicals or affixes having been assessed both from the corpus of theoretical patterns and, more vitally, from processed texts, i.e. real data. Only by examination of a substantial amount of processed data can decisions be made as to whether certain rare patterns or oddities should be dealt with by the sort algorithm or by a look-up list. This problem is considered further later on.

Abundant data was available from the word frequency count side of the project on which sampling work proceeded concurrently. Previous word frequency counts in Arabic have suffered from certain drawbacks connected with not only the type of material sampled (i.e. newspapers, books, plays, poetry, etc.), but also with the geographical range of the sample, the overall size of the sample, and the chronological period of the material sampled. In the past no attempt has been made to correlate range of occurrence (i.e. dispersion) with frequency of occurrence of the words sampled. In this project the emphasis has been on modern Arabic, that is, the Arabic which is the *lingua franca* of international communication and pan-Arabism, and, accordingly, the first criterion established was that only material published within the past twenty-five years should be sampled. Secondly, in view of research in progress earlier at Durham University, material displaying colloquial characteristics was avoided as far as possible; thus, plays were excluded. Modern Arabic poetry was not included because its new style and format are neither established nor published enough yet to provide a wide enough range for sampling. Newspaper Arabic was excluded because of the difficulty of satisfying the criterion of nationality of authorship which was one of the cardinal features of the sample. For the only effective way in which a sample of modern printed Arabic prose can be taken evenly over the entire Arab world is by considering the nationality of the author.

There were two alternatives for deciding how to select passages of text for sampling: by random selection or arbitrary stratified selection. Both must be dependent on other criteria governing the corpus or universe from which the sample is being taken. Random sampling involves the use of a table of random numbers, such as that of Tippett, but does imply that a multitude of publications – with wide subject coverage – is available. Owing to the disproportion in subject coverage of books published in Arabic this approach could not be adopted. Instead, a stratified sample was made of texts which satisfied the criteria of date of first publication, nationality of authorship and subject coverage. The latter was determined by consideration of two further criteria: proportionate coverage of subjects in Arabic publication and type of subject coverage encountered by students of Arabic. Eight subject groups were chosen but it proved impossible to meet the requirements of sampling in one of these, that of Fine Arts. The remaining seven comprised Religion/Philosophy, History, Literary Non-Fiction, Literary Fiction, Popular Geography/History, Social Sciences I and Social Sciences II. 168 texts were sampled to the extent of 875, 1,750, 3,500 or 7,000 running words from each, stratified by arbitrary parameters of page numbers, e.g. 26–35, 51–60, etc. It has been demonstrated by Herdan that stratified sampling of this kind does not produce statistically inadmissible deviations compared with results produced by random sampling.[1]

The sampled texts were key-punched on paper tape for computer input. The keyboard character set of the machine used, though standard, was limited and owing to the great variety of typographical features in Arabic some compromises had to be made. They included a limitation on the types of punctuation mark, and an inability to show short vowels, even when given in print. The transliteration scheme used was on a letter-for-letter basis, digraph representation being unacceptable owing to the further complexity it would give to the Arabic morphological argument. The argument sub-programs, i.e. those determining the morphological structure of the words, were written in Atlas Autocode, other facilities being provided by the Command functions available on the Cambridge Titan.

The results achieved confirm that efficient automatic alphabetization of Arabic words by this method is a feasible proposition both for linguistic analysis and for use in information storage and retrieval routines. Other users of the computer for natural language analysis will be familiar with problems of compatibility (even within a university campus), of limited availability of compilers for suitable programming languages, of access to computing time, and of efficiency of computer service operation. It re-

---

[1] G. Herdan, *The Advanced Theory of Language as Choice and Chance*, Kommunikation und Kybernetik in Einzeldarstellungen, 4 (Berlin, 1966), pp. 95–9.

mains to be seen how much more efficiently this particular operation could be run in another programming language and whether it would be better to prepare an alphabetization procedure as a software package available for a particular range of common computers.

The development of programs for automatic alphabetization of Arabic words is a battle between theory, that is, pattern prediction on an 'objective' basis, and reality, that is, the variety of pattern occurrence in sampled prose, including idiosyncracies or irregularities requiring 'subjective' solutions. The full range of words or patterns that require subjective solutions – inclusion on a look-up list – can only be determined by a very large sample. Moreover, the items requiring subjective answers can only be isolated when the great majority of patterns susceptible to objective solution have been catered for in the programs. Thus processing of the sample proceeded on the basis of running a batch of several thousand words, checking the print-out for radicalization errors, amending the master programs and then running another batch. This has the inherent disadvantage that the programs acquire several layers of amendments or additions and one rapidly reaches the point where a laborious re-working of the entire program, to achieve smaller compiled program storage space and more efficient argument, is vitally necessary. Most Arabists would settle for an efficiency of 99.5% in computer programs used for radicalization of Arabic words, but it would require a sample of several times half a million words to do better than that.

Remarks on programs so far have been confined to the radicalization part of the alphabetization process. That is, selecting two, three or four radical letters for the word sampled and treating these as the etymological headword under which the sampled word would be found in an Arabic dictionary. In practical terms this has meant that for every word sampled the chosen radicals have been printed out followed by the sampled word in context, and supplemented by a book/page/line reference, a diagnostic stating which sub-program had chosen the radicals, and a serial line number. The second part of the alphabetization process is a string-handling operation, that of shunting the lines about – one for each word sampled – so that they are alphabetized by the radicals given on the left of the line. This brings together all words derived from the same radicals, complete with context and book/page/line reference. With a corpus of almost 500,000 such lines on magnetic tape most of the more sophisticated alphabetization techniques are too impractical to use. At the time of writing no substantial effort has been made to experiment with various methods, but for the sake of producing the word-frequency count within a reasonable period of time a simple fishing job has been done. The radicalized data is transferred from existing magnetic tapes to others by taking lines in turn according to the alphabetical value of the radicals at the left of each line.

The cost of the project has been met by a grant made by the Department of Education and Science on the recommendation of the Committee on Research and Development in Modern Languages.

Some Oxford projects in oriental languages

ALAN JONES*

The aim of this paper is twofold: first, to describe briefly the main projects in oriental languages at present being carried out in Oxford with the aid of computers; secondly, to draw attention to some of the ways in which remote console facilities may be conveniently employed in dealing with literary and linguistic material, once such facilities become more widely available to workers in these fields.

Since June 1969 my college has been linked by a remote console to the Atlas Laboratory at Chilton, Berkshire, and I have been fortunate enough to have had extensive use of this link. The Atlas multi-access system makes it possible to create and manipulate files of information from remote consoles and to use these files for the initiation of jobs on the Atlas computer. The file handling and console servicing is carried out by an SDS Sigma 2 computer using a Data Products disc, shared with the Atlas machine, for the storage of files.

The system allows for the immediate running of jobs that take no more than thirty seconds of Atlas time (this is an operations limit not a systems limit), and the results of these runs are normally available in a few minutes. One can thus develop programs with a minimum of anguish owing to the possibility of rapid testing and editing.[1]

There are several other features which are invaluable to the orientalist who wishes to deal with awkward scripts by means of transliteration. It is possible, by means of editing and – where necessary – by processing texts in small batches, to ensure that the material concerned is efficiently checked for accuracy and is completely reliable. It is also possible to use the editing commands to switch from a commonly used form of transliteration, which for reasons of accuracy it may be desirable to use for initial punching, to one more suitable for computer processing. With these facilities it is rela-

---

* St Cross College, Oxford.
[1] For fuller details see J. C. Baldwin and R. E. Thomas, *Multi-Access Manual*, Atlas Computer Laboratory (Chilton, May 1969).

tively easy to solve any special problems inherent in a large-scale project before the main runs are put through the computer.

I am at present engaged on three projects which I consider to be of importance. The first of these is an analysis of samples of modern Turkish. For a variety of reasons – official policy, Western influence, and the like – enormous changes have taken place in Turkish since the alphabet was romanized in 1928. Thousands of Arabic and Persian loan-words have been dropped after being used in Turkish for hundreds of years. Their places are being taken either by newly coined 'genuine Turkish' words formed from old Turkish roots and suffixes or by loan words from western European languages, principally French. The syntax of the language has also been affected.

There are initially to be two groups of samples: (a) 320,000 words taken from newspapers and magazines from the period June 1968–June 1969; (b) an equivalent sample from literary works written during that period. The newspaper and magazine samples have been sorted and are now being punched up. They have been chosen from seven newspapers (*Adalet, Cumhuriyet, Dünya, Hürriyet, Son Havadis, Tercüman* and *Zafer*) and one magazine (*Hayat*). These papers form a good cross-section of the Turkish national press, though it is possible to think of other alternatives. It so happened that when I wanted material it was the editors of these publications that were first contacted on my behalf. They were all good enough to send me a year's issues. 40,000 words are being taken from each publication. 52 issues of each newspaper, chosen at random by a program put through Atlas, have been taken to cover the whole year. The material in each paper is divided into three categories: (a) home news, (b) foreign news, (c) editorials, sports and advertisements; approximately 250 words are taken at random from each. With *Hayat* 1,000 words have been taken from each of 40 copies, all major articles and features being covered.

The system we are using for processing the material is the COCOA concordance generating system developed by Donald Russell for the Chilton Atlas.[1] In addition to general sorting, the samples from each publication are being sorted separately when necessary. This is being done because when one reads Turkish newspapers one gets the impression that the political outlook of a publication affects not only its political vocabulary but also its general vocabulary and the way in which its material is presented. For example, the more conservative newspapers appear to retain more Arabic

[1] D. B. Russell, *COCOA Manual*, Atlas Computer Laboratory (Chilton, November 1967).

and Persian vocabulary and to resist to a greater extent the introduction of neologisms. Tests will be made to see whether or not this is so.

My present intention is to repeat the operation in five years' time, and also, if funds are available, to extend the sampling to earlier years. If possible, I should like eventually to go back to 1928, thus covering the whole of the modern period.

To examine the vocabulary of the samples is the most obvious and immediate task. The results will serve not only as a guide for teachers of Turkish in universities outside Turkey, but also in the improvement of literacy programmes in Turkey itself. One will, however, be able to go much further than this. With the archive of material we are building up it will be possible to make large-scale investigations into some of the syntactic peculiarities of modern Turkish and to examine some of the changes at present taking place in the language. Here, in fact, we shall be using the computer to make up for the paucity of Turkologists. The problems to be investigated are known, but the few scholars working in the field simply have not had the time to deal with them. Postpositions and pronominal suffixes, for example, are imperfectly understood. Collection of all the examples in our archive will be a substantial step towards rectifying this.

Modern Turkish, with its Latin-type alphabet, is much easier to deal with than most oriental languages. This is not the case with the next two projects, which are in Persian and Arabic respectively. In both cases we are working in transliteration at the input and sorting stages, but the final output will be produced in Arabo-Persian script by the SC4020 graphics machine, as described in this volume by Dr Churchhouse and Mrs Hockey.

The Persian project is a concordance of the poems of Hafiz, Persia's major lyric poet. This is also being processed by the Atlas COCOA system, while the poems are being punched in transliteration by a research associate, Miss Inger Karlsson. Ensuring the accuracy of the transliteration is a considerable problem, as I mentioned earlier. To overcome this we produce a concordance of each individual poem *via* the console and the line-printer. These individual concordances take about two seconds of Atlas time. Mistakes stand out clearly in the concordance format, and they can then be corrected by using the editing facilities available on the console. When we are satisfied that the text is correct, it is transferred to magnetic tape ready for final processing. After the complete concordance has been produced, we intend to use the stored text as the basis of a critical edition of the poems of Hafiz. Variants, of which there are a great many, will gradually be collected and added to the magnetic tape.

The third major project – or rather group of projects – is in many ways the most ambitious. It concerns my main field of research, the Qur'ān. I am gradually feeding the most widely used version of the text into my files, and carrying out various analyses of vocabulary, phraseology and grammar that would be extremely laborious, if not impossible, without a computer. My main aim in these analyses is to throw new light on the earlier, more problematical part of the text – the chapters composed between A.D. 610, when Muhammed began to preach, and A.D. 622, when he moved from Mecca to Medina.

More valuable to me, however, is the possibility of having a satisfactory way of producing a *variorum* edition of the text. In addition to the text most widely used, there are six other versions which are recognized as canonical and which are vital for any full study. There are several key manuscripts from a relatively early period which list all the variants of the seven versions. However, at the time that they were written, paper was still a scarce commodity, and so the record of the variants is condensed as much as possible. This is inconvenient for the production of a *variorum* text. For example, it is easy enough to remember a comment at the beginning of one of these manuscripts saying that Nāfiᶜ reads *mūmin* wherever Ḥafṣ reads *mu'min*. It is quite different to make the requisite note in the 230 places where *mūmin/mu'min* occurs, if one has to do this by traditional methods. If one can edit the text whilst it is stored in files or on magnetic tape, no such problems arise.

Another Quranic topic which has long required investigation is that of rhythm patterns. Again, this is tiresome and difficult without special aids. To deal with it I am creating a secondary version of the text, which is a simple reduction to long and short syllables.[1] 1 represents a short syllable, 2 a long syllable, while the beginning and end of verses are marked by A and Z respectively. With this version it is easy to search for rhythm patterns by using the file-editing facilities, the results being printed out at once.

Fig. 1, for example, shows a few lines from the beginning of chapter 80 and from the end of chapter 81.

---

[1] At present I dictate this version, and it is then punched. However, the Atlas Laboratory hopes to produce a compiler which will convert text into long, short and doubtful syllables. It is intended that the compiler should be applicable to the widest possible range of (natural) languages.

```
SURA-80
A    1111122   Z <80 : 1>
A    221222   Z <80 : 2>
A    122211211222 <80 : 3>
A    222111211222 Z < 80 : 4>
                  .
                  .
                  .
                  .
                  .
                  .
                  .
                  .
A    1212121   Z <81 : 26>
A    211222222121   Z <81 : 27>
A    12212222121   Z <81 : 28>
A    121221222212221222121   Z <81 : 29>
```

FIGURE I

I now give three very simple examples using these two chapters to show how patterns can be isolated in this version. They are:

(1) A search for the pattern *short long short long* at the beginning of verses.

(2) A search for the pattern *short short short long* at the end of verses.

(3) A search for the pattern *long long short short long* in any position.

The following points should be noted: R80-81 is the name of the file in which the syllabic version of chapters 80 and 81 is stored; in each search 3 is substituted for 1 and 4 for 2 to make the required pattern stand out more clearly.

```
      EDIT R80-81 GIVING R80-81A

***A
G L/A    1212/   E/1212/3434/
    80 A    3434122222   Z <80 : 7>
   110 A    34341122 Z <80 : 10>
   130 A    343411111   Z <80 : 12>
   530 A    34342112 Z <81 : 9>
   700 A    3434121 Z <81 : 26>
   730 A    343421222212221222121   Z <81 : 29>

***Z


      EDIT R80-81 GIVING R80-81B

***A
G L/1112    Z/   E/1112/3334/
   160 A    1223334 Z <80 : 15>
```

```
170 A   1223334   Z <80 : 16>
410 A   1122211121223334   Z <80 : 40>
420 A   21123334   Z <80 : 41>
430 A   12111211123334   Z <80 : 42>
490 A   112123334   Z <81 : 5>
520 A   1122213334   Z <81 : 8>
540 A   112113334   Z <81 : 10>
550 A   112123334   Z <81 : 11>

***Z


        EDIT R80-81 GIVING R80-81C

***A
G  L/22112/    E/22112/44334/
    40 A   124433411222 <80 : 3>
    90 A   122443342   Z <80 : 8>
   120 A   222144334   Z <80 : 11>
   180 A   11244334111   Z <80 : 17>
   250 A   221443341211   Z <80 : 24>
   380 A   1221224433422221   Z <80 : 37>
   390 A   12443342112   Z <80 : 38>
   400 A   211244334   Z <80 : 39>
   410 A   112443341221112   Z <80 : 40>
   460 A   112144334   Z <81 : 2>
   530 A   12144334   Z <81 : 9>
   570 A   114433412   Z <81 : 13>
   590 A   144334211   Z <81 : 15>
   610 A   44334211   Z <81 : 17>
   620 A   443341211   Z <81 : 18>
   640 A   221221443342   Z <81 : 20>
   650 A   12443342   Z <81 : 21>
   660 A   1443341222   Z <81 : 22>

***Z
```

FIGURE 2

It took under five minutes to enter the system, make the three searches, have the results printed out (see Fig. 2), and leave the system again. The amount of time used on the Sigma 2 computer was six seconds, and there was no need to use the Atlas machine.

The examples I have given are searches for strings of numbers, but searches for strings of words are equally simple and the results are produced just as rapidly. This facility is therefore an extremely useful tool for the worker in the humanities.

I hope that this brief outline has given an idea of the use that can be made of some computing techniques in a comparatively difficult field. The problems involved, both of script and of grammatical structure, mean that advances are likely to be slow, but the advances will undoubtedly take place. In addition to the languages I have already mentioned, for example, I have successfully tried small experimental runs with transliterated specimens of Armenian, Japanese and Sanskrit, to show other orientalists how they might start to make use of computers.

The pressures of specialization make it difficult for orientalists to become as skilled as they should be in computing. I should like to make it clear that it is very largely due to members of the staff of the Atlas Laboratory, Chilton, that I have been able to undertake the projects I have mentioned. Many of them, too many to name, have given me unstinting help. I find it most encouraging that with such assistance it is possible for someone like myself, with very little time available, to deal with unwieldy and daunting material in ways that my colleagues and I find very fruitful.

VI

Problems of input and output

What to tell the programmer

J. G. B. HEAL*

I hope that in the following paper I shall say nothing that will not, retrospectively, seem obvious. However, it is just the specifying of the apparently obvious which is vital if a problem is to be well defined for computer solution, and it is often the omission of such details which is responsible for the comparative failure of many computing projects in the humanities, as well as for strained relations between scholar and programmer. I shall give examples to show the unfortunate consequences of leaving the specification of seemingly trivial details either to an un-learned programmer or by default to the contingent behaviour of the computer. I ought perhaps to admit here that my experiences have been gained solely in making orthographically complex concordances, but most of what I shall say will be applicable to any machine handling of text.

The first point to stress is that one should decide what it is one wants out of the computer, before one sets about preparing the text to feed in. Once one has a machine-readable text, one can of course process it in many different ways, but the range of things one can do will be largely determined by the way it has been coded. Punching texts is seldom as simple as merely re-typing them, but involves many decisions as to which details of the printed copy are worth preserving in the machine version, and how they are to be encoded. Thus it is unlikely that one will record the presence of watermarks; one will probably omit footnotes and indexes, but title-pages, and use of italics are quite possibly worth retaining, and almost certainly most of the punctuation should be preserved. Which details are retained is invariably a compromise between the requirements of the scholar, and the expense and complexity of coding the less important attributes: deciding what should be kept is the province of the scholar; how it is to be coded is that of the programmer.

It is important to keep clear the distinction between the features one is

* Literary and Linguistic Computing Centre, University of Cambridge.

trying to record, and the symbols used to do so. One too often hears as an excuse for badly prepared computer-readable texts, say all in capitals with little punctuation, that they were prepared on a 44-character card punch which did not have the requisite signs. As one could transmit *Paradise Lost* in morse code, using only dots and dashes, it should surely not be beyond the wit of man to represent a variety of printed characters employing 44 signs, using groups of symbols to stand for the missing characters. Thus one might represent an exclamation mark by two paragraph signs, or, mnemonically, by *EXCL, but there is no reason whatsoever why any features of the text should not be represented if wanted, given sufficient effort in planning the code. Of course care must be taken that the codes chosen should not be mistakable for part of the text, but otherwise the choice of coding is to a large extent arbitrary, although it should take account of ease of recognition by programs, and ease of keyboarding – either by minimizing the number of key-strokes required or by being easily remembered.

Fairly similar considerations apply when outputting a text to a device which has a limited character set. If the text includes signs which the line-printer, say, does not, such as lower case, underlining or diacritics, one can again represent these by combinations of the characters it does have. For example, the exclamation mark we had to punch as *EXCL may be printable in its normal form, but the printer may lack characters such as query which were on the punch. These will have to be specially printed, say as *QUERY. The conventions used may or may not be the same as those used at the input stage, depending on the disparity of character sets and the convenience of proofreaders and users. Thus both at input and output, an unusual character can be represented using the symbols available in combinations, whilst preserving for programs the ability to treat it as a single character. If one had simply omitted, for example, all the diacritics on input, the distinctions they represented would be lost to programs, whereas if they have been specially coded, the fact of their presence could be put to good use. It is always easy for any distinctions present in the machine-readable text to be ignored, but it is impossible to re-create them once they have gone.

We have now seen that the character sets available on mechanical equipment offer no barriers to the coding of anything at all, given sufficient effort. We may therefore turn back to considering what is likely to justify such an effort. Clearly decisions must be reached about features such as type-founts, diacritics and ligatures. What are more often forgotten are details of page and text layout. If one intends the computer to do calculations or output text references based on canto, page or line numberings, these must somehow be indicated. Though all paper tape equipment includes an explicit newline character, a convention will be needed if cards are used to distinguish a card which begins a new line from one which continues a previous line. Actual line numbers seldom need to be explicitly recorded, as they can be deduced by counting newline symbols from the beginning – a trivial program feature. However, editors of scholarly editions have sometimes miscounted lines, and their line numbers have been canonized by usage. In such cases, where the required numbers are not in strict sequence, details must be coded to enable the program to keep in step, or rather out of step, with the original text. Page numbers similarly could be coded explicitly, or assumed to be sequential, but even then some indication of page ends must be made. Codings of page, act or poem numbers must in all cases be quite unambiguously distinguishable from anything that occurs as part of the text. Also, as the conversion of a text to either punched cards or paper tape is essentially a conversion from a two-dimensional medium to a one-dimensional medium, anything which depends for its meaning on this two-dimensionality will need separate treatment. For instance tabular material must be coded in such a way that it can still be treated as a table, and processed either by rows or columns, even though recorded in a medium where 'beneath' has no meaning.

We are now in a position to be able to record, and enable programs to refer to, any orthographical mark anywhere on a page. At this point one might well think one could proceed with the designing of programs. However, what we have done is merely to make accessible to the machine all the printed signs which the author and printer use to communicate with us, and it is not always the case that orthographies suitable for human use are also suitable for machines. In English, a single sign is used for the functions of apostrophe and quotation, and the full stop serves the functions of delimiting sentences, indicating abbreviations and representing broken-off utterances. Therefore if the computer is to do even something as apparently simple as counting sentences, it must be given additional information to help it resolve such ambiguities. The simplest solution is to remove the ambiguities entirely, by using different signs for the different functions. This would involve extensive pre-editing of the text, or elaborate punching instructions, but would make programming straightforward. Alternatively, one could leave the ambiguities in the text, and build the resolution criteria into the program. These would probably be rather *ad hoc* in nature, say based on the typical shortness of abbreviations, or the fact that they very often begin with a capital letter. Such choices between time-consuming pre-editing of texts, and increasingly complex but *ad hoc* programming, are common in computer text-handling, as soon as anything other than the most mechanical operations on language are attempted. The time to make such choices is clearly before any text has been punched, and not when programs prove not to work.

Most literary computing will at some time involve the notions of both 'word' and 'alphabetical order', and both are more troublesome than might be suspected, particularly when they interact. Splitting a text up into words – that is distinct written forms – is in most cases fairly straight-forward. Any sequence of letters bounded by spaces, punctuation or new-line symbols is usually an acceptable word. A decision must be made about hyphenated words: they could be split or not, or in a concordance perhaps counted in both split and unsplit forms. This would usually depend on the compound in question, but unfortunately the computer requires instructions in general terms. Though MOI-MÊME might usefully be placed both under MOI and MÊME, this can only be done at the price of generating the word T from A-T-ELLE. Apostrophes usually cause complications, and no simple rule applies equally naturally in all cases. If they are ignored, WE'LL is confused with WELL. If counted as part of the word, L'HOMME may not be recognized as an instance of HOMME, but if the apostrophe is made to terminate the word, like a space, word lists will include spurious WONs and TS, through mistreated WON'TS. Again one has a choice between pre-editing the source, before punching, and adding rules to the program, and perhaps including lists of special cases. Very often the most fruitful scheme is manually to rearrange the computer output, in which case one can take account of the oddities of particular words. Sometimes editorial markings in the text will be used in defining the notion of a word. If italics or under-lining in a text represent some editorial decision, say a disputed reading, it may be useful to treat forms containing italics distinctly from those without. Usually, as in most concordances, such features are ignored entirely.

Given a text in a form that can easily be broken into words, one is very likely to want some of those words arranged in alphabetical order, and here the programmer, if not the scholar, will certainly require advice. Not that he will need help putting CAT before DOG, but words including non-letters such as hyphens, apostrophes and ligatures will certainly create problems. In the case of hyphens there are two options open – the hyphen can be ignored for purposes of alphabetizing, or it can be treated as a letter, with its own place in the alphabet. The former, that of ignoring it, is very often the most natural, and is that usually used in hand-compilations. Thus Chambers's Dictionary places A-WING between AWHILE and AWKWARD. The other approach, of treating hyphen as a letter, is marginally easier to program, and is probably what will happen if the programmer is not given instructions otherwise. The main advantage is that it brings together all hyphenated compounds sharing the same first part. It would place ROUND-ARM and ROUND-WINGED close to each other, where ignoring the hyphen would separate them widely putting words like ROUNDEL between them. If this approach is used, the position of the hyphen in the alphabet must be decided. It is usually placed just before A or after Z. Howard-Hill in his recent Shakespeare concordances[1] places it after Z, but without proper warning, so one may easily miss A-HUNGRY which comes after AWAY. Cargo in his Baudelaire concordance[2] chose to put it before A, making VA-T'EN precede VALLON. No alphabetical order is inherently superior to any other, but whichever is chosen should be carefully explained to potential users, as a misunderstood arrangement makes the overlooking of words embarrassingly easy. In fact, in the two cases quoted, I suspect that no conscious decision was taken, either to treat hyphens as letters, or, if so, where to place them in the alphabet. I would guess that the order produced was determined solely as a side-effect of the way the program was written, and the contingency that one computer represented the hyphen by a number less than that representing A, whereas the other did not.

Apostrophes unavoidably cause difficulties, as unlike hyphens, their meaning depends on their context. A hand-produced concordance can easily arrange CAN'T under CANNOT, and SHAN'T under SHALL (NOT), but the computer program will probably have to have one rule for all occurrences. I assume of course that we have already decided that SHAN'T is to be a single word. If it is to be split, there is clearly no problem. The COCOA concordance system on the Chilton Atlas cunningly avoids this problem by the use of 'guide-letters'. These are letters which are punched in the text, to be used when sorting, but not in the final print-out. Using lower-case as guide letters, we could punch CAN'T as CANno'T, which will sort correctly, and still print in the contracted form. The disadvantage is that every occurrence of the word must be punched in full with the guide letters. If there has to be one treatment for all occurrences of apostrophe, one can

[1] *Oxford Shakespeare Concordances*, ed. T. Howard-Hill (Oxford, 1969 ff.).
[2] *A Concordance to Baudelaire's 'Les Fleurs du Mal'*, ed. Robert T. Cargo (Chapel Hill, 1965).

again choose between ignoring them for the purposes of order, and giving them their own position in the alphabet. I have no doubt that it is usually best to ignore them, although most concordances do not. One should not confuse the ignoring of apostrophes and the like for sorting purposes with their omission altogether. Thus although Howard-Hill, I think wisely, sorts SPIRIT'S as if it were SPIRITS, he also prints it as such, thus confusing the two. Cargo, individual as ever, chooses to treat apostrophe as a letter before A, and thus puts J'UNIS before JADIS. I should perhaps say that Cargo's concordance is of the KWIC or Key-Word-In-Context variety, where it is not so much words as whole lines that are sorted. The intention is that one should be able to look up complete phrases. Under MON, MON AME precedes MON COEUR, and under MON COEUR, MON COEUR EST BON precedes MON COEUR EST TOMBE. However, he forgot to remind the programmer that alphabetical order usually applies only to letters of the alphabet, so the computer has solemnly sorted complete lines, punctuation and all. Thus COEUR followed by a comma is some distance from COEUR followed by a space, which is itself distinct from COEUR followed by an exclamation mark. Two instances of the line

J'ai vu parfois au fond d'un théâtre banal

– identical except that one has a comma after PARFOIS, are separated by fifteen lines in the concordance. He is not even consistent, as the alphabetical position of apostrophe also depends on whether it occurs in the first word of context or not. If the former, it comes before A, and otherwise after O. Thus L'ABIME and L'UTILE precede LOURDS, but DE LOURDS precedes DE L'ABIME. So much for machine intelligence.

All the oddities we have seen so far could have been avoided, or at least lessened, by some editorial forethought. I would like now to examine a few difficulties which are less easily solved, where character-identity interacts with alphabetization. Consider alphabetizing words which contain ligatures and diacritics. There is far from universal agreement, even in hand-produced lists, on the correct order, so the need for clear instructions is vital, or the programmer may pick up some very odd ideas. Ligatures are usually treated as if written out in full. Aeolian is always sorted as if spelt AE, even when written with a ligature. However, Medieval German dictionaries often treat it as A. They also sometimes sort V as F, so the dangers of letting the programmer guess are obvious. I should like now to distinguish two sorts of diacritic which can affect alphabetical order. First, there is what I call a simple diacritic, as in French which is usually added to letters to show stress or pronunciation, but which is not strictly necessary to the spelling. Thus PATE and PATÉ both consist of the same four letters. In ordering such words, attention is paid firstly to the letters, and only if all letters are the same are the accents considered. Therefore DÉ precedes DES solely on account of the letters, and not because of the accents. Few dictionaries agree on the ordering of words which thus differ only in accents, and I know of no statement of general principles. Usually the form with fewer diacritics comes first, so OUTRE precedes OUTRÉ, but why Cassell's French Dictionary (23rd edition, 1952) should put COTÉ before COTÈ is not explained, as ZÈLE precedes ZÉLÉ. One could base an ordering on numbers of diacritics on each word, their position in the word, or assign an arbitrary lexicographical ordering to the diacritics. Whatever decision is made should not affect the final result materially, as the words will anyway be adjacent.

The second kind of diacritic can never be omitted as it is used to distinguish two different characters in the alphabet which are written similarly. In Spanish, for example, Ñ is a completely different letter from N, and has its own place in the alphabet – between N and O. Thus NON comes before NEQUE. As Spanish also uses simple diacritics, programs must be able to cope with both kinds. Another feature Spanish demonstrates is that of using combinations of letters as distinct members of the alphabet. Thus CH and LL behave as single characters, ordered after C and L respectively. This must be taken into account when sorting, so as to place CURAR before CHE. Fortunately this is not too difficult, as the constituent letters C and H never occur adjacently except in the digraph CH, so in effect the computer can replace them both by a single sign while sorting. This would not be the case in German if one had been rash enough to transcribe umlaut as E, as words like SAUER and FEUER contain a UE which must not be treated like U-umlaut, and the machine has therefore no way of recognizing umlauts.

This use of several letters to represent one character is a common feature of transliterations from one alphabet into another. Thus Russian contains characters which are usually written in the Roman alphabet SH, CH and SHCH. Clearly, if one now alphabetizes on Roman principles, the order will certainly not be Russian alphabetical order. In effect what one has to do is to sort on the Russian characters themselves and not on their Roman representation. The machine must therefore be able unambiguously to divide up the text symbols into groups, each representing a single character of the original script. If the transcription is intelligently chosen this should be trivial. Considering the above three characters, a human could tell in any word whether SHCH represented one or two characters, and therefore how to order the word. A computer could not, as this information has been lost by the poorly chosen transliteration. Another example is the common transliteration of both the Greek omicron and omega to the Roman o. Once the distinction has been lost, the transliteration is irreversible. It is therefore vital to remember that what may be an excellent transliteration for human purposes can be woefully inadequate for machine use.

Indeed if the above catalogue of errors has any moral, it would be that though it is fairly straightforward to represent any printed sign in machine terms, serious difficulties will arise if sufficient attention is not given to making explicit the function or meaning of the symbols used.

The use of a formally defined structure for the input of data from the British Museum Catalogue of Printed Books

EVELINE WILSON*

1. Aim of the project

This project was originally started as an experiment to determine to what extent and with what facility the techniques of syntax analysis could be applied to complex, conceptually structured bodies of data. These techniques have had revolutionary effects in the design of artificial languages. Also, they have led to an increased understanding and appreciation of those languages which were in use before such analysis was an accepted part of the implementation procedure. The retrospective application of a new technique to an old tool has thus not been a sterile operation.

The British Museum Catalogue of Printed Books provides a parallel situation in the field of data banks. It is almost self-evident that if one were starting a new fund of information which one knew was to be processed by mechanical means, it would be possible to provide for this information a strict definition which could be unambiguously expressed in some kind of formalized notation. Such an unambiguous structure would obviate any necessity for fixed-field format, and facilitate machine processing and error recovery procedures. It would also prevent impulsive *ad hoc* decisions being taken if it were necessary to process an irregular item, or if it were decided to introduce a new subfield into the existing format. However, in the BM Catalogue, a book is described by a method, which, although applied consistently and logically to each book, was devised many years ago on the assumptions that not only would it be put into effect by men of a high degree of intelligence, but also that the resulting file would be used, maintained and updated by men of a similar stamp. Despite this, it has been possible to analyse this structure so that its inherent syntactic features are made explicit, and to use this analysis to process catalogue entries with a mindless machine. An attempt has been made to measure the extent to which it is possible to automate the routine checking and maintenance of the BM Catalogue. Obviously once the data is in a form which can be read

* Documentation Processing Centre, Department of Education and Science, Manchester.

and manipulated by machine then more advanced projects such as the creation of new files or bibliographic searches become immediately possible. It is hoped that these techniques will also find application among other data bases of a similar nature.

2. Description of the tool used

The syntax analyser used for this experiment is the Syntax Improving Device (SID). This was developed in 1966 at the Royal Radar Establishment by J. M. Foster to improve the syntax rules of artificial languages; it accepts as data a definition of a context-free grammar written in a form which is similar to Backus-Naur. This definition it attempts to transform into an equivalent definition which can be parsed by a one-track algorithm. If it succeeds, SID can be made to generate this parsing algorithm. By 'one-track' is meant the ability to analyse a string at any point in terms of the next character and the previous analysis record. If the syntax rules submitted to SID are augmented by the insertion of 'actions' which the user wishes to associate with the syntax analysis, these will be carried through SID's transformation and embedded in the transformed rules at the appropriate places. The syntax-directed program thus produced has no need to refer back to the original form of the rules before carrying out actions. For a more complete description of SID, see J. M. Foster, 'A Syntax Improving Program', *The Computer Journal*, XI (1968), 31.

In the summer of 1969 it was decided to investigate the feasibility of using SID to analyse data. To do this, it must be provided with four sets of information:

   (i) the basic symbol sets of the source data;
  (ii) the names of the actions embedded in the rules;
 (iii) the rules describing the source data;
 (iv) the name of the entity whose structure is defined.

3. Description of the source data

The British Museum Catalogue of Printed Books was chosen as the data source for a number of reasons. It is easily accessible and quite familiar to many people. In addition, it has a complex format, which was not intentionally designed to accommodate machine processing. Entries from the Catalogue fall into two main groups, main entries and cross-references. The complexity of the defining structure for an entry can be adjusted within very wide limits: it is not necessary to have as many divisions as will be illustrated in some parts of this report; conversely, what is shown here as a single division may be capable of further subdivisions. Three analyses have been made in the course of the experiment:

(i) a very crude analysis of a simplified main entry;
(ii) a much more detailed analysis of a main entry;
(iii) a detailed analysis of a general entry, which could be either a main entry or a cross-reference.

For the sake of clarity and comprehension of the project as a whole, the experiment is explained below by reference only to an analysis of a simplified main entry. This is sufficient to illustrate all the technical points. For completeness, the example of more complex main entries and cross-references are given and the results of processing such entries shown in the Appendix.

The types of cross-references which the program attempts to recognize are:

(i) ordinary cross-references
(ii) cross-references of form
(iii) finding cross-references
(iv) annotations
(v) main title cross-references
(vi) analytical cross-references.

For a fuller description of these, see *Rules for Compiling the Catalogue of Printed Books, Maps and Music in the British Museum,* revised edition, 1936.

Main entries are usually indexed under author(s), or under a place name and subordinate institution. When the program is unable to decide which of these it is processing, it indicates this. See Appendix.

A main entry containing the minimum constituents to form a complete record comprises:

(i) Name of the book's author
(ii) Title of the book
(iii) Description of the book. This may be several sentences long or merely the pagination
(iv) Imprint of the book. This can contain the name of the publisher, the place of publication and the date of publication
(v) Format of the book
(vi) Shelfmark of the book.

Typical main entries are shown in Fig. 1. These illustrate the use of several

617

NICHOLSON (Cregoe Donaldson Percy)
—— The Genealogical Value of the Early English Newspapers.
pp. 20.   *C. D. P. Nicholson: London,* 1934.   8°.
09917. ee. 2.

NICHOLSON (D. E.)

——   Fertilizers and Manures.
See London.-*III.*—— *Royal Horticultural Society.*
Four Essays, *etc.* 1913. 8°.   07077. i. 68. (6.)

NICHOLSON (Daniel)

——   Laboratory Medicine. A
guide for students and practitioners, *etc.* pp. 433.
                              Henry Kimpton : London ;
printed in America, 1930.   8°.   7462. cc. 39.

—— Laboratory Medicine . . . Second edition, thoroughly
revised, *etc.* pp. xv. 566.   *Henry Kimpton: London ;*
printed in America, 1934. 8°.   20017. d. 24.

NICHOLSON (Daniel Howard Sinclair)

——   *See* Lopukhin (I. V.)
·Some Characteristics of the Interior Church ... Translated from the French by D. H. S. Nicholson, *etc.*
1912. 8°.   03558. df. 23.

——   *See* Scaramelli (G. B)
A Handbook of Mystical Theology. Being an abridg-
ment of "Il Direttorio mistico" . . . By D. H. S.
Nicholson. 1913. 8°.   04376. de. 5.

——   The Marriage-Craft. A
novel.] pp. 238.   *Richard Cobden-Sanderson :*
London, [1924.] 8°.   NN. 9912.

——   The Mysticism of St.
Francis of Assisi...Illustrated with reproductions of
etchings by Laurenzio Laurenzi. pp. 393.
Jonathan Cape: London, 1923. 8°.   4829. dg. 23.

——   Poems. pp. vi. 75.
Methuen & Co.: London, 1913. 8°.   011649. de. 25.

——   The Shortest Way Home.
pp. 315. *Arrowsmith: London,* 1926. 8°. NN. 12245.

——   Sweet Grapes. pp. 288.
Arrowsmith: London, 1927. 8°.   NN. 13097.

NICHOLSON (Daniel Howard Sinclair) and **LEE**
(Arthur Hugh Evelyn)

——   The
Oxford Book of English Mystical Verse. Chosen by
D. H. S. Nicholson and A. H. E. Lee. pp. xv. 644.
Clarendon Press: Oxford, 1916. 8°.   011604. g. 13.

—— Another copy.] The Oxford Book of English Mystical
Verse, *etc.* *Oxford,* 1916. 8°.   011604. ee. 13.
Printed on India paper.

NICHOLSON (Dorothy) *Lady.*
—— *See* Brooke (Dorothy) *Lady,* afterwards Nicholson
(Dorothy) *Lady.*

NICHOLSON (Douglas Nairn)

——   Medical Diseases
of Children. pp. 74.   *E. & S. Livingstone :*
Edinburgh, [1929.] 8°. [*Catechism Series.*]
07306. e. 1/27.

618

NICHOLSON (Douglas Nairn)

—— Medical Diseases of Children . . . Second edition.
pp. 76.   *E. & S. Livingstone: Edinburgh,* [1947.] 8°.
[*Catechism Series.*]   07306. e. 1/27.

NICHOLSON (E.) *See* Auerbach (B.) Spinoza. A
novel . . . From the German, by E. N. [*Collection
of German Authors.* vol. 42, 43.] 1882. 8°.
12250. k.29.

—— Chronological Guide to English Literature.
London, 1878. 8°. *   11851. cc. 1.

—— Student's Manual of German Literature. pp. 209.
Sonnenschein & Co.: London, [1882.] 8°. 11851. df. 10.

NICHOLSON (E. E. G.)

——   The Leyland Hydro-
Calculator. [1923.] 4°.   1880. d. 1. (71.)
A revolving card.

NICHOLSON (Edgar)
—— A Burmese Scene. Pictures to colour . . . Drawn by
Joan Chamberlin from photographs provided by E.
Nicholson who also tells the story. (Cut-out painting
book.) pp. 24.   *Edinburgh House Press: London,*
1954. 8°.   12838. cc. 17.

NICHOLSON (Edith Maud)

——   Bent on Conquest.
[A novel.] 3 vol.   *Hurst & Blackett :*
London, 1892. 8°.   012637. l. 7.

——   Darthula. pp. 299.
Drane's: London, [1925.] 8°.   NN. 11129.

——   The Fugitives. A
sketch of B.C. 75, in verse. pp. 32.   *A. H. Stockwell :*
London, [1928.] 8°.   011644. eee. 74.

NICHOLSON (Edward) *Assistant Surgeon, Royal Artillery.*
Indian Snakes. An elementary treatise on ophiology,
with a descriptive catalogue of the snakes found in
India, *etc.* *Madras,* 1870. 8°.   7290. b.25.

—— Report on Filter-Carts and Barrack-Filters. pp. 46.
E. Keys: Madras, 1875. 8°.   8777. e. 6.

NICHOLSON (Edward) *F.I.C.*

——   Men and Measures.
A history of weights and measures ancient and modern.
pp. xii. 313. *Smith, Elder & Co.: London,* 1912. 8°.
08548. de. 24.

NICHOLSON (Edward) *M.A.* A Method of Charity-
Schools, recommended, for giving both a religious education and a way of livelihood to the poor children in
Ireland. With a prefatory discourse about the practice
of charity in alms-deeds. *Dublin,* 1712. 4°.
8364. aa. 14.

NICHOLSON (Edward) *of Owthorne, Yorkshire.* Report
of the case of the Queen at the prosecution of Williams
v. Nicholson, for removing shingle from the foreshore at
Withernsea, heard . . . at the Police-Court, Hull, on the
31st May, 1870. *London, Hull* [printed], 1870. 8°.
6325. aaa. 24.

NICHOLSON (Edward Max)

——   *See* White (Gilbert)
The Natural History of Selborne...Edited, with an
introduction and notes, by E. M. Nicholson, *etc.*
1929. 4°.   *of Selborne.* 7003. dd. 4.

FIGURE I

```
RECORD=AUTHOR TITLE DESCRIPTION IMPRINT DATE FORMAT
SHELFMARK TERMINATOR;
        AUTHOR=SURNAME FORENAME EPITHET;
            SURNAME=RUL CHAR3RED CONTSURNAME;
                CONTSURNAME=$,CHAR3RED CONTSURNAME;
            FORENAME=BORB CONTFORENAME BCRB;
                CONTFORENAME=$,CHAR1BLACK CONTFORENAME;
            EPITHET=$,CHAR1RED EPITHET;
        TITLE=BDD CONTTIT;
            CONTTIT=ETC,BFULST BQUOTE,BQUEST BQUOTE,BFULST
            BQUEST,
                    CHAR2BLACK CONTTIT;
        DESCRIPTION=$,CHAR3BLACK DESCRIPTION;
        IMPRINT=$,IMPRINT1;
            IMPRINT1=PUBLISHER RCOLON IMPRINT2,IMPRINT2;
            IMPRINT2=PLACE RCOMMA CONTIMPRINT,
                    PLACE RSEMI IMPRINT1;
                CONTIMPRINT=$,IMPRINT2;
                PUBLISHER=PLIST;
                PLACE=PLIST;
                        PLIST=CHAR4RED,CHAR4RED PLIST;
        DATE=INTEGER,ROSB INTEGER RCSB;
            INTEGER=DIG1 DIG2 DIG3 DIG4 RFULST;
        FORMAT=FOL,EVENINT TO;
            EVENINT=B4,B8,B1 B6,B3 B2,B6 B4,B1 B2 B8,B1
            B2,B2 B4,B4 B8,B1 B8;
        SHELFMARK=CHAR2RED CONTSHELFMARK;
            CONTSHELFMARK=$,CHAR2RED CONTSHELFMARK;
                    CHAR3RED=RUL,RAPOST,RHYPHEN,RFULST;
                    CHAR4RED=CHAR3RED,RLL,RAMP;
                    CHAR1RED=CHAR3RED,RID;
                    CHAR2RED=CHAR1RED,RSLASH;
```

FIGURE 2– (partial—for continuation see foot of Fig. 4)

```
BID (0 1 2 3 4 5 6 7 8 9)

B0 (0)
B1 (1)
B2 (2)
B3 (3)
B4 (4)
B5 (5)
B6 (6)
B7 (7)
B8 (8)
B9 (9)

BUL (33 34 35 36 37 38 39 40 41 42 43 44 45 46 47 48
     49 50 51 52 53 54 55 56 57 58)

BLL (65 66 67 68 69 70 71 72 73 74 75 76 77 78 79 80
     81 82 83 84 85 86 87 88 89 90)

BAPOST (23)
BHYPHEN (29)
BCOLON (10)
BCOMMA (28)
BFULST (30)
BOSB (59)
BCSB (61)
BORB (24)
BCRB (25)
BAST (26)
BQUOTE (18)
BQUEST (15)
BAMP (22)
BSEI (11)
BSLASH (31)
BHASH (19)
DIG1 (97)
DIG2 (100 101 102 103 103 105)
RID (96 97 98 99 100 101 12 103 104 105)
RUL (129 130 131 132 133 134 135 136 137
     138 139 140 141 142 143 144 145 146 147 148 149
     150 151 152 153 154)
RLL (161 162 163 164 165 166 167 168 169
     170 171 172 173 174 175 176 177 178 179 180 181
     182 183 184 185 186)
RAPOST (119)
RHYPHEN (125)
```

FIGURE 3 (partial listing of basic symbols)

```
RECORD=SKIPOUT TERMINATOR,
INI- AUTHOR TITLE PRNTTIT DESCRIPTION PRNTDES IMPRINT
     DATE PRNTDAT FORMAT PRNTFOM SHELFMARK PRNTSHE TERMINATOR:
AUTHOR=SURNAME PRNTSUR FORENAME PRNTFOR EPITHET PRNTEPI;
     SURNAME=RUL CHAR3RED CONTSURNAME;
          CONTSURNAME=$,CHAR3RED CONTSURNAME;
     FORENAME=BORB CONTFORENAME BCRB;
          CONTFORENAME=$,CHAR1BLACK CONTFORENAME;
     EPITHET=$,CHAR1RED EPITHET;
TITLE=BDD CONTTIT;
     CONTTIT=ETC,BFULST BQUOTE,BQUEST BQUOTE,BFULST,BQUEST,
          CHAR2BLACK CONTTIT;
DESCRIPTION=$,CHAR3BLACK DESCRIPTION;
IMPRINT=$,IMPRINT1;
     IMPRINT1=PUBLISHER RCOLON PRNTPUB IMPRINT2,IMPRINT2;
     IMPRINT2=PLACE RCOMMA PRNTPLA CONTIMPRINT,
          PLACE RSEMI PRNTPLA IMPRINT1;
          CONTIMPRINT=S,IMPRINT2;
     PUBLISHER=PLIST;
     PLACE=PLIST;
          PLIST=CHAR4RED,CHAR4RED PLIST;
DATE=INTEGER,ROSB INTEGER RCSB;
     INTEGER=DIG1 DIG2 DIG3 DIG4 RFULST;
```

```
FORMAT=FOL,EVENINT TO;
EVENINT=B4,B8,B1 B6,B3 B2,B6 B4,B1 B2 B8,B1 B2,B2 B4,B4 B8,B1 B8;
SHELFMARK=CHAR2RED CONTSHELFMARK;
    CONTSHELFMARK=$,CHAR2RED CONTSHELFMARK;
    CHAR3RED=RUL,RAPOST,RHYPHEN,RFULST;
    CHAR4RED=CHAR3RED,RLL,RAMP;
    CHAR1RED=CHAR3RED,RID;
    CHAR2RED=CHAR1RED,RSLASH;
    CHAR1BLACK=BUL,BLL,BAPOST,BHYPHEN,BFULST,BAST;
    CHAR2BLACK=BUL,BLL,BAPOST,BHYPHEN,BAST,BCOLON,
               BCOMMA,BQUOTE;
    CHAR3BLACK=CHAR1BLACK,BCOLON,BCOMMA,BORB,BCRB,
               BOSB,BCSB;

    DIG3=RID;
    DIG4=RID;
    ETC=RE RT RC RFULST;
    FOL=BF BO BL BFULST;
    TO=BO BFULST;
    BDD=BHYPHEN BHPHEN;
```

FIGURE 4

4
RECORD

```
SURNAME IS                    NEWMAN
FORENAME IS                   (ROBERT P)
EPITHET IS
TITLE IS                      --RECOGNITION OF COMMUNIST CHINA?
DESCRIPTION IS                A STUDY IN ARGUMENT. PP. XII. 318.
PUBLISHER IS                  MACMILLAN CO.:
PLACE OF PUBLICATION IS       NEW YORK
DATE IS                       1961
FORMAT IS                     80
SHELFMARK IS                  X. 708/660.

SURNAME IS                    NEWMAN
FORENAME IS                   (WILLIAM)
EPITHET IS                    M.D.
TITLE IS                      --NOTES ON THE SANITARY STATE OF STAMFORD
DESCRIPTION IS                PP.17
PUBLISHER IS                  HENRY JOHNSON:
PLACE OF PUBLICATION IS       STAMFORD.
DATE IS                       1870.
FORMAT IS                     80.
SHELFMARK IS                  X. 329/546.

SURNAME IS                    NEWSOM
FORENAME IS                   (CARROLL VINCENT)
EPITHET IS
TITLE IS                      --MATHEMATICAL DISCOURSES: THE HEART OF MATHEMATICAL SCIENCE.
DESCRIPTION IS                PP.121.
PUBLISHER IS                  PRENTICE-HALL:
PLACE OF PUBLICATION IS       ENGLEWOOD CLIFFS.
DATE IS                       (1964).
FORMAT IS                     80.
SHELFMARK IS                  8509. I. 28.
```

FIGURE 5

styles of type to serve as visual aids to comprehension. Some of these changes are also of syntactic significance, i.e. they act as delimiters for the various components of the record. More delimiters are provided by the punctuation marks, many of which are standard and compulsory, e.g. the publisher's name must be followed by a colon.

4. Description of input to the syntax analyser

If two character sets are adopted which for convenience are here called RED (used largely to replace italic and bold script) and BLACK, a main entry can be formally described as shown in Fig. 2. All names are class names; sequential class names are separated by a space; alternatives to rules are separated by a comma (,); $ denotes the empty alternative; and semicolon (;) denotes the end of the rule. These rules form section 3 of the program to be processed by SID. All class names which are not defined in terms of other class names (i.e. names which do not appear on the left-hand side of a rule) are the names of basic character sets. These must be declared, with their values in internal code, in a preceding section of the program labelled 1, part of which is shown in Fig. 3. The final part of the program, labelled 4, tells SID the class-name of the entity whose structure is to be checked – in this instance RECORD, see foot of Fig. 4.

These three pieces of data are all that is required for a preliminary run of SID. When the definition of RECORD is found to be one-track, the rules are extended by inserting the names of actions at appropriate points in the syntax rules. (Compare Fig. 4 with the actionless version Fig. 2.) These action names must be listed in the section of SID input labelled 2. Since the insertion of actions could result in the definition no longer being single-track, SID is rerun with section 2 following section 1 in the input data.

The programs to implement the actions are written as ALGOL procedures, and routines are supplied to read in the source data and to output the results. These routines, and the analyser generated by SID are assembled into a complete program, which is compiled and run.

A specimen of output from this program is shown in Fig. 5.

This work originated from a suggestion by Mr A. G. Price of DPC. It would not have been possible without the cooperation of Mr J. Jolliffe of the British Museum and the considerable technical assistance of the Mathematics Laboratory at the Royal Radar Establishment, Malvern.

APPENDIX

SHELFMARK IS	X.108!1998.
FORENAME IS	(THOMAS ALLEN)
SURNAME IS	DOREY
	AND
FORENAME IS	(ALLISON)
SURNAME IS	LEON
TITLE IS	--THE NORMAN KINGS.
DESCRIPTION IS	
BRACKETNOTE IS	[A MEDIEVAL LATIN READER.]
PAGINATION IS	PP.84.
PUBLISHER IS	KENNETH MASON:
PLACE OF PUBLICATION IS	LONDON.
DATE IS	1964.
FORMAT IS	80.
SHELFMARK IS	X.989!658.
FORENAME IS	.(DAPHNE)
SURNAME IS	DU MAURIER
TITLE IS	--THE SCAPEGOAT.
DESCRIPTION IS	
PAGINATION IS	PP.319.
PUBLISHER IS	PENGUIN BOOKS:
PLACE OF PUBLICATION IS	HARMONDSWORTH,
DATE IS	1962.
FORMAT IS	80.
SERIES IS	[PENGUIN BOOKS.NO.1723.]
SHELFMARK IS	12208.A.1!1723.
FORENAME IS	(ANTHONY EDWARD)
SURNAME IS	DYSON
TITLE IS	--THE CRAZY FABRIC.
DESCRIPTION IS	ESSAYS IN IRONY.
PAGINATION IS	PP.XIV.233.
PUBLISHER IS	MACMILLAN & CO.:
PLACE OF PUBLICATION IS	LONDON;
DATE IS	1965.
FORMAT IS	80.
SHELFMARK IS	X.909!3220.
FORENAME IS	(ALICE MARIA)
SURNAME IS	EKERT-ROTHOLZ
	--[MOHN IN DEN BERGEN.]
TITLE IS	MARIE BONNARD
DESCRIPTION IS	.. TRANSLATED ... BY MICHAEL BULLOCK.
PAGINATION IS	PP.510.
PUBLISHER IS	NEW ENGLISH LIBRARY:
PLACE OF PUBLICATION IS	LONDON,
DATE IS	1965.
FORMAT IS	80.
SERIES IS	[FOUR SQUARE BOOK. NO.1244.]
SHELFMARK IS	012212.A.1!1244.
AMBIGUOUS NAME IS	ENCYLOPAEDIAS.
	--[L'ENCYCLOPEDIE LAROUSSE DES ENFANTS.]
TITLE IS	LEARN ABOUT PEOPLE.

```
DESCRIPTION IS
PARTHETICAL NOTE IS              (TRANSLATED AND ADAPTED BY MAURICE MICHAEL
                                   FROM L'ENCYCLOPEDIE LAROUSSE DES  ENFANTS,
                                 BY RENE GUILLOT.)
BRACKETNOTE IS                   [WITH ILLUSTRATIONS.]
PAGINATION IS                    PP.112.
PUBLISHER IS                     GOLDEN PLEASURE BOOKS:
PLACE OF PUBLICATION IS          LONDON;
PLACE OF PUBLICATION IS          PRINTED IN CZECHOSLOVAKIA.
DATE IS                          [1962.]
FORMAT IS                        40.
SHELFMARK IS                     X.972!12.

AMBIGUOUS NAME IS                ENGLAND.
SUBHEADING IS                    [MISCELLANEOUS OFFICIAL PUBLICATIONS.]
TITLE IS                         --TREATY ESTABLISHING THE EUROPEAN ATOMIC
                                 ENERGY COMMUNITY, EURATOM,ROME,25TH MARCH,
                                 1957,ET

C.
DESCRIPTION IS
PAGINATION IS                    PP.1V.108.
PLACE OF PUBLICATION IS          LONDON,
DATE IS                          1962.
FORMAT IS                        80.
SHELFMARK IS                     B.S.14!429.

SUBORDINATE INSTITUTION IS       -MINISTRY OF HEALTH.
PLACENAME IS                     ENGLAND.
TITLE IS                         --NATIONAL HEALTH SERVICE SUPERANNUATION
                                 SCHEME, ENGLAND AND WALES.
DESCRIPTION IS
                                 AN EXPLANATION.
                                 REVISED 1963.
PAGINATION IS                    PP.III.27.
PLACE OF PUBLICATION IS          LONDON,
DATE IS                          1964.
FORMAT IS                        80.
SHELFMARK IS                     B.S.17!73. (248.)

SUBORDINATE INSTITUTION IS       -POST OFFICE.
PLACENAME IS                     ENGLAND.
TITLE IS                         --BROADCASTING.
DESCRIPTION IS
                                 DRAFT OF ROYAL CHARTER FOR THE CONTINUANCE
                                 OF THE BRITISH BROADCASTING CORPORATION
                                 FOR WHICH THE POSTMASTER GENERAL PROPOSES
                                 TO APPLY,ETC.
PAGINATION IS                    PP.17.
PLACE OF PUBLICATION IS          LONDON,
DATE IS                          1963.
FORMAT IS                        80.
SHELFMARK IS                     B.S.31!119.

SUBORDINATE INSTITUTION IS       -SUGAR BOARD.
PLACENAME IS                     ENGLAND.
TITLE IS                         --NOTICE S.S.3[ETC.]
DESCRIPTION IS
PLACE OF PUBLICATION IS          LONDON,
DATE IS                          1963- .
FORMAT IS                        80.
SHELFMARK IS                     B.S.3!255.
```

The use of an SC4020 for output of a concordance program

R. F. CHURCHHOUSE* and SUSAN HOCKEY**

1. Introduction

At the Atlas Computer Laboratory we have been using the computer to produce concordances and indexes for three years mainly by use of the COCOA program. Until last year the only form of hard copy output was that produced by a conventional line-printer operating at 1,000 lines per minute. Whilst this form of output is quite acceptable for most scientific work, the restricted character set, consisting of upper case Roman letters, numerals and a few other characters, imposes artificial limitations in some types of project.

In 1968 the graphical output facilities of the Laboratory were enhanced by the purchase of an SC4020. The SC4020 records on microfilm and/or photorecording paper digital information received from a computer via $\frac{1}{2}$ inch (IBM) magnetic tape. The information is displayed on the face of a special cathode-ray tube known as a Charactron Shaped Beam Tube.

When used in the high-speed plotter mode any of 64 characters may be displayed at any point on a 1024×1024 position matrix. The normal character set contains the 26 capital letters, the digits, various punctuation marks and signs, brackets, a few Greek letters and a small number of special symbols such as the integral sign. The SC4020 system is available to users of both the FORTRAN and ALGOL systems and many subroutines and procedures are available which allow the user to make more sophisticated use of the facility. The programs for this work have been written in ALGOL using GROATS, the Graphic Output package for Atlas using the SC4020.[1]

Using the COCOA program we had produced concordances of Greek texts, including Homer and the New Testament. Because of the limited input/output facilities available all of this work had been done using an anglicized form of the Greek letters. It was, however, our long-term aim to

---

* Now at University College, Cardiff.   ** Atlas Computer Laboratory, Chilton.
[1] F. R. A. Hopgood, *Algol Groats Manual*, Atlas Computer Laboratory, SRC (Chilton, Didcot, Berkshire, August 1969).

provide something better than this and the SC4020 now makes it possible to produce output in Greek characters, diacritical marks included – assuming of course that this extra information has been provided in the original data. Mr Alan Jones of St Cross College, Oxford, has been using Atlas for work on Arabic and Persian texts (see his article in this volume) so we have also looked at the problem of reproducing Arabic characters on the SC4020. Theoretically one can program the SC4020 to produce any alphabet or collection of symbols and output them in any size one likes.

2. Input and output of Greek text

The Greek text is at present input as Roman capitals using a simple one for one substitution. The letters are as far as is possible represented by their Roman equivalents, e.g. B for beta, L for lambda. Some letters whilst not represented by their Roman equivalent in sound are denoted by a character which resembles them in appearance, e.g. W for omega. The codings that are not so obvious include the use of Q for theta, J for eta and Y for psi. The two forms of sigma are represented differently, V being used for the final form. A table of codings follows:

α	A	κ	K	σ	S
β	B	λ	L	ς	V
γ	G	μ	M	τ	T
δ	D	ν	N	υ	U
ε	E	ξ	X	φ	F
ζ	Z	ο	O	χ	C
η	J	π	P	ψ	Y
θ	Q	ρ	R	ω	W
ι	I				

Until recently the text has been key-punched without any diacritical marks, but with the inclusion of punctuation, the Greek colon being represented as either a comma or a full stop depending on the force of the stop. The absence of diacritical marks of any kind has led to the confusion of certain words, and grammatical forms. Of these one of the most important is the iota subscript which is written below the vowel when an iota forms a diphthong with a long vowel, e.g. ῳ. While it can be argued that the chances of confusion in the second declension between the dative singular ending in -ω and the dual are slight because of the rare occurrence of the latter forms, there is a much greater chance of confusion in the first declension between the nominative and dative singular.

The omission of the rough or smooth breathings which occur on initial vowels and initial rho in Greek has also led to some confusion in the interpretation of words. Initial rho and upsilon are always aspirated in Greek but the other vowels may or may not take a rough breathing. Several common words are written in exactly the same way except for the breathing which is the only sign of a difference in meaning. Examples include:

αὐτόν   him – not reflexive
αὑτόν   himself – reflexive

ἰέναι   to go
ἱέναι   to send

Many more pairs of words become identical when the accents as well as the breathings are removed, e.g.

εἰς   into
εἷς   one, masculine

ἐξ   out of
ἓξ   six

οὐ   not
οὗ   of which

αἴρω   I rise
αἰρῶ   I take

Simple omission of the accent on words that do not begin with a vowel or rho and therefore do not have a breathing can lead to confusion. A notable example is the interrogative pronoun τίς and the indefinite pronoun τις.

When all diacritical marks are omitted confusions arise between the following:

ἤ   'or', 'than'
ἡ   nominative feminine singular of the definite article
ἥ   nominative feminine singular of the relative
ἦ   particle meaning 'verily', 'in truth'
ᾖ   3 singular, present subjunctive of εἰμί (I am)

Iota subscripts have been punched as an I after the alpha, eta or omega, e.g. TWI as indeed they are written in Greek inscriptions. This means, however, that two characters have been punched for what is going to be output as one. This method is preferable if the text is to be output on the line-printer as it has been up to now.

Two alternative methods of input are possible if the text is to be output on an SC4020 with all its diacritical marks. One is to use a simple one-for-one substitution and thus involve many other characters for input coding.

This would mean that α, ά, ἀ, ᾳ and ᾷ would all have a different input coding which would have to be converted to A for the concordance program and then restored for the SC4020 output. The alternative is to follow each card of text by a card containing information concerning the diacritical marks or to follow each letter by a character indicating the diacritics to be placed on that letter. At the present stage of the program the first method has been used, as our primary objective was to perfect the character shapes. This method of input is easiest when the data is to be output without any processing into concordances. However, the other methods are being examined with a view to the concordance programs.

The shapes of the Greek letters available as software characters were obtained from the Bell Telephone Laboratories, New Jersey.[1] Two founts of both upper and lower case Greek letters were obtained and fount 1 was found to be preferable. The fount 1 characters are constructed initially out of straight lines on a grid 18 × 24 raster positions in size. On the whole a single line produces a character which is too thin and inelegant and rather faint. Two parallel lines one raster position apart throughout a character produce a letter which is too thick, though the slight blur which appears on either side of a line drawn by the SC4020 makes these two lines appear as

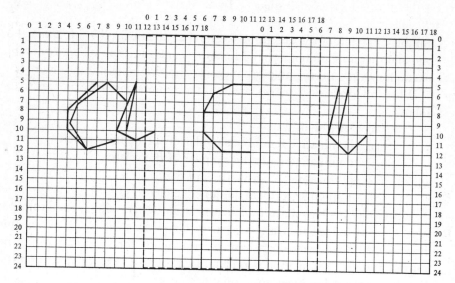

FIGURE 1. The broken line indicates the box for ε and the unbroken lines the boxes for α and ι. The overlapping brings the characters nearer together

[1] M. V. Mathews, Carol Lochbaum, Judith A. Moss, 'Three Fonts of Computer Drawn Letters', *Communications of the Association for Computing Machinery*, x (1967), 627–30.

one thick single line. A compromise between double and single lines in the form of lines drawn across the curves produces a more pleasing character and one which resembles printed type more closely. Sufficient space is left at either side of the letter to allow for room in between letters. It was found that this space was rather too much for normal spacing, but this was easily remedied by overlapping the rectangle boxes which contain the characters so that the grid is in effect 12 × 24 (see Fig. 1). This makes it possible to represent one complete card (80 characters) full of data across the width of the tube. At the present stage of the program, the narrow characters appear to be further apart than the wider ones. Omega and mu are almost touching whereas epsilon and iota are further apart than one would like. A procedure to introduce variable width typing is at present in an experimental stage. A call of this procedure will make all the letters appear the same distance apart. This includes Roman letters as well as Greek ones. The possibility of superimposing diacritics on a basic vowel was considered but rejected as this would make it necessary to reset the character spacing every time a diacritic is encountered.

The character shapes form the data to a program which reads the definitions of up to 256 characters and stores them on the disc. The data for the most straightforward character we have created, the Arabic letter alif, which is usually transliterated as A is

$$33 \ V12,4,12,12,F$$

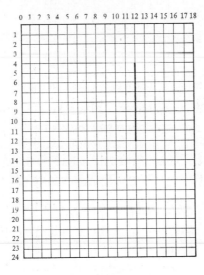

FIGURE 2. The Arabic character alif on a grid 18 × 24

This means that the character whose GROATS number is 33 is represented by a straight line whose coordinates are 12,4 and 12,12 on the grid – see Fig. 2. It must be emphasized that the origin of the grid is in the top left-hand corner, i.e. x increases from left to right and y from top to bottom. This character sits on a line half-way down the grid thus leaving enough space below for those letters which come below the line.

The letters provided by the Bell Telephone Laboratories did not include the final form of sigma which is represented by the Roman letter input coding of V. Several attempts were necessary before a character was produced which fitted the size, shape and general appearance of the other lower case Greek letters. Fig. 3 shows the new character on a grid 18 × 24.

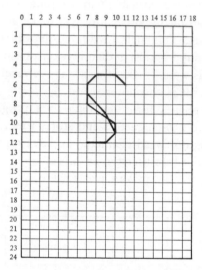

FIGURE 3. The Greek letter ς on a grid of 18 × 24

The new character is formed by calling the procedure
define new character;
This procedure reads from the currently selected input stream the vectors which make up the shape of the character. In this case the data is

54 V7,12,9,12,T10,11,T10,10,T7,8,V10,11,9,9,T7,8,V9,9,7,7,V7,8,7, 6,T8,5,T10,5,T11,6,F.

54 is the GROATS number of the character. V7,12,9,12, indicates a vector joining the points 7,12, and 9,12 and T indicates a line from the previous point, i.e. 9,12 to 10,11.

Slight alterations were also made to delta and theta to make them sit on the line as the other characters do and nu was thickened slightly to distinguish it more from upsilon. The shapes of all the lower case Greek letters have now been perfected and additional characters have also been plotted. At the moment these include all seven Greek vowels with rough breathings on them, the three vowels that can take an iota subscript and rough breathing. Rho has also been plotted with a rough breathing which it carries when it is the initial letter of a word. It is hoped in time to plot the Greek vowels with all the combinations of accents breathings and iota subscripts.

Whereas the procedure

define new character;

simply adds the character to the existing font, a complete new font of 256 characters can be defined by calling the procedure

define font;

which reads the definitions of 256 characters from the currently selected input stream. The size of the grid for each font must be declared at the beginning of the font and can be any size up to 31×63. All undefined characters are interpreted as 'space'. The Greek font which we have defined includes upper and lower case Greek and Roman letters together with those Greek letters which can carry diacritical marks as mentioned above as well as a few punctuation marks and other symbols such as + and / and the numerals – the punctuation includes the Greek question mark and the Greek colon which is now being punched as &. Computing time for the creation of the new font was 16 seconds on Atlas. A short program calls the font down from the disc and outputs the characters.

Because of the limited input character set it is only possible to produce up to 64 characters in any one conversion table, but a call of the procedure

displacement is (I);

will access the character numbered I + the number of the input character. This procedure is useful for capitals and Roman letters when the normal output is in Greek lower case, e.g. upper case Roman L input to the Greek font will be output as λ which is GROATS number 44. With a call

displacement is (64);

L will be output as l which is GROATS number 108, i.e. 64 + 44. A call of

displacement is (192);

will output L (GROATS number 236) with the same input character.

A recent revision of the system has reduced computing time for the output program. The time taken to produce the SC4020 orders for the sample extract from Thucydides (see Appendix) was 48 seconds on Atlas. A run of 20 seconds was required to execute the orders on the SC4020.

3. Arabic

Work has also begun recently on the output of Arabic script on the SC4020. As most of the 28 letters of the Arabic alphabet have more than one form (some have four and hamza in various combinations has seven) many more character shapes are necessary. It has been decided to follow an Arabic typewriter which does not have some of the rarer letter forms or ligatures but even this has over sixty different characters. Some preliminary work has been done on the character shapes. Though the vowels are not to be included, as they are usually omitted in the script, shadda, the sign which denotes the doubling of a letter, and the various combinations with hamza are to be plotted. The problem of writing the script from right to left has been solved and first attempts at joining up the letters have been made by, to a certain extent, imitating the Arabic typewriter. The present font of Arabic letters consists of all the Arabic letter forms found on the type-writer and the Arabic numerals. The final forms are accessed by a call of

$$\text{displacement is (64)};$$

in a similar way to the Greek capitals. It is hoped to have one font of Arabic letters and another of Persian to allow for the slight differences between the two alphabets.

4. Final stage, linking with COCOA[1]

When all the character shapes are complete the SC4020 will be used for the output of concordances in non-Roman alphabets. The text will be input with all its diacritical marks and then go through a pre-processor before being input to COCOA. When the concordance program has done its work the output from it will go through a post-processor to restore the diacritical marks and will then be output on the SC4020.

5. Automatic input

Of course it remains true that preparation of the input is the worst bottle-neck and the real explosion in the use of computers in the literary field is only likely to occur when we have some form of automatic input. This, in effect, calls for sophisticated Optical Character Recognition equipment.

[1] D. B. Russell, *COCOA Manual*, Atlas Computer Laboratory, SRC (Chilton, Didcot, Berkshire, November 1967).

The signs in this area are becoming more favourable but the appropriate equipment is not with us yet and it is likely to be very expensive when it does come. Conceivably, however, some manufacturer may offer the use of his OCR equipment on a bureau basis. There are in fact reports that at least one manufacturer is contemplating doing so.

We are grateful to F. R. A. Hopgood of the Atlas Computer Laboratory for expert advice on the use of the Atlas Algol Graphics System (GROATS)[1].

1 See note 1, p. 221.

APPENDIX

Examples of Greek and Arabic output on the SC4020

αβγδεζηθ ικλμνξοπρστυφχψω άέίόύήῶφήφᾷῄβ . . ;

ΑΒΓΔΕΖΗΘΙ ΚΛΜΝΞΟΠΡΣΤΤΦΧΨΩ

Greek characters

ه غ ع ج ـ اأإ ، ز ، ، ، د و ي ن م ل ك ق ف غ ع ظ ط ض ص ش س ز ر ذ د خ ح ج ث ت ب ا

Arabic initial and medial forms

ء ش س ه ن م ل ق ف غ ع ظ ط ض ص ش س ز ر ذ د ن ت ة

Arabic final forms

Θουκυδιδης αθηναιος ξυνεγραψε τον πολεμον των πελοποννησιων και αθηναιων,
ως επολεμησαν προς αλληλους, αρξαμενος ευθυς καθισταμενου και ελπισας μεγαν
τε εσεσθαι και αξιολογωτατον των προγεγενημενων, τεκμαιρομενος οτι ακμαζοντες
τε ησαν ες αυτον αμφοτεροι παρασκευη τη παση και το αλλο ελληνικον ορων
ξυνισταμενον προς εκατερους, το μεν ευθυς, το δε και διανοουμενον. κινησις
γαρ αυτη μεγιστη δη τοις ελλησιν εγενετο και μερει τινι των βαρβαρων, ως δε
ειπειν και επι πλειστον ανθρωπων. τα γαρ προ αυτων και τα ετι παλαιτερα σαφως
μεν ευρειν δια χρονου πληθος αδυνατα ην, εκ δε τεκμηριων ων επι μακροτατον
σκοπουντι μοι πιστευσαι ξυμβαινει ου μεγαλα νομιζω γενεσθαι ουτε κατα τους
πολεμους ουτε ες τα αλλα. φαινεται γαρ η νυν ελλας καλουμενη ου παλαι βεβαιως
οικουμενη, αλλα μεταναστασεις τε ουσαι τα προτερα και ραδιως εκαστοι την
εαυτων απολειποντες βιαζομενοι υπο τινων αιει πλειονων. της γαρ εμποριας ουκ
ουσης, ουδ' επιμιγνυντες αδεως αλληλοις ουτε κατα γην ουτε δια θαλασσης,
νεμομενοι τε τα αυτων εκαστοι οσον αποζην και περιουσιαν χρηματων ουκ εχοντες
ουδε γην φυτευοντες, αδηλον ον οποτε τις επελθων και ατειχιστων αμα οντων
αλλος αφαιρησεται, της τε καθ' ημεραν αναγκαιου τροφης πανταχου αν ηγουμενοι
επικρατειν, ου χαλεπως απανισταντο, και δι' αυτο ουτε μεγεθει πολεων ισχυον
ουτε τη αλλη παρασκευη. μαλιστα δε της γης η αριστη αιει τας μεταβολας των
οικητορων ειχεν, η τε νυν θεσσαλια καλουμενη και βοιωτια πελοποννησου τε τα
πολλα πλην αρκαδιας, της τε αλλης οσα ην κρατιστα. δια γαρ αρετην γης αι τε
δυναμεις τισι μειζους εγγιγνομεναι στασεις ενεποιουν εξ ων εφθειροντο, και
αμα υπο αλλοφυλων μαλλον επεβουλευοντο. την γουν αττικην εκ του επι πλειστον
δια το λεπτογεων αστασιαστον ουσαν ανθρωποι ωκουν οι αυτοι αιει. και
παραδειγμα τοδε του λογου ουκ ελαχιστον εστι δια τας μετοικιας ες τα αλλα μη
ομοιως αυξηθηναι. εκ γαρ της αλλης ελλαδος οι πολεμω η στασει εκπιπτοντες παρ'
αθηναιους οι δυνατωτατοι ως βεβαιον ον ανεχωρουν, και πολιται γιγνομενοι ευθυς
απο παλαιου μειζω ετι εποιησαν πληθει ανθρωπων την πολιν, ωστε και ες ιωνιαν
υστερον ως ουχ ικανης ουσης της αττικης αποικιας εξεπεμψαν.

VII
Programming the computer for literary and linguistic research

A versatile concordance program for a textual archive

N. HAMILTON-SMITH*

In 1964 Paul Bratley of the Edinburgh University Computer Unit and
Mr A. J. Aitken[1] of the *Dictionary of the Older Scottish Tongue* (*DOST*)
began setting up an archive of Older Scottish texts in machine-readable
form. Paul Bratley wrote three programs (in Atlas Autocode and Atlas
machine language) which could be applied to these texts to produce:

   (i) alphabetically arranged word-indexes with frequency counts;

   (ii) excerpts for specified word-forms found in particular texts on
6″ by 4″ slips for dictionary use; each slip contains the keyword,
a three line context, the reference and some other information,
including, where applicable, rhyme-words;

   (iii) conventional concordances.

These programs were for a number of years the main means of utilizing the
archive for dictionary purposes. The second of them was able to excerpt
selectively from an archive on a magnetic tape containing many different
works, but the third program was suitable for only rather short stretches of
text, at most a single complete work.

    Later Dr D. B. Russell, of the Chilton Atlas Laboratory, wrote (in Atlas
machine language) a program known as COCOA for generating word counts
and concordances. Before writing the program he visited scholars in many
British universities to discuss with them the particular facilities they would
hope to see in a general purpose computer program for literary work. In the
event, COCOA has proved and is proving an invaluable aid to scholars,
including those in Edinburgh and elsewhere who are working on texts in
Older Scots. It enables users to generate word-counts and concordances of
selected sections of given texts. The texts may be in any language that can
be transliterated into an alphabet of 44 or less characters. The texts may be
presented on punched cards, 7-track paper tape or magnetic tape: the size

* Edinburgh Regional Computing Centre.

1 The writer is grateful to Mr Aitken for correcting details of this paper and for writing the paragraphs on the particular needs of *DOST*.

of texts is limited only by the amount which may be filed on an Ampex one inch magnetic tape, i.e. the upper limit is about 20 million characters or 2–3 million words.[1]

In 1968 it was decided to add to the facilities offered by the Edinburgh Regional Computing Centre (ERCC) a program modelled on Dr Russell's COCOA. When this was being planned Dr Russell kindly described how he had planned his own program, but he is in no way responsible for any short-comings of the Edinburgh program which is written around a modified form of a sorting routine provided by D. R. McCann and D. D. M. Ogilvie of ERCC. Like COCOA this program, known as CONCORD, generates word counts and concordances.[2] The program is written in IMP, a high level programming language of ALGOL type developed in Edinburgh from Atlas Autocode. The program originally ran on an EELM KDF-9 computer and is currently in service on an IBM 360/50 and being tested on an ICL System 4/75. The transfer of the program in 1969 from the KDF-9 to the 360/50 necessitated the alteration of a few instructions owing to the difference in length of computer word in the two machines and to the use of magnetic tapes for backing storage on the first machine and discs on the second.

The output from a word count consists of three tables, each giving the number of occurrences and form of every orthographic word in the selected text. The three tables differ only in the order in which the information is presented. The first table lists the words in reverse alphabetical order, the second in dictionary order and the third table in descending order of frequency with words in alphabetic order if two or more have the same frequency. A fourth table is a frequency profile giving the number of words which appear only once, twice and so on, with cumulative totals of different orthographic words and occurrences of orthographic words: the cumulative totals are additionally expressed as percentages of their grand totals.

The output from a complete concordance consists of one record for every occurrence of every word containing:

(i) a reference enabling that occurrence to be located easily in the original text;

---

[1] Full details of the facilities provided by COCOA are set out in the manual: *COCOA – A word count and concordance generator for Atlas*, by D. B. Russell, The Atlas Computer Laboratory (Chilton, Didcot, Berkshire).

[2] Full details of the facilities provided by CONCORD are set out in a program description which may be obtained from: The Edinburgh Regional Computing Centre, The King's Buildings, Mayfield Road, Edinburgh, 9.

(ii) a certain amount of the context of that occurrence. The exact amount of context is limited to a maximum specified by the user (never more than two output lines) and may also be restricted to all context up to but not including some symbol in the text, which allows the context to be restricted to one textual line, sentence or any other stylistic unit.

The records are ordered in one of two ways so that all occurrences of a particular word (keyword) are grouped together and then the citations are ordered under each keyword, again in one of two ways:

		Order of keywords	
		Dictionary	Reverse alphabetic
Citations ordered under keywords by:	Reference	√	√
	Context to	Right	Left

There is a facility for pre-grouping the keywords according to the root of each. Further facilities allow one to limit the concordance either by excluding listed keywords or by including only these; alternatively to limit the keywords selected to those within a stated alphabetical range and within a particular range of frequency of occurrence.

Markers for text selection or reference purposes are placed in the text by printing an opening angle bracket followed immediately by an upper case Roman letter, which defines the type of reference, followed by the reference itself and concluded by a closing angle bracket: thus a title could be < T RAUF COILZEAR >. Fortunately this is also the method by which Paul Bratley's programs and Russell's program recognized such information so the texts which had been prepared for the former, including all texts in the Older Scottish archive originally prepared for *DOST*, could be used without alteration for this purpose, although there were other markers between stanzas and works that had to be eliminated. A number of types of reference have been inserted in the texts, e.g. authorship, date, title of collection, title of individual work, alternative reference to other edition or other title, literary mode, stanza form, date and locality, as well as folio or page and line, so that texts may be selected by various criteria. References of a type not used either for text selection or reference in the output are ignored by the program. As far as is possible a full set of references is always given for every text: this means that occasionally the authorship will be of the form < B ? DUNBAR > if it is only probable but not certain that the author was Dunbar or < B ANON > when the text cannot be attributed with certainty to any one author.

With this completeness of references one can for example analyse either the whole of the Bannatyne manuscript (one of the collections in the *DOST* archive) or only works within the collection written by Dunbar: Dunbar is one of the 32 authors contributing to this collection and he wrote 52 of its 453 works.

When the user comes to generate a word count or concordance he has to define the purpose of every character used in the text, otherwise the character will be treated as an interverbal space. At its simplest this means the user must define the characters and sorting order of his alphabet and punctuation. For a word count the program has to be informed which characters in the text are parts of keywords and all other characters can be treated as interverbal spaces by implication: keywords will usually be the lexical words of the chosen text or texts, but the program can alternatively treat punctuation or diacritical marks as keywords if this is one's particular interest.

It was mentioned earlier that there is a facility for pre-grouping the keywords of a concordance by the root of each keyword. This facility was originally provided (by COCOA) for scholars working on Semitic languages, since in these languages the lexical roots are essential. The user can of course edit pseudo-roots into his text if he so desires. CONCORD is informed which characters contribute to the roots, and it can then extract not more than the first four root letters from every word of the text and sort them. The user will probably, if not necessarily, be interested in the complete lexical word in addition to the root so he will declare which characters can contribute to the non-root part of each word. The program then uses these and possibly the root letters to sort the various complete keywords under their appropriate root heading. Finally the citations under each keyword are sorted by either the context of the keyword or the reference associated with the keyword. The sorting of roots, then keywords and finally context can be exemplified by taking one stanza of a poem by Dunbar and assuming that the five vowels contribute to the root:

> sum gevis for pryd and glory vane
> sum gevis with grugeing and wtq pane
> sum gevis in practik for supple
> sum gevis for twyis als gud agane
> in geving sowld discretioun be.

(*Note: wtq* represents *w* followed by superscript *t*)

The root sort gives 12 sets of words:

3	A	and, and, als
1	AAE	agane

2	AE	vane, pane
1	AI	practik
1	E	be
5	EI	gevis, gevis, gevis, gevis, geving
4	I	with, in, twyis, in
1	IEIO	discretioun
5	O	for, glory, for, for, sowld
5	U	sum, sum, sum, sum, gud
1	UE	supple
1	UEI	grugeing

The second sort is on the keywords under each root, e.g. under O the order becomes:

5   O   for, for, for, glory, sowld

The third sort is on the reference to the textual source or on the context to one side of the keyword and in this example will determine the order of the three instances of keyword *for*.

CONCORD recognizes eight different types of character, known as types o to 7. The type number of each character is the decimal number corresponding to the binary number made of ones and zeros according to whether the character is to be included in the Root, Key and Context or not:

Type	R	K	C
1	0	0	1
2	0	1	0
3	0	1	1
4	1	0	0
5	1	0	1
6	1	1	0
7	1	1	1

The eighth type, type O, is the set of characters which separate words and are to be printed in the citations: this will usually be the punctuation. A type number is assigned to a set of characters by stating the type number and then listing the set of characters within a pair of angle brackets, e.g.

3 < A&BCDEFGHIJKLMNOPQRSTUVWXYZ >

If two or more of character types 2 to 7 inclusive are being used and different numbers of characters appear in the separate declarations then spaces must be included where necessary to make the declarations of the same length. This is because the type declarations also determine the sorting order of the various characters: when two or more characters occupy the same column (counted from the left-hand angle bracket) they are equal for sorting purposes but the uppermost character in that column will appear in the output for all the characters in the column, e.g.

```
3 <ABCDEFGHIJKLMNOPQRSTUVWXYZ>
7 <a     e    i      o     u        >
```

Upper case and lower case vowels will be equal for sorting purposes (except that the lower case vowels will be used for the root sort), but all vowels will be printed in upper case in the output.

CONCORD has next to be informed of the maximum length of word that will be accepted as a keyword. Any word which is longer than this maximum is ignored in its entirety.

In order to select from the archive the works required for the analysis CONCORD has to be instructed which types of reference properties are being used to distinguish works and the number of symbols that will be used to define each of the particular properties. The works to be analysed are then listed exactly in terms of the chosen references and the type of analysis is specified. CONCORD will then start at a chosen point (a particular data set) in the archive and by reading sequentially locate each work in turn.

Since the last work to be analysed is not necessarily the last work in the archive there is provision for terminating the search when a particular work which is not to be analysed is encountered. The sequential nature of the search through the archive means that time could be wasted if there were a number of unwanted works between the ones for which CONCORD was searching. For example, a small program written to check an archive on the Chilton Atlas took approximately 15 seconds to read 20,000 lines of text and print every reference encountered. This wasted search time may be minimized in some cases by careful arrangement of the order of works in the archive, say by the juxtaposition of all works by one author within a collection which is written to the archive as a single data set. However, this may not necessarily benefit all analyses, e.g. Henryson, Dunbar *et al.* have contributed to the Asloan, the Bannatyne and the Maitland manuscripts; one scholar may be interested in the works by Dunbar in all of these collections and so this scholar would prefer all works by Dunbar to be the first in the collections. Another scholar may be interested in all works by Henryson and so must necessarily read the whole of the Dunbar in the first two collections, unless each collection is written to the archive with a separate data set for each author. The number of authors contributing to the collections mentioned, as well as the general use of the archive, render it impracticable to have a separate data set for every author.

The facilities so far mentioned reproduce in the main those originally offered by COCOA. However, although CONCORD was not written solely for *DOST*, the particular needs of this dictionary have led to the inclusion in CONCORD of facilities additional to those of COCOA.

DOST is using the computer to study exhaustively a number of texts mainly to supply examples of the use of words other than the most common in several texts which make up part of the dictionary's basic collection.[1] Composite concordances to these texts are supplied routinely to the dictionary's editors in small batches which correspond as nearly as possible to the stretch of the alphabet being edited at that time. This makes it possible to eliminate (for the texts concerned) a rather cumbersome feature of the dictionary's original system; by this a quotation slip which had been used for one keyword had then to be 'posted forward' to a later alphabetic position in the dictionary's files if it contained a keyword for that position (e.g. after having been used for a word beginning with A, it might be posted forward to one beginning with B, and so on). The computer concordances thus save some unnecessary re-reading and re-sorting.

Examples of the commonest words are, it is believed, already adequately provided for in the dictionary's original manually compiled files. It is the responsibility of the dictionary's editors to note any exceptional instances of these very common words occurring in slips which, by the old system, would have been 'posted forward', but which would otherwise, by the new computer-assisted system, have been discarded; these exceptional slips – but only these – continue to be posted forward. As a rule, then, citations for the more common words are not included in the batch-concordances supplied to the dictionary, but the items themselves are listed with their frequency in each text: this enables the dictionary editors to check that the original collections do indeed adequately represent these items and that, for example, early occurrences of these items are not overlooked.

This requirement is probably unique to this particular dictionary and is an outcome at once of the 'posting forward' system and of the fact that the dictionary is already nearly two-thirds edited. Formerly this need was supplied by means of the first two of Bratley's programs (p. 235): after editing a batch of copy the editors consulted the word-lists and requested

---

[1] See pp. 4ff. above, where A. J. Aitken gives an explanation of the concept 'basic collection'.

I

citations, in the form of slips, for those keywords which seemed to be missing or poorly represented. However, it has proved much more convenient to have the lists presented in composite concordance form and with contexts for the less common items; this enables the editor to judge at once whether he requires a particular quotation or not. If he does so, he could, if he wished, obtain his quotations printed out as slips by the computer, using Bratley's second program. In fact, since it is only occasionally that he needs an additional example from this source it is much more convenient and less wasteful of paper to copy out his citations manually from the computer concordance and so add them to his files at once. Consequently the aim is to produce a program which will generate concordances and to give the user a degree of control over how the citations are printed out.

The output from a concordance consists of a statement of the first keyword and its frequency of occurrence in the first text specified and under this heading the various citations for the first keyword in that text; this is followed by similar statements and citations for the same keyword in each successive specified text. This procedure is then repeated for each subsequent keyword.

If the keywords selected are restricted by an inclusive alphabetical range the user must also specify an inclusive frequency range. CONCORD counts the frequency of occurrence of every keyword selected; if the frequency of any keyword violates the chosen range a statement of the keyword and its frequency of occurrence are printed but none of the citations of this keyword are printed. It is also possible to apply this frequency limitation to the frequency of each keyword in subdivisions of the works selected. For instance if one were generating a concordance to a collection of works such as the Bannatyne manuscript one could instruct CONCORD to separate the use of each keyword by the author of the work from which the word came. In this case if a keyword used by any author violates the frequency range the detail of the author is added to the statement of keyword and frequency.

CONCORD is designed to analyse concurrently a number of texts from the *DOST* archive. This necessitated the provision of a facility whereby the reference to source text in the output could be varied from selected text to text, e.g. one can refer to a poem from the Bannatyne manuscript by Folio and line and to a poem from the Maitland manuscript by Item and line, but not vice versa.

Older Scottish is one of the languages which has more variant spellings and homographs than does, say, Latin. A facility has been provided to enable the computer to lemmatize variants under a single headword. The user provides a list of the words he wishes to have lemmatized and states the headword under which these words are to appear: the headword does not have to appear in the text. This facility could also be used for grouping the various tenses of any particular verb under one head, or any other such grouping of related words. A further facility enables the computer to search for particular collocations of words, such as set phrases or similar compound lexical items. The user specifies a pair of words and also the number of other words in the text which may separate them before they are no longer considered to be a pair. The pairs appear in the output under the first word, the adjacent pairs being cited first and the most widely separated pairs last.

The Older Scottish Textual Archive is on magnetic tape, but is not yet available to the general user. This is because it contains some known errors which were caused by the original paper input tapes being torn during the creation of the archive. There are also the special markers between stanzas, works and texts which Paul Bratley's programs required and which now must be removed: these markers are letter triplets which therefore appear as items in word counts and concordances when the archive is used with the current program. Once the faults have been removed from the archive it will be documented and made available to scholars other than those associated with *DOST*.

We hope that any user will then be able to retrieve whatever information he requires, by means of CONCORD and any subsequent programs which may be added (for example, one for delivering concordance material in slip form). All the user will need to do, in effect, will be to specify the criteria for selecting the part(s) of the archive to be accessed, state the exact nature of his requirements in terms of the facilities described above, and pay the charges for computing time. We hope thus to approach the ideal of a generally accessible computer archive, as proposed elsewhere in this volume (pp. 15ff. and 23f.).

The archive contains at present eleven major works in Older Scots and these are arranged as 17 different data sets. The larger number of data sets than works has arisen because a separate data set has been created for each volume of source text. The computer system can concatenate any stated selection of these data sets so that CONCORD need search only those parts of the archive which will yield the works in which the user is interested. Every work is adequately provided with markers for selection and reference purposes (p. 237) so that the archive has great flexibility of access. All subsequent additions to the archive will be provided with similar sets of markers. One such addition, which will be added shortly is a data set containing all the works by Dunbar found in all the collections used by *DOST*. It is not intended to follow a similar policy for every author but it is felt that more scholars than the one for whom this data set is being prepared might be interested in the works of Dunbar alone.

FORTRAN as a language for linguists

A. COLIN DAY*

1. The status of FORTRAN

A program carefully written in standard FORTRAN can be run without any alteration on more machines than a program in any other language. The compatibility of FORTRAN is due to two separate factors:

(a) More computers have compilers for FORTRAN than for any other language.

(b) FORTRAN has been well defined by the USA Standards Institute (USASI), and almost all compilers accept as a subset the language of one or other of these two standards.

As FORTRAN is not such a high level language as, say, SNOBOL, the programmer has a greater burden to bear. On the other hand, this means that the resulting object code can be considerably more efficient. Very high-level languages may in fact prevent a programmer from employing efficient techniques.

The most compatible form of FORTRAN is American Standard Basic FORTRAN, as described in the USASI publication X3.10-1966. To this must be added format code A in order for this language to be of use to linguists. Many compilers which accept Basic FORTRAN do in fact also accept format code A.

The failings of FORTRAN are obvious to all those who program in it. Languages have been devised which are much more satisfying aesthetically; in particular, it was not designed to facilitate character manipulation. (Performing character manipulation in FORTRAN has been likened to shelling peas whilst wearing boxing gloves – J. M. Sykes, *Computer Bulletin*, XI, 2, 147.) However, with the aid of appropriate techniques, programs for linguistic work can be written in FORTRAN. Once written, there is considerable probability that they will not need to be rewritten, and that they

* Computer Centre University College London.

245

will serve a far greater number of linguists than programs produced in any other form.

2. Programming techniques for linguists

FORTRAN has been used extensively at the Computer Centre of University College London for linguistic programs. In this way experience has been gained concerning techniques which would be of help to other programmers. The particular problems which have been considered in the past difficult to program in FORTRAN have been list processing and character manipulation. At the risk of being condemned for introducing obscure technicalities, or for repeating what is very well known in some circles, or for being excessively practical (which is almost a crime these days), I will describe some of the techniques which we have used. It is true that these techniques can quite easily be used in other languages besides FORTRAN. The point is, however, that they may be used in FORTRAN to take the place of some facilities which other languages already have.

(a) List processing

This term is used in its widest sense here. It seems to be common for programmers to regard list processing as something quite out of the ordinary, requiring the help of special subroutine packages. Such packages (of which SLIP is an example for FORTRAN users) are designed to tackle the most intricate list processing problems which can be conceived, and the full power is supplied even to the user who has a trivial problem. This inevitably results in a great loss of efficiency, both with regard to time and space.

Most list processing problems can be directly and simply coded in FORTRAN, without the need for complex packages. In order to do this, it is necessary for pointers to contain the index of a cell in a certain array, rather than the machine address of that cell. It is always important to keep list structures as simple as possible (in order for the programmer to keep track of what is happening, if for no other reason). There are at least three levels of complexity in the techniques to be used in FORTRAN list processing. The data structures represented by a simpler technique can be represented using a more complex technique, but not necessarily vice versa. These three levels are as follows:

(i) *Stacks.* All that is needed for a stack (or last-in-first-out list) is a vector and a pointer. When the stack is empty, the pointer is set to zero. For example, the stack can be set up as follows:

```
DIMENSION LIST (1ØØ)
DATA LNG/Ø/
```

An item is added to the stack in this way:

```
LNG = LNG+1
LIST (LNG) = ITEM
```

An item is removed from the stack in a similar way:

```
ITEM=LIST (LNG)
LNG=LNG−1
```

I have omitted statements to test for attempts to place more than 100 items in the stack, or to remove items from an empty stack.

If the items to be kept in the stack occupy more than one cell, then a single pointer may be used to control several vectors, or an array of the appropriate width.

(ii) *Circular buffers*. A circular buffer is sufficiently powerful for the storage of lists which may have items added or removed from either end. This means that stacks, queues and deques (double-ended queues) may be implemented in this way. The requirements are a vector and two pointers, one for the head of the list and one for the tail. Whenever a pointer is incremented beyond the length of the vector, it is set to one. Whenever a pointer is reduced to zero, it is set to the length of the vector. This means that in effect the vector is bent round until its ends meet. The tests for the list overflowing the size of the vector, or being accessed when it is empty, are now slightly more complicated.

(iii) *Chained lists*. If a list is to be amended anywhere along its length, and not just at its ends, then it must be kept as a chained list. This means that for every datum there must be a pointer. In FORTRAN this may be accomplished by means of two vectors, one for the pointers and one for the data items. An additional pointer will be required apart from these vectors for every list which is to be kept. This pointer will hold the index of the start of the list. It is usually most convenient to have a list of available space. This will initially consist of all the elements of the vector, chained together. As lists are set up, they are created from elements set free from the available space list. Lists (or parts of lists) which are deleted are returned to the available space list. 'Garbage' collection need not be any more complex than this.

For the storage of trees, or more generally, graphs, more pointers will be needed. A binary branching tree may be stored as three vectors, two of them being used for pointers, and one for the data. In Appendix A an example is given of a subroutine to perform a list processing sort (or tree sort, or monkey-puzzle sort) written in this way. No originality is claimed for this: it is simply included to show how economically programs can be written in FORTRAN to perform quite complex list processing.

(b) Character manipulation

(i) *Storage of characters*. Linguistic data to be manipulated must be read in FORTRAN under A1 format code. The variables into which the characters are read may be of any type. It has been found much more convenient to read characters into integer variables than into any other type, and this will be assumed throughout the rest of this section.

Characters read in A1 format are placed in the higher (leftmost) end of the cell, with the rest of the space padded with blanks. Considered as integers, the characters usually produce very large numbers, which may be positive or negative. Alphabetical comparison cannot be performed unless the characteristics of the machine are known (in particular, unless it is known whether negative integers are stored in complement form, or as sign and modulus). There is, however, a way to reduce these enormous numbers into positive integers between 1 and 513. This is by means of a statement function:

$$\text{KRUSH (I)} = \text{I} - (\text{I}/257)* \ 257 + 257$$

The resultant numbers are believed to differentiate the characters uniquely on most machines. A discussion of this statement function is given in Appendix B.

For most purposes integers between 1 and 513 are still too large, when the character set may be no more than 50 characters. The number may be reduced further by means of table look-up. A vector of length 513 is used. In it are placed numbers between 1 and (say) 50, at places corresponding to the characters in the set. By this means characters may not only be represented by the integers 1 to 50, but the numbers used may reflect the collating sequence required, which may differ from the computer's collating sequence. Another vector of length 50, filled with the characters as read under A1 format, may be used to transform the integers back to the appropriate characters once more, for printing purposes.

With the large amounts of data processed by linguists, it is very wasteful to use one computer cell for the storage of only one character. When the characters have been reduced to small integers, several may be packed in one cell by means of multiplication. For example, if the result of reducing a character lies between 1 and 50, then the cell can hold several of these numbers treated as digits to the base 51. The number of characters held in one cell is computer dependent, but this can be read in as a parameter for a general program. Usually more characters can be packed in a cell when they are reduced to integers in this way than could be read into a cell by A format. Also the cells containing packed integers may be compared arithmetically when sorting the characters according to the linguist's chosen collating sequence.

(ii) *Storage of words.* The storage of words brings particular problems for the programmer. They are variable in length, and considerations of efficiency forbid that each word be stored in the amount of space needed for the longest. Furthermore, it is necessary to be able to look up a word easily, to see whether a certain word has been stored, and if so, where it is.

The first problem, that of storage, may be overcome by placing the characters (optionally reduced to small integers and packed) in a vector, with pointers to the beginning of each word. For each word, one cell of the vector gives a count of the number of cells used for that word. An example may be given diagrammatically:

2	TH	E	4	SI	XT	EE	N	1	AT

The second problem, that of dictionary look-up, may be solved by storing the pointers in a 'hash' table. This is best explained by way of an example. Let us suppose that a vector 170 cells long is to be used as a hash table. When the word SIXTEEN is first encountered, it is reduced to small integers which are packed in successive cells of some work vector. The first block of characters (say SI) may be treated as a large integer number. The remainder on dividing this number by 170 may be found, and will lie in the range 0 to 169. By adding 1 to it, it will now lie in the range 1 to 170, and may be used as an index to the hash table vector. Let us suppose that the remainder plus one comes to 58. Then if position 58 of the hash table is empty (zero) the word SIXTEEN is placed in the character vector (as shown in the previous paragraph) and the pointer to it is stored in position 58. If this position already contains a pointer, a test is made to see whether this pointer leads to the word SIXTEEN in the character vector. If it does not, position 59 in the hash table is similarly considered, and so on.

Hash tables enable the programmer to use part of the data as an address of the location at which information about the data is stored. At the same time they eliminate the need for reserving space for data with every possible address.

Hash tables may also be used to store the sparse matrices which sometimes arise in linguistic programs. Suppose that the frequencies of co-occurrence of words are required. By means of the dictionary look-up given above, every input word in the text may be translated into a small integer (the index of the pointer in the hash table vector may be used for this). If there are 2,000 word types in the text, then the number of possible co-occurrence types is 4,000,000. No present computer could handle such a large number of cells. Very few of the 4,000,000 co-occurrences would actually be found, so that most of the numbers stored would be zero even if we could store them. By using hash table techniques all of the data may be stored adequately. If there are 5,000 co-occurrences altogether, then two vectors at least of length 5,000 are needed, one for the hash table, and the other for the frequencies. If a word whose look-up number is m is found before a word of look-up number n, then let the value $i = (m \times 2001) + n$. The remainder on dividing i by the length of the hash table (with one added) is used as the entry point into the hash table. If this location is zero, then i is stored in it, and the count of co-occurrences is kept in the corresponding cell of the other vector.

(iii) *Storage of patterns*. A problem which is commonly met in linguistic programming is the storage of information concerning structures in a form in which it can easily be applied. A simple yet powerful technique which may be used here is that of symbol–state tables. A fuller description of these tables is given in my article on 'The Use of Symbol–State Tables' (*Computer Journal*, XIII, 4, 332–9). An example can be given here to show an application to linguistics.

Recently one of our language departments in University College asked my advice. Its members have coded some texts according to grammatical categories and wish to count various features. The problem was to count the frequencies of occurrence of the following eight types of clause:

1.	IO	S	V	
2.		S	IO	V
3.		S	V	IO
4.	IO	V	S	
5.		V	IO	S
6.		V	S	IO
7.	IO	V		
8.		V	IO	

Elements of the clause other than the verb, subject and indirect object are to be ignored, as are clauses which do not fit any of these eight patterns. The solution adopted was to use a symbol state table of 16 rows and 3 columns. At the start of each clause a row pointer, N, is set to 9. Each time a subject, verb or indirect object is encountered the column pointer is set to

	S 1	V 2	IO 3
1			
2			
3			
4			
5			
6			
7	4		
8	5		
9	10	15	13
10		11	12
11			3
12		2	
13	14	7	
14		1	
15	16		8
16			6

FIGURE I

1, 2 or 3 respectively. The intersection of row and column in the table gives the new row pointer. The symbol–state table used is shown in Fig. 1. Some cells of the table are left blank for readability. These are filled with negative numbers, which then are used for detecting errors in the data (e.g. a clause with two subjects). At the end of a clause, if N is less than 9, N gives the type of clause identified.

Let us suppose that a clause with structure V IO is being examined. N is initially 9. When the V is encountered, column 2, row 9 of the table is taken as the new value of N, which then becomes 15. On finding the IO, column 3, row 15 of the table replaces N, which becomes 8. At the end of the clause the clause type is therefore 8. Note that if an S had been found after V IO, N would have become 5.

Pattern matches for characters can be stored in a symbol–state table. For instance, Fig. 2 shows part of a table which will match the pattern ABA, or

	A 1	B 2	C 3	D 4	E 5
1	3	2			
2					o
3		4			
4	o				o

FIGURE 2

the pattern ABE, or the pattern BE. A more complicated system will be required to handle patterns such as AB and ABA (where one string is completely contained in another) or where it is desired not simply to match the patterns, but to know which pattern proved to be a match. Some of the techniques given in the paper on 'The Use of Symbol–State Tables' may be employed here. If the symbol–state table happens to be sparse, then hashing techniques may be used for storing it.

At UCL Computer Centre a project has been undertaken to produce the final volume of Sir Ralph Turner's *Comparative Dictionary of the Indo-Aryan Languages*.[1] The main part of the dictionary contains approximately 19,000 Sanskrit headwords, with their cognates among present-day Indo-Aryan languages. The final volume is to be an index to certain sound patterns, giving for each sound pattern a list of all the Sanskrit headwords in

[1] This work has been done under a grant from the School of Oriental and African Studies. Alan Shaw did the programming, and conceived the idea of using a symbol-state table for pattern matching.

which it is to be found. Proofreading of the headwords and sound patterns was made easier by using a symbol-state table which only permitted sequences of characters found in Sanskrit. Searching for 1,600 patterns at every position of 19,000 headwords appeared at first sight to be a prohibitively large task. It was made much more efficient by storing the sound patterns as a symbol-state table similar to that shown in the last paragraph.

3. Work at UCL Computer Centre

At University College London Computer Centre Alan Shaw and I have been working on a package of programs for linguists. These programs are written in Basic Standard FORTRAN (plus A format), and are designed to be easily used by those who have no knowledge of programming. One program has already been written for dictionary production. This will produce mono-, bi- or tri-lingual dictionaries in one to three columns across the page. Sub-entries which cannot be printed in one line are continued on successive indented lines. The user may specify a title for each page, subtitles for the columns, the alphabetical order to be used, the order of subentries across the page, and several other parameters. After one set of data has been read in, a number of dictionaries may be produced from the data in different formats. Sets of data with control cards may be batched to produce dictionaries of several languages in one run.

It is hoped that other programs in the package will perform (*a*) word/ morpheme frequency counts, (*b*) charting of phoneme distribution, (*c*) concordance production, (*d*) random generation of sentences according to the user's grammatical rules, and possibly (*e*) parsing.

In addition to the linguistic package of programs, I have done some research on automatic syntactic analysis. The aim of this work is to write a computer program which will read in a corpus of text material, and will produce information concerning the syntax of that language. The first step in the strategy I have followed is to group together certain words which are very likely to belong to the same word class. Then various strings of classes may be grouped together as structures which belong to the same paradigmatic class, and so on.

Words are compared by comparing their environments. A record is kept for each word of those words which have been found immediately preceding it, and those found immediately following it. If two words show considerable overlap in their preceding contexts, and also in their following contexts, then they are grouped together. The results of one trial run are shown in Appendix C. The program which produced these results was not written wholly in FORTRAN. In order to speed up the comparisons, part of it was written in Assembler language. This is, however, only a research project at the moment. The value of writing production programs in standard FORTRAN is very great. In the next decade it is to be expected that linguists will be using the computer very much more than in the past. It is not to be expected that many of them will be able to delve into programming to any great depth. The only answer appears to be the use of compatible programs (and subroutines). As the medium for these programs and subroutines I heartily recommend standard FORTRAN.

APPENDIX A

```
1              SUBROUTINE SORMP(LIST,N,INDX,KOMP)
        C
        C  PURPOSE - SORTS THE INDICES OF N ITEMS
        C
        C  DESCRIPTION OF PARAMETERS
        C     LIST - A TWO-DIMENSIONAL WORK ARRAY OF SIZE (2,N)
        C     N    - THE NUMBER OF ITEMS TO BE SORTED
        C     INDX - A VECTOR INTO WHICH THE ORDERED INDICES ARE TO BE PLACED
        C     KOMP - AN INTEGER FUNCTION KOMP(I,J) WHICH RETURNS A POSITIVE
        C        VALUE IF ITEM I SHOULD PRECEDE ITEM J, AND NEGATIVE OTHERWISE
        C
        C  EXPLANATION
        C     THE FIRST ITEM IS MADE THE HEAD OF THE TREE, AND THE OTHER ITEMS
        C     ARE THEN ATTACHED ONE BY ONE. FOR ANY ITEM I, LIST(1,I) IS USED
        C     AS THE LEFT POINTER, AND LIST(2,I) AS THE RIGHT POINTER. THE LEFT
        C     POINTER OF AN ITEM MAY BE ZERO, OR MAY POINT TO AN ITEM WHICH
        C     SHOULD PRECEDE IT. THE RIGHT POINTER OF AN ITEM WILL BE ZERO IF
        C     IT IS THE LAST ITEM OF ALL, POSITIVE IF IT POINTS TO AN ITEM
        C     WHICH SHOULD FOLLOW IT, OR NEGATIVE IF THE ITEM WHICH SHOULD
        C     IMMEDIATELY FOLLOW IT IS FURTHER UP THE TREE. IN THE LAST CASE
        C     THE RIGHT POINTER IS CALLED A BACKTRACK. AFTER BUILDING THE TREE,
        C     THE INDICES ARE STRIPPED OFF IN ORDER.
        C
2              DIMENSION LIST (2,N), INDX (N)
        C  SET ALL THE POINTERS TO ZERO
3              DO 1 I=1,2
4              DO 1 J=1,N
5            1 LIST(I,J) = 0
        C  FIT THE ITEMS ON THE TREE ONE BY ONE
6              DO 10 I=2,N
        C  START THE COMPARISONS ON THE FIRST ITEM
7              J=1
8            2 IF(KOMP(I,J).LE.0)GO TO 4
        C  ITEM I PRECEDES ITEM J - DOES ITEM J HAVE A LEFT BRANCH
9              IF(LIST(1,J).EQ.0)GO TO 3
        C          IF SO, FOLLOW THE LEFT BRANCH AND COMPARE AGAIN
10             J=LIST(1,J)
11             GO TO 2
        C          IF NOT, MAKE A LEFT BRANCH FROM ITEM J TO ITEM I
12           3 LIST(1,J)=I
        C          AND A BACKTRACK FROM ITEM I TO ITEM J
13             LIST(2,I)=-J
14             GO TO 10
        C  ITEM I FOLLOWS ITEM J - DOES ITEM J HAVE A RIGHT BRANCH
15           4 IF(LIST(2,J).LE.0)GO TO 5
```

```
            C           IF SO, FOLLOW THE RIGHT BRANCH AND COMPARE AGAIN
16                J=LIST(2,J)
17                GO TO 2
            C           IF NOT, COPY THE BACKTRACK OF ITEM J INTO ITEM I
18              5 LIST(2,I)=LIST(2,J)
            C           AND MAKE A RIGHT BRANCH FROM ITEM J TO ITEM I
19                LIST(2,J)=I
20             10 CONTINUE
            C
            C NOW STRIP THE TREE, PLACING THE ORDERED INDICES IN INDX
            C SET THE VALUE OF THE NEXT INDEX TO BE FOUND
21                IND=1
            C           AND THE NODE OF THE TREE WHICH IS TO BE CONSIDERED FIRST
22                NODE=1
23                GO TO 12
            C FOLLOW THE LEFT BRANCH
24             11 NODE=LIST(1,NODE)
            C IF THERE IS A LEFT BRANCH, FOLLOW IT
25             12 IF(LIST(1,NODE).GT.0)GO TO 11
            C THE PRESENT NODE IS THE NEXT IN ORDER, SO KEEP A REFERENCE TO IT
26             13 INDX(IND)=NODE
27                IND=IND+1
            C IS THE RIGHT BRANCH OF THE PRESENT NODE NEGATIVE, ZERO OR POSITIVE
28                IF(LIST(2,NODE))14,16,15
            C           IF NEGATIVE, FOLLOW THE BACKTRACK
29             14 NODE=-LIST(2,NODE)
30                GO TO 13
            C           IF POSITIVE, FOLLOW THE RIGHT BRANCH
31             15 NODE=LIST(2,NODE)
32                GO TO 12
            C           IF ZERO, THE SORTING IS DONE
33             16 RETURN
34                END
```

APPENDIX B

Reducing characters to small integers

Let us consider machines which hold positive integer numbers as binary integers, i.e. excluding those which hold an integer as a non-normalized floating point number. On such machines, some characters read in under A1 format code into an integer location will correspond to positive integers. When this is so, the function

$$I-(I/257)*257+257$$

corresponds to the function

$$I \ (\text{modulo } 257)+257$$

Let the bit pattern corresponding to a certain character represent the integer number i, and another such bit pattern represent the integer number j. Let the number of characters which will fit into one cell on this machine be n and the number of bits used for one character be b. The characters read under A1 format code are placed in the higher end of the cell padded with blanks to the right. The contents of two locations I and J may be represented as follows:

Let the integer number corresponding to the $n-1$ blanks be B. Then the integer value of I may be written as

$$i \cdot 2^{b \cdot (n-1)} + B$$

and that of J as

$$j \cdot 2^{b \cdot (n-1)} + B$$

By the laws of congruences, if $I \equiv J$ and if $2^{b \cdot (n-1)}$ is relatively prime to m then $i \equiv j$ (modulo m). By choosing m as 257, we ensure that $2^{b \cdot (n-1)}$ is relatively prime to m whatever the values of b and n. This means that if the function returns the same value for two characters, the bit patterns of the two characters represent integers which are congruent, modulo 257. This means that the bit patterns are equal, since present computers use no more than 8 bits per character (so i and j will be in the range 0–255).

Those characters which correspond to positive integers will thus be reduced to unique integers between 257 and 513. Now let us consider 'negative' characters. If integer division causes rounding towards zero, the 'negative' characters will be reduced by the function to unique integers lying between 1 and 256. They will, therefore, not clash with any of the 'positive' characters. On a machine which rounds down on integer division, the results for 'positive' and 'negative' characters again do not in fact clash, but all lie between 257 and 513.

APPENDIX C

Word classification

The following initial grouping of words into classes was made after one pass through approximately 17,000 words of text from the book *Frontier Ways*:

Group 1   THE, A
Group 2   IN, ON
Group 3   IT, THEY, HE, THERE, THEM
Group 4   FOUND, BECAME, GAVE
Group 5   THAT, WHAT
Group 6   THE, THEIR, HIS
Group 7   MANY, SOME, MOST
Group 8   PEOPLE, CATTLE, SETTLERS, LAND, WATER, WORK, FOOD, TIME, CHILDREN, HOME, MONEY, LANDS
Group 9   TIME, REGION, HELP
Group 10 MONEY, HOMES, TABLE, DEEP

Group 11 HAD, MADE, OFTEN, BUILT, CAME, FOUND, BROUGHT,
         USED, CALLED, HELD, GIVEN, KEPT, SOLD
Group 12 WORK, MONEY, NEIGHBORS, SPEECHES
Group 13 DUGOUT, GARDEN
Group 14 NEW, PRAIRIE, WESTERN, WILD

Designing a programming language for use in literary studies

M. F. PORTER*

The benefits of writing programs in a high-level language are too familiar to require enumeration here, and one would like to think that they can be reaped by the programmer engaged in literary studies together with everyone else. Unfortunately the languages most often at his disposal are not usually very appropriate. SNOBOL is the obvious candidate for meeting his needs, but it has two serious disadvantages. One is that its range of symbols is essentially that of the computing system in which the language is implemented: this is not usually general enough for his purposes (more will be said about this later). The other is that for various reasons SNOBOL is slow to run, which prohibits its use in large applications. Other languages are often designed for quite different purposes and prove to be of little assistance to him. FORTRAN is in this category. Consequently there appears to be a definite requirement for a language designed specifically for literary applications, in which the basic concepts of the language correspond to the basic needs and activities of the literary programmer.

I have implemented a programming language on the Titan computer at the Computer Laboratory, Cambridge, which could be useful in this respect, and which is described in this paper. The present implementation produces programs which are somewhat slow working, but the language itself has the potential of being sufficiently fast to be of practical use.

The nature of the problem

Before designing a language to aid the programmer engaged in literary computing, we must first decide what his particular problems are. To begin with, let us consider a topic characteristic of his activities, namely concordance making. From his point of view this falls into two parts. The first of these includes such problems as deciding what a letter is, what a word is,

* Literary and Linguistic Computing Centre, University of Cambridge.

what contexts are suitable for each quoted headword, what line number or other such reference is to be given to each headword, and what the final format of the concordance is to be. Having found suitable answers to these problems, most probably under the direction of a scholar, the programmer will then have to embody these answers in the programs he writes. The second part consists of sorting all the words, with the information about them, into alphabetical order. We will call these parts of concordance making analysis and sorting.

The programmer will soon realize that, of the two tasks, sorting is by far the less troublesome. The program to do the sorting will often be quite large and will take a fairly long time to run; it will also have to take into account the limitations of the computer and make the best use of its various facilities. But once written, such a program can be used over and over again. The rules for word order may be different at each run, but this will usually only necessitate rewriting the orders that determine word order, or giving the program some data determining word order, or even putting the material to be sorted into some slightly unusual form for the purposes of the program.

The analysis, on the other hand, will involve fresh work for each concordance. Even when texts are of similar form, in the same language, of the same period, and punched out using the same conventions, considerable extra work can be expected with each. If the works are dissimilar, the analysis will have to be done afresh in every case. The programmer will eventually find that it is the analysis which calls for his main programming effort, although the majority of machine time may be devoted to sorting.

Concordance making is characteristic of many aspects of literary computing. In one phase certain forms in which we are interested are extracted from the text. (For a concordance this is every word together with reference and quotation.) In the next phase they are sorted into the desired order and then they are printed out in an appropriate format.

If a programming language is to aid the programmer engaged in literary computing, it is not vital that it should do the sorting for him. It should of course be possible to sort in such a language, but rapid sorting of very large quantities of information need not be a priority. If the programmer can write programs for the analysis phase in the language, he will be using it for 90% of his effort.

As another very different example, consider paginating a document for the benefit of a line-printer or a typesetting machine. Here the problem is to construct the algorithm by which the width of the gap between adjacent words is determined. This could depend upon the lengths of the words, the presence and nature of a punctuation mark between them, and the distribution of gap widths in the preceding lines. Now this is similar to the analysis in concordance making. Both processes can be thought of as collections of operations which search for a syntactic form in a given region of text.

To clarify these ideas let us suppose that T is a specimen of text and S is a description of some syntactic form. S could be thought of as 'the next word', 'the next pair of blank lines', 'the pair of adjacent words in the next line which comprise the maximum number of letters', and so on. We could think of a command

T   S

as being an attempt to find in T the syntactic form described by S. The commands of the language I have been developing all grew out of this idea. It is of course not novel: SNOBOL and, in a more rudimentary form, COMIT are based upon it.

What the language does not do is to suppose that S decomposes T in some way and that T is then reassembled into a new form by some further rules, U. COMIT, for instance, works in this way. I have chosen not to do this because it is not of much value in literary computing, where one wants to carry out very general searches throughout a piece of text, but not very general manipulations of the text itself. The emphasis in the language is therefore on the different forms of S.

We may now consider briefly a very thorny problem in literary computing – namely input and output. The programmer in the literary computing field has to deal with a range of characters from the printed page which will usually be far more varied and complex than the set of characters associated with the computer he is using. Various problems thus arise from the need to represent characters internally in the computer and externally in the various input-output devices; overcoming these difficulties can be very time-consuming in practice. Consequently the language must allow the representation of a wide range of characters by the more restricted character set of a teletype or flexowriter. The scheme actually adopted is as follows:

No problem exists if the characters to which we wish to refer appear on the machine on which we prepare the program.

Data	Representation
The Pupil.	'The Pupil.'

If the machine has no lower case letters we can use *C1 to indicate 'lower case letters follow' and *C0 to indicate 'capital letters follow'.

The Pupil.   'T*C1HE *C0P*C1UPIL.'   (1)

*C0 and *C1 only affect letters, and *C0 is assumed by default.

Since we may need space and new-line for layout purposes, we represent them as data by *S and *N respectively. So (1) is more properly written

The Pupil.   'T *C1 HE *S * 0 P *C1
              UPIL.'

If a character does not appear on the machine, we must refer to it by its code. So we might have

§ £ %   '*270 *S *192 *S *310'

A shift into a special font is marked by writing *Fn, where n is the number associated with that font. So

ITALICS **BOLD**   '*F1 ITALICS *F2 BOLD'

'Ordinary' font is *F0, which is assumed by default. If underlining is assumed to represent italicization, we see that *F can have immediate relevance for typewriter input.

Diacritics are represented by *Dn. Thus

déjà   '*C1 DE*D1 JA*D2'

where acute and grave accents have diacritic-numbers one and two associated with them.

Since asterisk and apostrophe have special functions in this scheme, we refer to them by ** and * ' respectively. Thus

* '   ' ** *' '

There is a code corresponding to this representation, which indicates the bit patterns by which text is represented within the computer. For different implementations of the language this code could of course vary widely, but we are assuming that for a given implementation it is fixed. Now the coded representation of text on the various devices external to the computer is not usually immutable. The typist has to represent a passage of text by the limited set of characters on the keyboard, and if left to herself she will probably choose some *ad hoc* way of doing so which will be different for each text. Consequently the input and output of text will have to be done by some flexible input-output routines which will transform the text to and from the standard internal form. The nature of these routines will depend upon the particular computing environment. The more flexible their design, the more valuable they will be, but they may, if made very general, begin to encroach upon the usefulness of the programming language. For instance, if the typist represents â by a∧ we might incorporate in the input routine the ability to do the transformation

' a ∧ ' → ' a*D1'

although this is just the type of transformation we would expect to be able to do in the language.

A short description of the language

The language deals with two types of data item, which we shall call *elements* and *strings*.

An *element* is a bit pattern which will usually occupy a word, or some other fixed unit of computer store. It can have the value of a store address, an integer or the coded representation of some printed character. In the last case the bit pattern is divided into different *regions* each of which records information about some different aspect of the character. The regions correspond to case, font, presence of diacritic, etc.

A *string* is an ordered sequence of elements. Typically, a string is a piece of text. But it can also be a sequence of integers or a sequence of store addresses, or a mixture of all these.

The language contains *variables* which can be written as a letter, or a letter followed by letters and digits, e.g.

A   B   C   CAT 1   CAT 2   KITTEN

The value of a variable is an element. When the value of a variable is a store address, it usually marks a position on some string. Strings are always referenced by pointers in this way, and do not themselves have names associated with them.

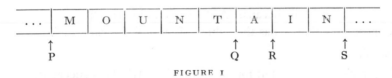

FIGURE I

For example, Fig. 1 shows a string containing the sequence of elements 'MOUNTAIN' with variables P, Q, R, S marking positions on the string.

We refer to different parts of the string by means of variables enclosed in square brackets. In the example of Fig. 1,

[P S] refers to 'MOUNTAIN'
[P R] refers to 'MOUNTA'
[Q R] refers to 'A'

We shall call these pointer pairs *string references*.

A program is made up of *commands*. With a few exceptions which we shall not be considering, all commands have the same general form, and cause one collection of elements to be processed with another. Every command begins with a variable or string reference which specifies one of the collections of elements. We shall call this the *left-component* of a command. Frequently this processing involves taking elements in pairs and testing them. The test may be for equality, for the same diacritic, or for alphabetical order, and each test will either succeed or fail. A command will also either succeed or fail, and this will depend upon the result of the tests made within the command.

A few examples will clarify these points. Suppose we have the situation of Fig. 1.

[P Q] 'MOUNT';

The elements of the string reference [P Q] are taken with the specified elements 'MOUNT' and tested in pairs for equality. Thus the pair of elements 'M' are tested, then the pair of elements 'O', and so on to the pair of elements 'T'. The test on each pair of elements succeeds, and so the whole command succeeds.

[P Q] 'MO';   (2)

This command succeeds similarly.

[P Q] 'MOAT';

This command fails because the 'A' of 'MOAT' is different from the 'U' of 'MOUNT', with which it is tested for equality.

[P Q] 'MOUNTAIN';

This command fails because 'AIN' lies outside [P Q].
Suppose now that X has the value 'M' and Y the value 'U'.

X 'M';

Here variable X is tested for equality with 'M'. This succeeds.

X 'U';   (3)

This fails.

[P Q] X 'O';

X has the value 'M' so this succeeds, cf. (2).

[P S] X 'O' Y 'NT' [Q R] [R S];

This command succeeds. The part of the command after the left-component simply gives the elements 'MOUNTAIN' and these are tested for equality with the left-component.

A *label* may be set at a command by putting the label name, preceded by a sharp, before the command, e.g.

   #CAT X 'U';

If a label name, preceded by a sharp, follows the left-component of a command, and if, during execution, the command fails, the program will take as its next command the one at which the label is set, e.g.

   X #DOG 'U';

Cf. (3). This causes a jump to the command at which label DOG is set.

Frequently we will want to consider alternative possibilities when testing the value of the left-component. To do this we use the system name ANY. ANY takes a list of arguments in brackets separated by commas. The arguments are taken in order and processed with the elements of the left-component until a success occurs. If no individual success occurs the final result is a failure, e.g.

   VOWELCHAR   #NOTAVOWEL ANY ('A', 'E', 'I', 'O', 'U');

This command, I hope is self-explanatory.

   [P Q] ANY ('C', 'F') ANY ('OO', 'OA') 'L';

This succeeds if [P Q] refers to any of 'COOL', 'COAL', 'FOOL' or 'FOAL'.

If we want to move down a string until we find a specific item we use HOPB

   [P Q] HOPB 'A';

This causes the string to which [P Q] refers to be scanned from left to right until an 'A' is found. If no 'A' is found the command fails.

   [P Q] #NOBRACKETS HOPB '(' HOPB ')';

This will cause a jump to label NOBRACKETS if [P Q] does not contain a pair of brackets. The second HOPB will search for a closing bracket between the opening bracket and the point of the string marked by Q.

The next example is the outline of a simple program.

```
#NEXT < Input a line of text as [A B] >
[A B] #NEXT HOPB ANY ('?', '!');                              (4)
< Print out [A B] and jump to NEXT >
```

In line 2 the argument of HOPB is ANY ('?', '!') and the whole command tests to see if [A B] contains a question or exclamation mark. If it does we go on to line 3. If it does not we jump to label NEXT which is set at line 1. Thus the program prints out those lines of a text containing question or exclamation marks.

As we have seen, commands cause two collections of elements to be processed together. ANY and HOPB described above cause the form of this processing to be modified in some way; and so we will call them *modifiers*. The language has about thirteen modifiers in all. Since there will not be space to describe them individually, I shall confine myself to some general remarks.

With a few exceptions modifiers can take quite general arguments made up of variables, string descriptions and other modifiers. (4) gave an example of a modifier with a modifier as argument.

The argument of a modifier may be put in round brackets. If these brackets are omitted, the modifier will take as argument the shortest non-empty group following the modifier which, in the definition of the language, can meaningfully be an argument. If the opening bracket is inserted and the closing bracket omitted, it will take as argument everything up to the end of the command. These rules are very useful. They prevent the language from having that confusing plurality of brackets which one tends to encounter in, say, LISP.

It may be of interest to mention the modifier MASK, since it is connected with my remarks on page 262. When an element represents a printed character, we shall often want to ignore some of its regions (see p. 263). We may want to test two letters for equality without regard for their fonts or cases, or may want to look for a diacritic independently of the letter it covers. We then use MASK, which restricts the processing of elements in a command to certain regions of the elements, e.g.

   [P Q] MASK [D] HOPB '*D2';   (5)

This tests for diacritic number 2 in [P Q]. '*D2' can be thought of as a null character with diacritic number 2 on it. MASK [D] confines the testing for equality to the diacritic region of the elements.

Note that without the bracketing conventions described above we would have had to write (5) as

   [P Q] MASK [D] (HOPB ('*D2'));

So far we have only considered one type of operation between pairs of elements in a command, namely testing for equality. Many more are available, and they can be set by the use of *operators* which, syntactically, resemble modifiers. Operators can be divided into two classes.

(a) Test operators

The test for equality, which the language will assume by default, is a test operator, and can be set explicitly by the equals sign, i.e.

[P Q] = (< some construction >);

is equivalent to

[P Q]   < some construction > ;

Together with = there are available ╪, >, ≧, <, ≦. These have obvious uses if the elements are interpreted as integers, e.g.

A #NOTPOS > 0;

This causes a jump to label NOTPOS if variable A is not greater than zero.

They are also useful when the elements are interpreted as printed characters, since the internal codes of the printed characters are arranged in the following numerical order,

lowest   space

⌄   punctuation characters

      digit 0 to digit 9

highest   letter A to letter Z

and then the command

A > B;

is a good test for alphabetical order between the character-values of variables A and B.

A further test operator is TYPE, with which we can test to see if an element of the left-component belongs to some such category as letter, digit, punctuation mark, either letter or digit, neither letter nor digit, and so on.

(b) Setting operators

These are used to alter the values of elements. If the operator begins with a colon, the elements of the left-component are set to some new value, e.g.

A := 1;   Set A equal to 1.

A :+ B;   Add the value of B to A.

If the operator begins with a full stop, the elements of the left-component are used to give new values to the other elements, e.g.

A .= B;   Set B equal to the value of A.

A .+ B;   Add the value of A to B.

The colon and stop operators go in corresponding pairs, and operators are provided to do subtraction, multiplication, division, shifting and logical operations. These operators provide the programmer with all the apparatus he needs for doing integer arithmetic, although arithmetic instructions can look unfamiliar. Thus an instruction that one would naturally write as

A := ((B ∧ 31) + C) x D

would be written

A := B :∧ 31 :+ C :x D;

On the other hand these operators deal with strings very neatly. Thus the command

SUM :+ [P Q];

will cause all the elements of [P Q], interpreted as integers perhaps, to be added to SUM.

The command

F .+ [P Q];

causes F to be added to every element in the string [P Q]. If F indicated italic font, the command could indicate italicization.

In the situation of Fig. 1 the command

[Q S] := 'ING';

would change the elements 'AIN' to the elements 'ING' on the given string.

We will now give a more substantial example which illustrates some of the power of the language. It is a command to print out all the palindromes in a segment of text.

The modifier REV changes the direction in which the elements of the left-component are processed. Thus

[Q P] REV [P Q];   (6)

tests to see if [P Q] is the same as [P Q] reversed. PRINTL is a command which causes one element of the left-component to be output. ALL is a modifier which causes repeated processing of its argument until a failure occurs. The command

[P Q] ALL PRINTL PRINT '*N';   (7)

causes [P Q] to be printed out, terminated with a newline. Under the test operator TYPE the numbers 1 and 6 signify the categories 'letter' and 'non-letter'. An exclamation mark preceding a variable in a command causes the variable to be set to the position of the last element of the string reference to be processed. The command

[A B] TYPE (HOPB 1 !P HOPB 6 !Q);

will cause P to point to the first letter in [A B], and Q to point to the first non-letter after position P. Then [P Q] is the first word in [A B]. Finally the following command causes all palindromes in [A B] to be printed out.

```
[A B] ALL (TYPE (HOPB 1 !P HOPB 6 !Q)
MOST :[Q P] REV (HOLD [P Q] ALL PRINTL
PRINT '*N'););
```

Commands (6) and (7) have been combined in lines 2 and 3. The modifier HOLD enables us to do this, but we will not give a complete description of its action here. The colon in line 2 indicates that a nested command follows, which is terminated by the first semicolon in line 3. Thus the action of the whole command is to find a word in [A B], to see if it is a palindrome, and if so to print it out. If the word is not a palindrome, the nested command will terminate without printing the word out and with the result failure. We do not want this failure to cause the whole command to be abandoned, since we want to go on and look for more palindromes in [A B]; and this is done by the modifier MOST which takes as argument the nested command, and which, in effect, turns the failure of the nested command into success. Finally the ALL of line 1 causes the whole process to be repeated, and this will cause every word in [A B] to be tested for being a palindrome.

If [A B] represented the text

I THINK THAT THE SUN IS REDDER AT SUNSET THAN AT NOON

the output from the command would be

```
I
REDDER
NOON
```

I will conclude by stressing that I have not given a complete picture of the language, but merely an outline. In particular I have skipped the question of input and output commands completely, because they could take many different forms; and no special claim is made for those in the language at the present moment.

POP-2 as a programming language for literary research

MICHAEL G. FARRINGDON*

The POP-2 programming language was designed by Rod Burstall and Robin Popplestone in the Department of Machine Intelligence and Perception at Edinburgh University. As a computer language it has several interesting features, the two most important of which are firstly that it can be used in on-line mode and secondly that it permits easy manipulation of non-numerical data. The conversational on-line mode enables a user to interact directly with his program while it is running, a very useful facility when developing a program or 'debugging'; in addition, POP-2 can be used in a normal batch-processing system. The language was designed for non-numerical as well as numerical applications and a variety of data structures are available, so that POP-2 combines in one programming language facilities for both types of programming. Some of the other design features are that the compiler should not occupy much storage and that the language is easy to learn and use, which should recommend it to potential users from non-scientific disciplines.

The fundamental concepts of a number of existing languages are contained in POP-2. For instance, it has

(*a*) the basic numerical facilities of ALGOL, with ALGOL-like expressions and statements, conditionals and jumps, functions and arrays;

(*b*) the list processing facilities of LISP with *words* roughly analogous to LISP atoms;

(*c*) the basic record handling facilities of COBOL and PL/I.

This does not mean, however, that POP-2 is just a mixture of ALGOL, LISP, COBOL and PL/I, since additionally POP-2 is flexible enough to allow the development of new features naturally.

At the present time there are implementations of POP-2 for the following machines: ICL 4100, 1900 and System 4, IBM 360. Control over the official form of the language ensures a high degree of compatibility between

* Department of Computer Science, University College of Swansea.

the various compilers so that a program written for one machine may be run on another type of machine with only minor alterations (if any).

Data

The objects on which POP-2 programs can operate are called *items* of which there are two kinds.

(*a*) *Simple items* which have no substructure and are directly represented by bit strings. There are two kinds of simple items *integers* and *reals*. In addition *characters*, *bit strings* and *truth values* can be regarded as simple items since they are represented by integers according to a defined code.

(*b*) *Compound items* which have structure and are represented internally by addresses or pointers. A compound item has as its *components* other items. A particular compound item is a member of a *class*, there being two kinds of classes called *records* and *strips*. Members of a record class have a fixed number of components and a function is associated with each component which may be used to select that component or update it. Members of a strip class have a variable number of components and there is a single function to select or update a particular component. Among the standard structures provided, together with functions to operate on them, are *pairs*, which are records with two components, *lists*, *strings*, *words* and *arrays*.

Lists

Lists are ordered sequences of items and in the following examples *words* will be used as the items in lists and the lists will be constructed by enclosing the *words* in square brackets. The composition of *words* in POP-2 is restricted since only the first eight letters of a textual word are significant when it is used as a *word*. In practice *strings*, held in *character strips*, which can contain textual words of any length, would probably be used.

Lists of words may be assigned thus

```
[ONCE UPON A TIME] → P;
[THE OWL AND THE PUSSYCAT] → Q;
```

The lists P and Q can now be printed

```
    P =>
**  [ONCE UPON A TIME]
    Q =>
**  [THE OWL AND THE PUSSYCAT]
```

One of the basic operations on lists is *concatenation* which joins two lists together using the < > operator to create a new list thus

```
    P <> Q =>
**  [ONCE UPON A TIME THE OWL AND THE PUSSYCAT]
```

or

```
    [ONCE UPON A TIME] <> [THE OWL AND THE PUSSYCAT] =>
**  [ONCE UPON A TIME THE OWL AND THE PUSSYCAT]
```

There are two standard functions, HD and TL, which can be used to access any item on a list. If the list R is assigned as

```
    [SIMON MET A PIEMAN] → R;
```

the function HD gets the first member or the head of the list

```
    HD(R) —>
**  SIMON
```

and the function TL gets the tail of the list

```
    TL(R) => >
**  [MET A PIEMAN]
```

Notice that the tail of a list is the list with the head removed. The second and third members of the list R can be accessed by

```
    HD(TL(R)) =>
**  MET
```

and

```
    HD(TL(TL(R))) —>
**  A
```

and so on.

To add an item to the head of a list another standard function CONS, also written as : : is used to construct a list. For example if

```
    "SIMPLE" › X
```

then

```
    CONS (X, R) =>
**  [SIMPLE SIMON MET A PIEMAN]
```

The same result would be obtained by

```
    X::R =>
```

and

```
    "SIMPLE" :: [SIMON MET A PIEMAN] =>
```

K

Functions

The POP-2 system has a number of standard functions, for example, SQRT for calculating square roots, EQUAL for testing the equality of two lists, LENGTH which given a list, produces the number of items in that list, and REV which reverses a list. A user may define new functions and so extend the basic set. In this way large programs may be built up from functions which are small complete programs in themselves.

An example of a *function definition* is

```
FUNCTION PRALLMEM L;
A:    IF  NULL(L)  THEN RETURN
                   ELSE  HD(L) =>
                         TL(L) → L;
                         GOTO A

        CLOSE
END;
```

Here a function called PRALLMEM is defined, which given a list L will test if L is an empty list and if so return to the main program, otherwise it will print the first member (the head) of list L, assign the tail of L to L and go back to the statement labelled A. In other words, this function will print all the members of a list, for example if

```
[SIMON MET A PIEMAN] → R;
```

then when the function is called

```
PRALLMEM(R);
```

the result is

** SIMON

** MET

** A

** PIEMAN

The elementary operations on lists and other data structures can be easily and precisely connected by control statements. This is important since many programs require certain operations to be executed only if some condition is satisfied. In the function PRALLMEM there is a *conditional*

IF condition THEN imperative sequence

(followed in this case by   ELSE imperative sequence)

(followed by)   CLOSE

If the condition (NULL (L)) is *true* then the imperative sequence following

THEN is executed, if the condition is *false* the imperative sequence following ELSE (if any) is executed. The language allows for quite complicated and long conditionals and for the nesting of conditionals.

Conditionals eliminate the need for labelling statements and for the use of *goto statements* in many cases but not in all. Program statements may be prefixed by a *label* so that after execution of a goto statement, the next statement to be executed is the one referred to by name in the goto statement.

Goto statements and their associated labels, and conditionals may only occur in a function definition.

Pattern matching

A fundamental manipulation often used by humanities programmers is pattern matching. For instance, to find if the pattern SLITHY occurs somewhere in the list [TWAS BRILLIG AND THE SLITHY TOVES], the function MATCH could be used to scan the list member by member to find if the pattern SLITHY occurs in it. If a match is found the function will return a truth-value *true* (printed as 1) and if no match is found a truth-value *false* (printed as 0).

```
FUNCTION MATCH MEM L;
   P:  IF  NULL(L)  THEN FALSE
                    ELSEIF HD(L) = MEM THEN TRUE
                    ELSE TL(L) → L;
                    GOTO P
       CLOSE
   END;
MATCH ("SLITHY", [TWAS BRILLIG AND THE SLITHY TOVES]) =>
** 1
```

The above is an example of a basic type of pattern matching. However, it is often necessary having found a pattern match to replace the pattern in the list with another pattern. Suppose that it is necessary to replace the word BITCH with an * in the list UNCUT.

```
[JIM IS A SON OF A BITCH AND SO IS BOB] → UNCUT;
```

then the function REPMEM, to replace a member of a list, may be defined

```
FUNCTION REPMEM L1 MEM L2;
IF  NULL(L1)  THEN NIL
              ELSEIF HD(L1) = MEM THEN L2 <> TL(L1)
              ELSE HD(L1) :: REPMEM (TL(L1), MEM, L2)

CLOSE
END;
```

and calling the function

    REPMEM (UNCUT, "BITCH", [*]) =>

results in

    **[JIM IS A SON OF A * AND SO IS BOB].

The function REPMEM is a simple example of the use of *recursion* where a function calls itself during execution. A recursive definition is often much simpler to write than its equivalent *iterative* definition using a goto statement, but the recursive definition is generally less efficient both in terms of execution time and storage.

If the pattern match requires searching for an ordered sequence of members of a list, say SON OF A BITCH had to be replaced by **** in the list UNCUT, then this could be done as follows:

```
FUNCTION REPLACEHD L1 L2 L3;
IF   NULL(L2)   THEN L3 <> L1
                ELSEIF NULL(L1) OR NOT (HD(L1) = HD(L2)) THEN
                "UNDEF"
                ELSE REPLACEHD (TL(L1), TL(L2), L3)

CLOSE
END;

FUNCTION REPLACE L1 L2 L3; VARS R;
IF   NULL(L2)   THEN L3 <> L1
                ELSEIF NULL(L1) THEN "UNDEF"
                ELSE REPLACEHD (L1, L2, L3) → R;
                    IF R = "UNDEF" THEN HD(L1) :: REPLACE (TL
                    (L1), L2, L3)
                                        ELSE R

                    CLOSE
CLOSE
END;
```

so that

    REPLACE (UNCUT, [SON OF A BITCH], [* * * *]) =>

gives

    * * [JIM IS A **** AND SO IS BOB]

Character strips

As mentioned above, the words of a literary text, and the punctuation if required, would probably be stored as strings in *character strips*. A strip is a data structure with a fixed number of components and each component of a character strip can be used to represent alphabetic or numeric characters or punctuation symbols. Suppose a textual word is to be read character by character and the whole word stored in a character strip. Until the end of the word is reached it is not possible to know what size of character strip is required. The characters can be initially stored in a list CHLIST and counted by CHCOUNT. Initializing the list and count by

```
NIL → CHLIST; 0 → CHCOUNT;
```

characters can be read in one at a time to a variable CHAR by

```
IN: CHARIN( ) → CHAR;
```

and after testing the character in CHAR to see if it is an alphabetic character, say, and not a word terminator, CHAR can be added to the list and counted and the next character read

```
CHAR :: CHLIST → CHLIST;
1 + CHCOUNT → CHCOUNT;
GOTO IN;
```

When a word terminator is found, the standard initiating function INITC (N) is used to construct a strip of N components and the standard function SUBSCRC(I, S) is used to access the Ith component of strip S. The word thus stored as a list of characters can now be transferred to a character strip CHSTRIP where it is held as a string by

```
          INITC (CHCOUNT) → CHSTRIP;
LOOP:  IF CHCOUNT = 0 THEN GOTO WDFIN CLOSE;
          HD(CHLIST) → SUBSCRC (CHCOUNT, CHSTRIP);
          CHCOUNT - 1 → CHCOUNT;
          TL(CHLIST) → CHLIST;
          GOTO LOOP;
```

Records, word counts and concordances

The author has written a POP-2 program which given a literary text will produce an alphabetically ordered word count and a concordance giving each word in a line of context together with the appropriate references. The words are read character by character and stored in character strips as described above; the relevant references for each word, say Act, Scene and Line are also recorded. An alphabetically ordered list of different words is gradually built up, together with their references. As each new word is read a search is made to see if it has already occurred, and if so only the new references are added. If the new word is not found then it is inserted into the correct position in the list together with its references.

The references are stored in *records*. A record class of REFS is first defined which creates a set of functions for handling records of that class:

RECORDFNS ("REFS", [0 0 0]) → LINE → SCENE → ACT → REFDETAILS → NEWREF:

NEWREF constructs a new record out of components, for example if the word 'article' occurred in Act 1, Scene 1, Line 133 a new record of these references would be constructed by

NEWREF (1, 1, 133) → TYPEREF;

The function REFDETAILS can be used to produce all the components of a record:

REFDETAILS (TYPEREF) =>
** 1 1 133

ACT, SCENE and LINE are used to access the appropriate components of a record and update them if necessary. For example

LINE (TYPEREF) =>
** 133

and to update or correct the line to 233, say (should this really be necessary!)

233 → LINE(TYPEREF);

the action of this can be seen by printing the components of the record again

REFDETAILS (TYPEREF) =>
** 1 1 233

The list of different word types and their associated references are stored like

[ARTERIES [<4 3 302>] ARTICLE [<1 1 139><1 1 133>] ARTS [<4 3 349> <4 3 231><2 1 45>]]

where a word type is followed by a *list* of records containing the Act, Scene and Line for the word. For the sake of clarity in this example, each record is enclosed by < and >. Lists like this, in which the elements alternate

entity – attributes – entity – attributes – . . .

are quite common and are called association lists. Thus, if a word already occurs in the list it is easy to add the record containing its references to the head of the attribute list.

When the complete text has been read the word-types can be retrieved from the alphabetically ordered list and the frequency of each type can be found by using the standard function LENGTH which given a list produces the number of members in that list, for example for the word 'article'

```
LENGTH ([<1 1 139><1 1 133>]) =>
** 2
```

To construct a concordance, using the attribute list, it is useful to reverse the order of the members of the list so as to print the lines of text containing the word in their order of occurrence. The reversing of members of a list can again be done using a standard function REV so that

```
REV ([<1 1 139><1 1 133>]) =>
** [<1 1 133><1 1 1 139>]
```

Postscript

POP-2 is a rich and versatile language and can give the researcher freedom to experiment with a variety of concepts. Its features ensure that the researcher using it can concentrate on his problem rather than on petty programming details – so often the case with other languages – and sophisticated programs for executing complex tasks can be written with a modicum of experience.

I wish to express my thanks to Professor D. C. Cooper and Mr Robin Milner for the extremely useful discussions we have had on POP-2 and for their encouragement.

POP-2 References

R. M. Burstall, J. S. Collins and R. J. Popplestone, *POP-2 Papers* (Edinburgh, 1968).

R. J. Popplestone, 'The Design Philosophy of POP-2', *Machine Intelligence*, 3, ed. D. Michie (Edinburgh, 1968).

A command language for text processing

B. H. RUDALL*

This paper describes the need for a 'purpose built' command language for the processing of texts and the design of one such language PROTEXT, for the limited manipulation of a textual corpus. This is discussed in relation to the needs of the non-programmer in the field of literary data processing. Consideration is also given to the use of PROTEXT as an environmental language for applications in this field involving the use of higher level compiler and symbol-manipulating languages.

General concept of a text processing language

The more sophisticated hardware, operating systems and languages now available, together with the introduction of real time working have made computers more accessible than ever before. This fact has, however, only served to emphasize the problems of communications which so many users who are not computer specialists encounter.

Computer systems, on the whole, are still geared to numerical computation and the non-specialist with a non-numerical problem, is, in a sense, as remote from the computing machine as ever. Fortunately, however, many symbol-manipulating languages have been designed and implemented, and the researcher in a particular field who has expert programming assistance or the capacity to learn programming is not entirely neglected. But does the scholar in the Humanities have to learn a language like PL/I – a suitable programming language for Humanities Research,[1] or a symbol-manipulating language like COMIT, developed at MIT for linguistic studies, before he can use a computer as an information processing machine?

Developments in natural language programming[2] allied to advances in

---

* Computing Laboratory, University College of North Wales, Bangor.
[1] See J. Heller and G. W. Logemann, 'PL/I:A Programming Language for Humanities Research', *Computers and the Humanities*, 1 (1966), 19–27.
[2] Discussed by F. H. George and P. A. Sarkar, 'Aspects of LIP Programming', *Journal of the Institution of Computer Sciences*, 1 (1970), 16–18.

string processing languages may well serve to produce the ideal, all purpose, communicating language for the non-specialist. Alternatively, of course, it is worth establishing what the non-specialist in any field requires from a computing system and initially at least attempting to meet his fundamental needs.

Such a field is that of Literary Data Processing, where most non-specialists in computing require the machine to store information in an easily accessible form, and for the system to provide the capacity to manipulate in a limited fashion, derived or stored data.

The need to store and retrieve information is accepted, and the development of information retrieval and interrogatory languages such as 'Easy English',[1] POSE, RECOL, SPECOL[2] and CLIC has resulted. Such languages, together with the limited facilities for information processing demanded by the particular field of application, may well provide the means of communication in Literary Data Processing fields as well as in other types of research where the computer user wishes to remain a non-programmer. Somewhere, therefore, between the extremes of a list processing language like LISP 1.5 and a simple enquiry language like SPECOL, a need exists for application orientated languages with simple command forms.

A language of this kind was required for the computer analysis of surviving Old English Poetry,[3] when in order to see whether traces of the oral techniques used by illiterate singers were still visible in extant Old English texts it was necessary to test each word of a particular poem against the rest of the corpus to determine its pattern of recurrences. Here as in most literary data processing it was necessary to create an archive of texts, prepared and stored in the computer in a defined manner, and to perform limited manipulations of the text strings in order to activate a set of standard algorithms for the production of the word lists needed by the scholar.

Such a language is also required by the computer specialist, as an environmental language which will allow him to organize and prepare texts, and to carry out routine processing before his more detailed algorithm in a higher level or list processing language can be executed.

[1] An example is given by M. Rubinoff, S. Bergman, H. Cantin and F. Rapp, 'Easy English – A Language for Information Retrieval through a remote typewriter console', *Communications of the Association for Computing Machinery*, XI (1968), 693–6.

[2] B. Smith, 'Developments in SPECOL – A Retrieval Language for the Non-Programmer', *The Computer Journal*, XIII (1970), 10, and XI (1968), 121.

[3] This involved the recognition of Anglo-Saxon character clusters in the text. B. H. Rudall and C. Hall, 'Literary Data Processing on a Small Store Computer', *Computer Bulletin*, XI (1967), 131.

Before defining the syntax of such a language it is worth noting the comments of M. V. Wilkes[1] in his ACM Turing Lecture – 'it would be more logical first to choose a data structure appropriate to the problem, and then look around for, or construct with a kit of tools provided, a language suitable for manipulating the structure'.

Design concept of PROTEXT

The Command Language PROTEXT[2] has been designed about a text data structure in an attempt to provide both the specialist and non-specialist computer user with the following facilities:

(*a*) Natural language commands of simple syntactic form.

(*b*) Text storage in a flexible, defined form.

(*c*) Creation of permanent archives for texts.

(*d*) Retrieval and filing of text or subtexts.

(*e*) Limited manipulation of stored texts.

(*f*) Activation of standard algorithms applicable to the field of Literary Processing.

(*g*) Integration with one or more higher level or information processing languages for numerical computation or more detailed string processing.

A typical command in PROTEXT for searching a stored text, by lines, for a given set of characters would be:

```
SEARCH (BY LINE) TEXT WANDERER/
PART 1/LINE 31–72 FOR 'FORLET', 'CWITH', 'ENGEL',
'GAEST' AND 'GEDAEL';
```

Any section of stored text is printed, using the command:

```
PRINTOUT TEXT HOMILETIC/LINE 10-50;
```

A new text ALPHA is created by

```
NAME 'WITHSTANDAN', TEXT ALPHA;
```

Real time computing provides the opportunity for interaction between user and machine, between a scholar and his texts. An interactive implementation of PROTEXT, called LITRATE is currently being designed for a time-sharing environment.

[1] M. V. Wilkes, 'Computers Then and Now', 1967 ACM Turing Lecture, *Journal of the Association for Computing Machinery*, xv (1968), 4.

[2] For a precise definition see B. H. Rudall, *Syntax and Semantics of* PROTEXT – *A Text Processing Language* (University College of North Wales Computing Laboratory Publication, 1969).

Basic features of the language

(a) Text strings

A text is defined as a string of symbols, which belong to a defined character set. The text string is further subdivided into standard subtext strings. For example a paragraph string consists of lines, lines consist of words, words consist of symbols. In addition, non-standard strings which may cut across the standard strings are also definable. All strings within a text are defined by a set of terminators which belong to a reserved character set. Field lengths for all strings are fixed initially.

Reserved character sets and the field parameters are input as data to the PROTEXT program. The following sets must be uniquely defined; the BACKUS notation (with the symbol / meaning 'or') is used throughout the syntactic and semantic definition of the language.

<P-Text symbol> defines the actual symbols allowed in the text, e.g. each of the symbols A/B/C/TH/DIV/2/ is represented in the computer by a unique binary pattern.

<Q-Reserved symbols> defines the reserved symbols for text control, e.g. word, line, terminators; they could be, space, comma (,), fullstop (.) to coincide with normal punctuation marks.

<S-String Field lengths> defines the maximum length of the string fields.

<N-Text name characters>, <D-Digit references>, <B-Language characters> define the reserved set of characters for creating text references and language symbols.

The use of these sets as parameters to PROTEXT allows a choice of typing conventions. Established conventions for Greek, Hebrew and Russian[1] could well be used, with an appropriate choice of string terminators. A symbol may be represented by several characters in some implementations, particularly when a text includes accents, scansion and literary markings. Comments in the text are also allowed.

The Anglo-Saxon character set chosen for storing the text of the *Wanderer*, Exeter Book (Knapp and Dobbie Poetical Records), with terminators, takes the form:

```
OFTq 1HIMq 1ANHAGAq 1AREq 1GEBIDETHq 1q 2
METUDESq 1MILTSEq 1THEAHq 1THEq 1HEq 1MODCEARIGq 1q 2q 3
```

[1] A. Q. Morton and M. Levison, 'The Computer in Literary Studies', *Information Processing 68*, II (1969), 1072.

Old English letter forms have been ignored to suit modern type-face and thus the symbols (ð) and (þ) are both represented by the two symbols now representing the sound (th). For the ICL 803 implementation: q_1 = space, q_2 = crlf, q_3 = fullstop. The symbol q_3 in this implementation was used as an end of text terminator.

The language allows each standard or non-standard string to be uniquely defined within a named text string. For example,

```
<word> :: = <symbol>q₁/<symbol><word>
<subtext name> :: = SYMBOL/WORD/LINE/PARAGRAPH/PART
<string name>  :: = STRING/COMPOUND STRING
```

The syntax allows reference to any particular <subtext name> or <string name> within a named TEXT, e.g.

```
TEXT JOHN
TEXT JOHN/PART 1-5
TEXT TENNYSON/PART 1/LINE 3/WORD 4-12
TEXT PETER/LINE 101/SYMBOL 10
```

Particular sets of symbols can be used as 'literals' by enclosing them in quotes, e.g.

```
'HT'    'FORLET'    'CWITH'    'YLD*A'
```

where * represents a missing symbol belonging to the set P.

(b) Result file

A set of common accumulator files for storing the results of a text analysis is defined

```
<Result File Name> ::=RESULT(<Digit>)/RESULT
```

Result files are regarded as Text files and take the form,

```
RESULT, RESULT(1)....... RESULT(n)
```

where n is a given positive integer.

(c) Commands

Commands of the type Control, Basic, Special and Procedure are available.

Control Commands such as SUMMARY, LIST, STOP, WAIT etc. allow simple control facilities within a program. The control commands LANGUAGE and ENDLANGUAGE allow specified, self-contained, language inserts within PROTEXT.

The result files can act as common storage between the independently compiled language inserts.

A Basic Function Command has as its arguments, named text strings, e.g.

```
INPUT TEXT WALDHERE/PART 1
RETRIEVE TEXT MAXIMS/PART 2/LINE 6-27
AND TEXT JOHN/PART 1
```

The definitions and implementations of the Basic Functions depend on the type of storage system available. In its defined form it is assumed that two store levels (fast access and backing) are available. Typical functions are:

```
<Basic Function> :: = STORE ARCHIVES(<Digit>)/
                      RETRIEVE/FILE/NEWFILE/RENAME/
                      NAME/READ/WRITE/CHECK/DELETE/
                      PRINTOUT/PRINT COMMENT/INPUT/
                      INPUT ARCHIVES(<Digit>)
```

STORE ARCHIVES refers to the protected backing store where new text files can only be created if the correct digit code is input. All other text files are regarded as temporary, although facilities for private files are normally implemented.

Functions are provided for Text storage, Text file control, the input and output from text files, and for printing out, e.g.

```
PRINTOUT TEXT JOHN/PART 1/LINE 111-135,
TEXT PETER/PART 2/LINE 31-72 AND
TEXT PAUL/PART 3/LINE 4/WORD 6-9
```

Special Function commands allow the use of standard text processing algorithms, the processing results are stored in the work file RESULT in the order of the execution of the special functions' text arguments. Typical algorithms incorporated within the system are named by:

```
<Special Function> ::= SEARCH/ORDERED SEARCH/
                       COUNT/COUNT AND SEARCH/SIMPLE COUNT
```

For example SEARCH searches a named text file or literal text, by given subtexts or strings for named texts, subtexts, strings or literal symbols. Hence the command,

```
SEARCH(BY LINE) TEXT COME DOWN O MAID/
LINE 1-31 FOR 'GHT', 'OLD', 'LOVE', 'THE',
'ING', 'SHEPHERD', 'MOAN', 'LONE', 'HUDDLING'
AND 'HE'
```

would give the result in the RESULT workfile

```
TEXT COME DOWN O MAID TENNYSON
STARTLINE REFERENCE NUMBER=1
        STRING No.              LINE No.
            1                       2
           10                       2
            1                       3
            4                       3
```

etc.

Similar Special Functions are defined, e.g.

```
COUNT (BY PARAGRAPH) TEXT KENTISH HYMN/
LINE 10-21 FOR 'DAEL', 'GODES',
'YLDRA' AND (BY LINE) TEXT HOMILETIC/LINE 3-9
```

Kentish Hymn is searched by paragraph for 'DAEL', 'GODES', 'YLDRA' and for the individual lines of the named text HOMILETIC. A table of the frequency of the occurrence in the subtexts is stored in the workfile RESULT.

Additional text processing algorithms, not already available as special functions, may be declared as procedure functions and incorporated within the system. A Procedure Function Command activates the algorithm.

Finally the command block specifies the order of execution of commands

```
<Command block> :: = <command>./
                     <command>;<command block>
```

Such a command block could constitute a program to search a Tennyson poem for the symbols and words of two given texts. Texts are prepared in the given character sets P and Q.

```
INPUT TEXT KEYWORD 32 AND TEXT CLUSTER 321;
INPUT TEXT COME DOWN O MAID;
COUNT AND SEARCH(BY LINE) TEXT COME DOWN O MAID/
LINE 5-20 FOR (BY WORD)
TEXT KEYWORD 321/LINE 3 AND (BY SYMBOL)
TEXT CLUSTER 321; RENAME RESULT, TEXT ANSWER 1;
FILE TEXT ANSWER 1;
PRINTOUT 'ANALYSIS REF 31', TEXT COME DOWN O MAID, TEXT
KEYWORD 321, TEXT CLUSTER 321 AND RESULT.
```

Two separate subtexts containing symbols to be searched for and counted are stored, the main text 'COME DOWN O MAID' is stored in a temporary text file (or in the Archives, in which case it need only be called by name). A frequency count and the location of the words and symbols respectively of the two subtexts occurring in the lines of the main text are stored in the RESULT file. The results are stored in a new text file ANSWER 1 for later use, and printed out for immediate analysis.

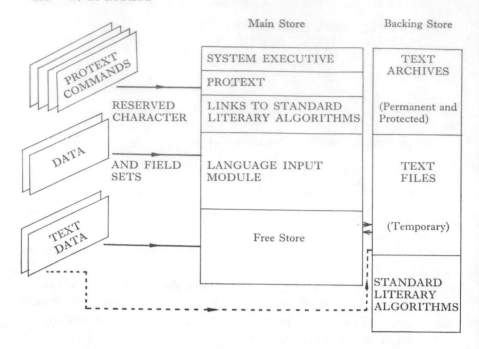

Implementation

Fig. 1 gives a storage map of a simple operating system accepting (i) data for the PROTEXT input module, that is, the reserved character sets for text preparation, the terminators, and field lengths of strings; (ii) commands for the PROTEXT program; (iii) text data, which can be input directly to the main store, the temporary text files, or the permanent Text Archives. Links to the standard literary algorithms are made with the appropriate parameters indicated in the Command Blocks of the language statements.

A subset of PROTEXT has been implemented on a small store computer (ICL 803) with paper tape files for storing the complete corpus of Old English Poetry. The language is currently being implemented on the ICL 4130 for Anglo-Saxon Texts, in a machine independent form, initially as a preprocessor in ALGOL and later in basic machine form. The problems of 'code inserts' are obviously considerably simplified if the PROTEXT preprocessor is written in the code of the insert.

The interactive version LITRATE is at the design stage and it is hoped it will be available in a conversational form on the ICL 803 and in the multi-access system of the ICL 4130.

A frequency count package for literary research: an example of literary program design

E. B. JAMES and CHRISTINE ALLWRIGHT*

The frequency count package discussed in this paper is a set of routines for assisting literary scholars in their work. Although it is not the main purpose of this paper to describe the package in detail, a brief description of its use will be given before going on to consider why the method employed is believed to be one of the most practical when undertaking the design of programs for literary applications, and particularly for those scholars whose experience is in literary studies and not in computing, and who do not have time available to learn to program efficiently.

The function of the package is to locate, in a single examination of a text, and in any language which can be encoded on punched cards, features chosen by the user of the program for their linguistic or stylistic significance and to record details of their occurrence.

For examination, the text is divided into sections of convenient size, partly because computer storage space would not allow any but the smallest text to be examined whole, but mainly because it is the pattern of the occurrences of each feature throughout the text which will be of importance to the user. The length of the sections must be decided by the scholar, this may vary according to the size of the complete text, and the expected frequency of the features, for important changes in the pattern of occurrences may be most clearly perceived only when the sections are sufficiently large or sufficiently small. Typical sections could be, for example, 100 words or 10 sentences in length.

Each feature may be a single letter, a combination of letters (which may or may not form a complete word), a word, or a combination of words, and its presence will be recorded only if its context is that prescribed by the user, who may wish to ignore it otherwise. A different context may be specified for each feature to be searched for in one examination of the text, or the same context for all; alternatively every occurrence of one,

* Department of Computing and Control, Imperial College, London.

several or all of the features, irrespective of context, may be recorded, if required. When the context conditions are satisfied in this search, the location of each feature is recorded, and its occurrence is noted in a table corresponding to the sections into which the text is divided.

The information thus collected can be presented graphically in several ways. A simple bar chart of the number of occurrences can be produced, while another useful possibility is the cumulative sum plot, which may show up more effectively the variations of occurrence of particular features. For this plot calculation is made of the average number of occurrences of each feature per section, based on the total in the text, and then of the total number expected at each section successively as a cumulative sum of the average is made. Then the difference between this expected total at the end of each section and the actual total number of occurrences to the same point is plotted. This method produces a smoother graph than if the occurrences themselves were plotted, whilst emphasizing fluctuations in the general pattern. The graphical output can also include a table listing the number of occurrences of each feature in each section of text.

If desired, it is possible to verify systematically throughout a complete text the belief that two or more features are used repeatedly in close proximity to each other, although not necessarily adjacent to each other. Once the features have been determined by observation, the package can be instructed to register every co-occurrence, as each section of the text is examined, and to print out the relevant sections of text.

Let us now consider the difficulties facing someone involved in literary studies who wishes to obtain these or similar details about his text, and who is going to use a computer for the first time. The so-called high-level languages which have been developed to meet precisely this situation may well appear too difficult and complicated to use. This is generally because the purpose for which a language such as FORTRAN has been designed is rather vague and generality of use gives rise to a need to specify many details. Literary and linguistic studies are likely to have much more limited requirements than those provided for by the FORTRAN language. This argument seems to point to the need for a special language for the literary user, but it is uncertain where the effort can exist to create such a language, and it is certain that there will be no general agreement upon its structure. We would suggest that there is an alternative between the use of a special language with its accompanying translating mechanisms on the one hand and the full FORTRAN language, for example, on the other – an alternative which allows the program to be written by a non-literary programmer and used by the literary scholar without needing to understand it.

The current situation is that the FORTRAN language is in very common use throughout the world; virtually all computers have available a compiler which will translate the language into machine-code; this is likely to be as good, if not better, than for any other language. It seems sensible to profit from the vast investment in this language and therefore it is clearly not sensible to write a translator from literary language directly to the machine-code for a particular machine.

We believe, therefore, that the most useful compromise is to make use of the concept of an 'interpreter' between the scholar and the program written in FORTRAN which actually produces the results. If such programs are written flexibly, incorporating many different facilities, they can be of assistance to a wide body of users, and the 'interpreter' allows the user to decide which of the particular options he wishes to select, in view of the results he has in mind. This 'interpreter' is itself a program, written in FORTRAN, which acts on statements, consisting of English words and phrases, which the user provides to specify his particular requirements. Given the existence of the 'interpreter', the statements can then be executed on any machine which possesses a FORTRAN compiler.

Typical statements which might be provided by the literary user are as follows:

```
TEXT NOVEL
SPLIT TEXT NOVEL INTO 100 WORD SECTIONS
PROCESSING 4 FEATURES
FEATURE 1 2 CHARACTERS IS ET WITH DELIMITERS 6 AND 6
FEATURE 2 3 CHARACTERS IS QUI WITH DELIMITERS 6 AND 6
FEATURE 3 3 CHARACTERS IS QUE WITH DELIMITERS 6 AND 6
FEATURE 4 3 CHARACTERS IS QU' WITH DELIMITERS 6 AND 0
DRAW CUSUM PLOT OF TEXT NOVEL
LIST OCCURRENCES OF FEATURES IN TEXT NOVEL
FINISH
```

These statements, which relate to our own literary package, can clearly be understood by literary users even if they are not familiar with the program. Technically, apart from stating very concisely the operations required, the main advantage is complete freedom from any restraining format which the statements must obey. In FORTRAN, programming statements must be laid out to a very precise positional specification, whereas in the above the only important factors are the relative occurrence of the words in the expected order and the fact that they are separated from each other by one or more spaces. Some programmers will recognize a resemblance

071069

```
TEXT IS    FIL STAR TØ 9999 9999
THE TEXT IS SPLIT INTØ 22    SECTIØNS ØF100 WØRD

FEATURE  1 IS ET WITH DELIMITERS 6 AND 6
FEATURE  2 IS QUI WITH DELIMITERS 6 AND 6
FEATURE  3 IS QUE WITH DELIMITERS 6 AND 6
FEATURE  4 IS QU' WITH DELIMITERS 6 AND 0
```

REFERENCE	0102	0111	0119	0129	0138	0205	0214	0222	0231	024
FEATURE 1	2	1	2	2	3	2	2	1	1	2
FEATURE 2	2	0	1	2	2	1	4	3	1	0
FEATURE 3	1	0	5	7	2	3	5	5	1	5
FEATURE 4	3	4	2	0	3	1	0	1	4	5

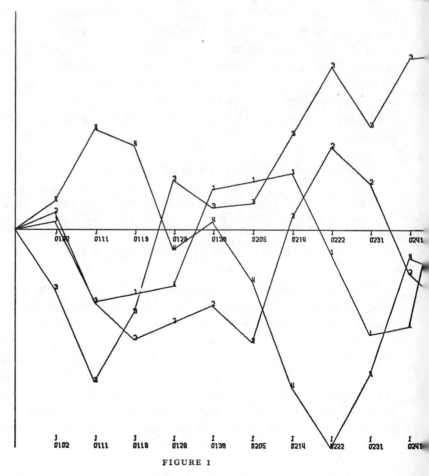

FIGURE I

0307	0317	0327	0337	0404	0414	0423	0433	0501	0512	0522	0530
4	1	1	1	3	1	1	3	3	2	2	2
1	3	2	1	5	1	2	3	2	0	0	1
3	2	5	2	2	1	5	0	2	3	1	3
2	1	3	2	3	3	1	4	1	3	4	2

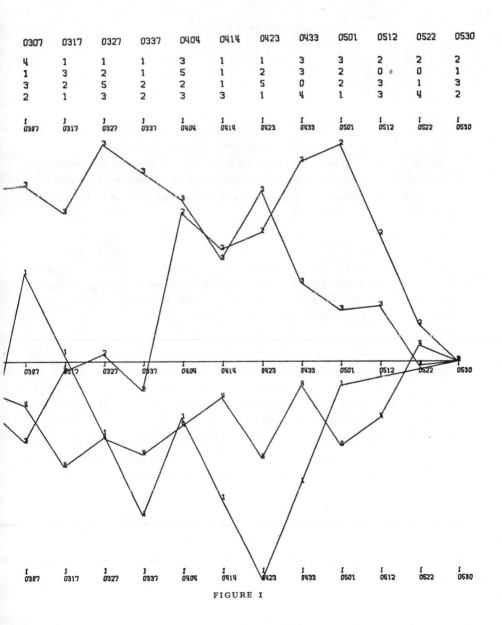

FIGURE I

to the COBOL language. The disadvantage of that language is generally in the excess of words required in the statements. In the literary package this is overcome by arranging for certain of the words to be optional; the experienced user can thus write the above statements in a more concise form, as follows, if it suits his purpose:

```
TEXT NOVEL
SPLIT TEXT NOVEL 100 WORD
PROCESSING 4
FEATURE 1 2 CHARACTERS IS ET 6 6
FEATURE 2 3 CHARACTERS IS QUI 6 6
FEATURE 3 3 CHARACTERS IS QUE 6 6
FEATURE 4 3 CHARACTERS IS QU' 6 0
DRAW CUSUM
LIST OCCURRENCES
FINISH
```

These statements in fact describe a particular set of measurements concerning a literary text, and the CUSUM results are shown in Fig. 1.

Although these statements are simple in form, certain of the operations involved in their performance are not directly specifiable in FORTRAN in a very efficient manner. It is necessary therefore to have certain routines available which are already written in machine-code for a particular machine, and these may be necessary for any program based on these principles. There are three of these used in our package, and they are very simple to specify and to program for any required machine. They arise because FORTRAN assumes that one piece of information will be stored in each computer location and that it will generally be a numerical value. In text processing the raw data is of course alphabetical characters and it is possible to store several of these in the same machine location. Machine-code routines are then required to access and replace the individual characters in the computer location. It is possible to arrange for the storage of only one character in each computer location and this will enable us to dispense with the machine-code routines. If graphical representations such as the CUSUM plot are required it is necessary also to have a special plotting package. This is a standard package developed by the manufacturers of the plotting equipment, and it should be available for all machines in common use. These issues do not, of course, affect the literary user.

Experienced users will recognize that nothing has yet been said about what is usually the main problem in text processing, that is, the preparation of the data. The form required by the current system is records of 80 characters with up to 72 characters of text and 8 characters for line identification in the last 8 positions of the record. It is simple to arrange for other formats. Extensive texts have been prepared in this form from originals in French and classical Hebrew. It is not considered useful to attempt any universal system of encoding and a method of transliteration to the standard set of keypunch symbols has been developed separately for these two types of text. The system of representation of the Hebrew text is naturally much more complex than that for modern European languages (details of the systems are available from the authors). It is a comparatively simple matter to convert modern English text to a suitable form.

It may be of interest to describe further developments of this package which are in hand at present. Firstly, there will be extensions to the literary statements so that sorted lists may be produced. Secondly, it is hoped to make the system available for use with a terminal display. The literary statements can then be specified by input from a teleprinter keyboard or graphical display. The program runs on the central computer and the results can be displayed or printed out almost immediately.

It is not claimed that the literary package provides any new and sophisticated method of dealing with literary problems. It is hoped, however, that because it may be used immediately by the literary scholar, on a large range of machines, it may help to release him from time-consuming manual counts, and enable him to concentrate on the assessment of results.

Index